T G I F

TODAY GOD IS FIRST

*365 Meditations on the Principles
of Christ in the Workplace*

OS HILLMAN

Destiny Image® Publishers, Inc.
P.O. Box 310
Shippensburg, PA 17257-0310

"Speaking to the Purposes of God for This Generation
and for the Generations to Come"

ISBN 0-7684-2049-0

For Worldwide Distribution
Printed in the U.S.A.

This book and all other Destiny Image, Revival Press, Mercy Place,
Fresh Bread, and Treasure House books are available
at Christian bookstores and distributors worldwide.

My message and my preaching were not with wise and persuasive words, but with a demonstration of the Spirit's power, so that your faith might not rest on men's wisdom, but on God's power (1 Corinthians 2:4-5).

Dedication

My Three Ladies

To the three most important ladies in my life: Angie, my wife; Lillian, my mother; and Charis, my daughter.

There I will give her back her vineyards, and will make the Valley of Achor [trouble] *a door of hope. There she will sing as in the days of her youth, as in the day she came up out of Egypt* (Hosea 2:15).

Acknowledgments

Writing a book is like being the quarterback on a football team. You get credit for a lot that many others are responsible for in your success. With gratitude, I wish to acknowledge the contribution of several people who assisted me greatly in this project.

My wife, Angie, was a constant encouragement to me to continue in this project and provided important feedback on individual devotionals. My mom has been a continued intercessor for my life going back as early as the late 60's when she had to pray me into the Kingdom. Jan Christie has been a faithful personal intercessory prayer supporter since 1996, and has been a prayer warrior on the front lines since the beginning. Along with other intercessors, she has been a strategic partner for God's purposes in my life.

Special thanks go to Billy Burke, an American English teacher living in Japan, who responded to a devotional that had weak grammar and suggested I have someone look at my work. I said, "How about you?" He agreed, and became my long-distance editor. God provided him at just the right time. Lisa Frigas, another reader who also made the same observation, became a contributor to this work as well.

Victor and Catherine Eagan with Workplace Wisdom Ministries came into my life in January 1999. They have been a tremendous encouragement to me to keep writing and have made it possible for me to give time to this and other writing projects. Steve Wike, founder of Goshen.net, now Crosswalk.com, asked to host my devotionals on his Web site. God used him to introduce Marketplace Meditations (now *TGIF: Today God Is First*) to the world. For that, I am eternally grateful to Steve.

Endorsements

The well-chosen title for Os Hillman's book illustrates the transformational paradigm shift from a temporal horizontal perspective (*TGIF*) to a timeless vertical perspective (*Today God Is First*) that is developed in each of its meditations. This book skillfully combines biblical insights with relevant and practical applications that speak to men and women who are seeking to manifest an eternal value system in a temporal arena.

Dr. Kenneth Boa
President, Reflections Ministries and Trinity House Publishers

Integrating faith and work starts with bringing God into our hearts in very intentional and personal ways. These devotionals are a daily springboard into the wellspring of God's truth on how to honor Christ in the marketplace.

Stephen Caldwell
Executive Editor, The Life@Work Co.

I have been a fan of Os Hillman's devotionals since day one. Few people have really understood the call on business people in the marketplace. Os not only understands, but has lived the issues his devotionals address. Few have captured the true heart and issues that marketplace leaders face in living out their faith. His firsthand knowledge and openness have created a book that illustrates his understanding of living out faith in the workplace. A must-read for anyone seeking to reconcile his or her faith with a call to the marketplace.

Dennis Doyle
Chief Executive Officer, Welsh Companies
President, Nehemiah Partners

Os Hillman's contribution to the marketplace-ministry movement is timely. We need to move from the 1970-80's grassroots experimentation and activism to reflection, prayer and much more Biblical fiber in our bones. We need to give God more of ourselves so that our work and witness is rooted in God-like character that brings the fruit of the Spirit into our relationships, workplaces and organizations. Then coworkers will be drawn to Jesus and the systems of our world will be more humane. Thanks, Os!

Pete Hammond
Vice President, InterVarsity Christian Fellowship-USA

Os Hillman has captured key lessons from the Scriptures and applied them in clear and concise devotional form for helping us in all facets of life. Start your day with inspiration and encouragement to meet the challenges facing every servant leader at home and in your workplace.

Dr. Carle Hunt
Professor, Regent University
Executive Director, Master Trainer International

In the often lonely environment of the marketplace, Os Hillman's devotions are a source of comfort and guidance. Os' background in business and his current calling of ministering to marketplace ministry leaders has uniquely equipped him for this task. I am confident that these meditations will bless you as they have blessed me.

Rich Marshall
RIO Ministries and Nehemiah Partners

Os Hillman's contribution to Christians serving God in the marketplace has been significant. His devotional, *TGIF: Today God Is First*, is on the cutting edge of this exciting global awakening of Christians in the marketplace. May his zeal be highly contagious!

Dennis Peacocke
President, Strategic Christian Services

In the world of business, little time is given to God. It seems that everyone is too busy designing, making and selling widgets in the perfect way, in order to advance one's position in the corporate world. So the tendency is to say "I will open the Bible tonight or in the morning" but the time comes and goes and the Word remains closed. How refreshing it is to have a daily devotion that provides the power of the Word in a short and concise way. *TGIF: Today God Is First* is a must for all workplace Christians.

Angel D. Rivera
Director, AT & T Christian Employees for Christ

Somehow, keeping Jesus as the first priority in our day is the last thing we make time to manage well! That's why I have loved being on the receiving end of the marketplace meditations included in *TGIF: Today God Is First*. I was introduced to them through the Internet and recommend that this hard copy format be augmented by the "cyber source" nuggets Os Hillman provides. The fresh spiritual reminders that come like clockwork through daily e-mails have been a great boost to my starting the day faithfully by putting Jesus first. Once you get "linked" to the life lessons found in *TGIF*, this resource will be the last thing you will want to drop from an overcrowded schedule!

John Rowell
Pastor, Northside Community Church
Author, *Magnifying Your Vision for the Small Church*

This book is powerful and practical. We have personally seen tens of thousand of lives throughout the world transformed by the daily marketplace meditations. This book is a must-read for every individual.

Dr. Jay Victor and Catherine Eagan
Directors, Workplace Wisdom Ministries

This author reminds me of Oswald Chambers in *My Utmost For His Highest*, in that he quickly moves past the symptoms to deal with root causes. For the crowded executive and time-conscience personality, *TGIF* touches us in the realm of the spiritual without verbosity or circumlocution.

Bob Mumford, M. Div.
Author and International Bible Teacher

Believers who are called to the marketplace must continuously discern the difference between God's ways and the ways of the world. These meditations are a powerful catalyst, prompting us to know and do God's will in our work day by day.

John D. Beckett
President, R. W. Beckett Corporation
Author, *Loving Monday: Succeeding in Business Without Selling Your Soul*

TGIF Today God Is First has been blessing men and women in the market place for the last three years, and I am excited about it because I truly believe that the workplace will be the primary mission field of the 21st century. God is raising up people who go to work everyday to be

His evangelist and disciples, and Os Hillman has been faithful to give all of us what God has given to him as a gift.

Tim Philpot
President, CBMC International

As the author of *Jesus, CEO, The Path,* and *Jesus in Blue Jeans,* etc. I have to tell you how much I am enjoying your new book *TGIF Today God Is First.* What a visionary writer you are! I'm sure that your advertising background helped you develop such clear and concise messaging. TGIF is my new favorite devotional book, and I felt compelled to write you and say "Well done!"

Laurie Beth Jones
Founder, The Jones Group

One of the most strategic places to serve Christ is in the market place. It is also one of the most challenging. I believe that these practical devotionals can be a source of great encouragement and help to anyone who our Lord has called to serve Him in the workplace.

Dr. Paul Cedar
Chairman and CEO, Mission America.

In the often lonely environment of the marketplace, God comes near as Os Hillman invades with a word of hope from the God of hope. Os' background in business and his current calling of ministering to marketplace ministry leaders has uniquely equipped him for this task. I have been blessed over the last year by reading these meditations on a daily basis. The very concept of this book—meditations for those in the marketplace—excites me. For too long, the church system has forgotten to equip and train her members for ministry in the very place where they spend the most time—the marketplace.

Os Hillman is a leader of the growing band of those committed to bringing about change in our world through very practical means. I am confident that these meditations will bless you as they have me.

Rich Marshall
President, ROI, Inc. ministries,
Author of *God@Work* and former Pastor for 35 years

Contents

Introduction

In March 1994, my world fell apart. The losses I incurred in my business and personal life led me to do things I would not have done apart from these experiences. One of those things was to begin writing and reflecting on the important lessons I gained through these hardships. In these few years, I have learned more about the Lord and the intimacy we can have with Him than in all of the combined 20 years since my conversion.

The theme verses of this book (First Corinthians 2:4-5) deal with the fact that so often we in the West have experienced a gospel that has been based on men's wisdom, rather than God's power. If the world is to see a difference in our gospel versus other religions, it will only be as a result of the power that is behind this gospel, not just in our moral behavior.

It is not often one has the privilege of "test marketing" a book before it ever gets on the shelf. But such is the case with *Today God Is First*. This book is a result of a leading from the Lord to begin writing a daily e-mail meditation to businesspeople I knew. For almost nine months I sent a daily meditation from my computer. It began with just a few people. Soon others asked if they could be added to my list of recipients. When it grew to 200 subscribers, Steve Wike, president of goshen.net, a major Christian Web site, asked to host the meditations on his Web site and manage the subscriptions for me. When this happened, the devotional subscriptions increased dramatically. I began to receive letters from marketplace Christians from every part of the world—China, Singapore, Malaysia, former Soviet Union, Philippines, Australia, and many other nations. The most common words I heard were: "Your words were just what I needed today." "I cannot believe how your devotional today spoke to my particular situation." "God bless you for allowing God to use you." Not a day goes by that such a letter does not come across my computer from one of God's children somewhere in the world. I give Jesus all the glory and honor for allowing me to participate in His work in this way. Each day, I have the privilege to hear how God is working in the marketplace among His children as a result of a devotional.

The messages in these devotionals are not mere principles; they are testimonies of how God has worked experientially in my life or some other life. Unless we can see and experience the reality of God in our daily lives, the gospel is mere talk. That is why you will hear me share in very personal and transparent ways. I have found that our readers determine this to be the most helpful aspect of the messages. They discover that I don't have it all together; I've just learned from my mistakes and share those experiences as a fellow journeyman walking down the Calvary road in work and life.

My prayer is that "my message and my preaching [are] not with wise and persuasive words, but with a demonstration of the Spirit's power, so that your faith might not rest on men's wisdom, but on God's power" (1 Cor. 2:4-5).

God bless you as you seek to know our Lord in a deeper and more intimate way.

Os Hillman

January 1

Dissolving Partnerships

So Abram moved his tents and went to live near the great trees of Mamre at Hebron, where he built an altar to the Lord.

Genesis 13:18

One day Abraham and his nephew Lot realized that the land they were living on could no longer support both families and all their flocks. It was decision time. They were going to have to split up. This meant someone had to go a different direction. But who should get first choice of the land? Obviously, Abraham was Lot's senior and by all rights should have that choice. Abraham could have pulled rank on Lot since he was the elder. This story is the model for splitting a business partnership. However, few businesspeople are willing to follow Abraham's example.

Abraham took a totally different approach to solving this problem. He told Lot to choose which land he wanted. Imagine, Abraham could have been dooming himself and his family if he was unable to find adequate land and water for them. He gave up his rights in the matter, and Lot took full advantage. "Lot looked up and saw that the whole plain of the Jordan was well watered, like the garden of the Lord, like the land of Egypt, toward Zoar" (Gen. 13:10). So Lot left and took up residence in the valley later to be known as Sodom and Gomorrah. Sometimes what seems good on the front end turns out to be disastrous later. Such would be the case for Lot and his family.

As for Abraham, he made a choice. He decided to take life's high road—a choice that didn't necessarily mean his life circumstances would benefit him. He was willing to leave that outcome to God. He made the decision based on an eternal measuring stick. Interestingly, the place where Abraham moved was called *Mamre*. In Hebrew, the name *Mamre* means "strength." How can choosing the weakest position become "strength"? Jesus must have asked the same question of His Father when faced with the proposition of going to the cross. How can the cross be a place of strength? The devil thought he had won, but the cross is what freed the captives for eternity. The Bible tells us that when we are weak, then we are really strong. To willingly choose the way of the cross becomes our strength.

January 2

Seeing the Big Picture

> …*"Everything is against me!"* Genesis 42:36

Jacob had come to the end of his rope. He had lost Joseph. Simeon was in jail in Egypt. Now, in order to free Simeon, Benjamin, Jacob's youngest son, would have to go to Egypt. It was more than Jacob could handle. Jacob could not see the years of preparation for what would be the most exciting time of his life and the life of a nation. The darkest hour is the hour just before daybreak. Jacob was in his darkest hour just before God's daybreak in his life. God's big picture is often too big for us to comprehend. The heartaches don't seem to add up, but Jacob was about to understand the big picture.

Eventually, Benjamin along with Jacob's other sons learned that their brother Joseph was second in command in Egypt. Joseph revealed his identity, and Jacob was reunited with his son whom he had not seen for more than 13 years. He had thought Joseph to be dead.

So often we believe our dreams are dead. There seems to be nothing left in our world to live for. Everything appears to be against us. During these times, God is doing His deepest behind-the-scenes work. During these times, God is performing a deeper work in each of us—a work that cannot be seen.

When clients began leaving my ad agency and it dried up for no apparent reason, it appeared "everything was against me." I could not see that God was orchestrating a whole new calling on my life. At the moment, it seemed like the worst thing in the world. It seemed that I had been a failure. But God said, "No." All the years before had been preparation for what God's ultimate calling would be. One of God's methods for directing His children's steps is through drying up resources: a job loss, a career change, or a disaster. In these times we are willing to listen more intently, and to seek God in ways we would not normally do. C.S. Lewis once wrote, "God whispers to us in our pleasures, speaks in our conscience, but shouts in our pains; it is His megaphone to rouse a deaf world." [C.S.Lewis, *The Problem of Pain* (New York: Macmillan Publishing Company, 1962), 93.]

January 3

Your Positioning

> *Let another praise you, and not your own mouth; someone else, and not your own lips.*   Proverbs 27:2

Many years of owning and operating an ad agency taught me that *positioning* was defined as a place or position that a product, service, or person held in the mind of the audience. We knew that often perception was reality for people, regardless of the truth. For years, I spent time and money seeking to position our company in the minds of our prospective clients. Although it would seem that is a natural and logical marketing function, I later discovered there is a dangerous flaw when we attempt to position ourselves by promoting our own attributes. I discovered that positioning is a by-product of who we are and what we do, not an end in itself.

King David was my first biblical lesson in coming to understand the difference. Here was a man who had committed adultery and murder, and failed many times in his family life. Yet, God describes David as a "man after God's own heart." Isn't that interesting? Why would God describe someone who had obviously failed in many areas as one who was after God's own heart? Throughout David's life, we find frequent descriptions made by God: "So David's fame spread throughout every land..." (1 Chron. 14:17). Although David did make many mistakes, his heart was soft toward God and sought to praise Him. David wrote the majority of the Psalms. God honored what was in David's heart, not his perfection. I believe that God's strategic placement of David was so that we may learn from and be drawn to the attribute of David that God primarily wanted him known for—a heart bent toward Him. His *positioning* was a by-product of who he was, not an end in itself. In our business and personal life, our positioning among those who will know us should be a by-product of our life and service, not an end itself.

What is your "position" today among your peers? I once asked my Bible study group to ask others, "What do you think of when someone mentions my name?" This exercise can bring some interesting revelations. It might motivate us to make some changes, or it might confirm that God is doing a great work in you.

January 4

Coming Out of the Stronghold

> ..."Do not stay in the stronghold. Go into the land of Judah"...
> 1 Samuel 22:5

David and his fighting men had been hiding in the cave of Adullam. He was fleeing Saul. Many of life's down-and-out had come and joined David's army. David was content to stay in the stronghold of safety. Then, God's prophet came to David and told him that he must leave the stronghold and go into the land of Judah.

When life beats down on us and we get to the place where we want to hide in a cave, God often places people around us who prod us into moving in the right direction. He does not want us to remain in the place of discouragement. He wants us to move into the land of "praise." *Judah* means "praise."

I recall when I went through a very difficult time. It seemed to drag on and on with no change until finally I wanted to retreat to a cave and forget pressing on. It was a great time of discouragement. A godly man came to me and said, "You must keep moving! There are too many who are depending on you in the Kingdom." I didn't totally understand what he meant at the time. Now I know he was saying that God is preparing each of us to be the vessel He wants to use in the life of another person, but we will never be that vessel if we give up and hide in our cave of discouragement. Not only must we keep moving, we must move into a new realm. Our attitude must move from discouragement to praise. It is when we move past discouragement to praise that we begin living above our problems. Make a decision today to go into the land of Judah.

January 5

Failure That Leads to Godliness

All those who were in distress or in debt or discontented gathered around him, and he became their leader....   1 Samuel 22:2

God uses broken things to accomplish His greatest work. When David was anointed to be the next king, he was just a boy, the youngest among all his brothers. Little did he know that the next several years would be years of fleeing from Saul whose successes turned into obsessions as a leader who had fallen from God's anointing. Perhaps David thought, *Why am I living a life as a fugitive? I am the next king of Israel.* Yet, his life was filled with adversity after adversity before he ever fulfilled the ultimate calling God had for him. Others began to hear of David's successes and identify with his plight. But, it wasn't the successful and polished who came to join him. It was "those who were in distress or in debt or discontented" who would be part of his army—and an army it was! His army would become known throughout the world as the greatest ever assembled, not because of their skill, but because of the God behind the army. God turned David's men into "mighty men of valor" (see 1 Chron. 11:10).

God often uses failure to make us useful. When Jesus called the disciples, He did not go out and find the most qualified and successful people. He found the most willing, and He found them in the market-place. He found a fisherman, a tax collector, a farmer, and a doctor.

The Hebrews knew that failure was a part of maturing in God. The Greeks used failure as a reason for disqualification. Sadly, in the Church, we often treat one another in this way. This is not God's way. We need to understand that failing does not make us failures. It makes us experienced. It makes us more prepared to be useful in God's Kingdom—if we have learned from it. And that is the most important ingredient for what God wants in His children.

January 6

Receiving Only From God

> *To this John replied, "A man can receive only what is given him from heaven."*   John 3:27

"God never gave you that property," said my friend who had entered my life at a time of great turmoil. These were hard words at the time. I was separated in my marriage, and my financial resources were drying up on all fronts. It was like rowing a boat with five big holes in it, not knowing which one to try to plug. My business, my personal finances, my marriage, all seemed to be drying up at the same time. My friend had made an observation about some land we had purchased years before. His point was that I had acquired something that God had never given me. In other words, it was not a Spirit-directed purchase that was blessed by God. It was not a by-product of God's blessing; it was a source of sweat and toil born out of the wrong motives of the heart.

When John's disciples came to him and asked if he was the Messiah, he responded that he was not and that one could only be what God had given him to be. He was a forerunner to the Messiah, and he was fulfilling a call God had given him. We cannot acquire and become anything that God has not given us. God gave John that anointing. We must ask whether we are trying to be or trying to acquire anything God has not given us. When we seek to acquire anything that God has not given us, we can expect God to respond to us like any good father would to a child. He will remove that which the child is not supposed to have.

David understood this principle. When he was preparing to furnish the temple, he told God in his prayer, "Everything comes from You, and we have given You only what comes from Your hand" (1 Chron. 29:14b).

January 7

The Purpose of the Desert

Therefore I am now going to allure her; I will lead her into the desert and speak tenderly to her.   Hosea 2:14

If you have an important message to convey to someone, what is the best means of getting the message through? Have you ever tried to talk with someone who was so busy you could not get him to hear you? Distractions prevent us from giving our undivided attention to the messenger. So too, God has His way of taking us aside to get our undivided attention. For Paul, it was Arabia for three years; for Moses, it was 40 years in the desert; for Joseph, it was 13 years in Egypt; for David, it was many years of fleeing from King Saul.

God knows the stubborn human heart. He knows that if He is to accomplish His deepest work, He must take us into the desert in order to give us the privilege to be used in His Kingdom. In the desert God changes us and removes things that hinder us. He forces us to draw deep upon His grace. The desert is only a season in our life. When He has accomplished what He wants in our lives in the desert, He will bring us out. He has given us a mission to fulfill that can only be fulfilled after we have spent adequate time in preparation in the desert. Fear not the desert, for it is there you will hear God's voice like never before. It is here you become His bride. It is here you will have the idols of your life removed. It is here you begin to experience the reality of a living God like never before. Someone once said, "God uses enlarged trials to produce enlarged saints so He can put them in enlarged places!"

He brought me out into a spacious place; He rescued me because He delighted in me (2 Samuel 22:20).

January 8

Blessing Those Who Curse You

…"Leave him alone; let him curse, for the Lord has told him to. It may be that the Lord will see my distress and repay me with good for the cursing I am receiving today."   2 Samuel 16:11-12

As David's enemies were increasing and he was fleeing the city from his son who was seeking to take his throne, a man named Shimei began heaving rocks and cursing him as he passed by. Cursing the king was against the law, so David had every right to cut off the man's head—as his generals were encouraging him to do. Here we see the difference between Saul and David in their response to those who would seek to do them harm. This is the defining difference between a leader who seeks to lead through a vertical dimension with God versus a horizontal fix-it mode. God knew David as a man after His own heart. Yet, David was a murderer, adulterer, and had failed in many areas of his life. But one thing separated this leader from all the rest: He had a heart that sought to please God and be in His will. When David blew it, he repented.

What is the purpose God desires to accomplish with the estranged relationship you may have with someone? Has He brought this affront to find out what is in your heart today? Will you seek revenge and solve the problem yourself? Or will you find the grace to allow God to carry out vengeance in His time if it is needed? When I learned this lesson to stay vertical with God and avoid the trap of fixing things in my own energies, it was a day of freedom. No longer was it my problem. We must examine our own heart in these matters. But if we are clean, then this affront is for character building. It is the only way God builds the deepest level of character in His saints. A.W. Tozer tells us, "It is doubtful whether God can bless a man greatly until he has hurt him deeply." God actually raises up storms of conflict in relationships at times in order to accomplish that deeper work in our character. We cannot love our enemies in our own strength. This is graduate-level grace. Are you willing to enter this school? Are you willing to take the test? If you pass, you can expect to be elevated to a new level in the Kingdom. For He brings us through these tests as preparation for greater use in the Kingdom. You must pass the test first.

January 9

God-Inspired Delays

Yet when He heard that Lazarus was sick, He stayed where He was two more days.   John 11:6

Delays in our life are not always easy to handle or to reconcile in our minds. Often, when God does not answer our prayers in the time that we feel He should, we appoint all sorts of characteristics to God's nature that imply He does not care. Such was the case with Lazarus' sisters when Lazarus became ill and died. Jesus was a close friend to Lazarus and his two sisters, Mary and Martha. (Mary, you may recall, was the woman who came and poured perfume on Jesus' feet.) When Jesus arrived two days later, Martha shamed Him by saying, "If You had come he would not have died." She implied that He didn't care enough to come when sent for. It was a matter of priorities for Jesus, not lack of love.

God often has to delay His work in us in order to accomplish something for His purposes that can be achieved only in the delay. Jesus had to let Lazarus die in order for the miracle that was about to take place to have its full effect. If Jesus had simply healed a sick man, the impact of the miracle would not have been as newsworthy as resurrecting a man who had been dead for four days. This is Jesus' greatest "public relations act" of His whole ministry. What many do not realize is that the key to the whole story is in the next chapter.

> *Many people, because they had heard that He had given this miraculous sign, went out to meet Him. So the Pharisees said to one another, "See, this is getting us nowhere. Look how the whole world has gone after Him!"* (John 12:18-19)

If Jesus had not raised Lazarus from the dead, there would have been no crowds to cheer the Lord when He came into Jerusalem riding on a donkey.

God often sets the stage so that His glory is revealed through the events that He orchestrates. He did this with Moses and Pharaoh, allowing delay after delay for release of the Israelites from Egypt. He did this with Abraham and Sarah for the promised child, Isaac. God granted Sarah a baby past the age of childbearing in order to demonstrate His power.

God did this in my own life. He delayed the fulfillment of what I believed He called me to do for several years. But the delays provided the necessary preparation and greater glory that God was to receive. My friend, don't take the delays lightly. Do not faint as God places you in what seems to be a holding pattern. God is at work. God knows the purposes for His delays. Don't give up, for they are for His greater glory; so we need to remain faithful.

January 10

Sudden Ghosts in Life

> *When the disciples saw Him walking on the lake, they were terrified. "It's a ghost," they said, and cried out in fear.*
> Matthew 14:26

Have you ever had some unexpected event happen in your life that caused great fear? Sudden calamities can result in great fear unless we know Who is behind the event. Such was the case for the disciples when they were out in their boat at night. Suddenly, they saw a figure walking on the water and assumed it was a ghost. They feared for their very lives. But as the figure got closer and closer, they could see that it was Jesus. Their fear turned to joy because now they knew whom they were confronting. This seemingly life-threatening event turned into one of the great miracles of the Bible. Peter was invited to walk on the water—and he did just that.

Many times we have events in our lives that appear to be ghosts. For me, it was a period in my life when I lost my marriage, my finances, and 80 percent of my business, all in a matter of a few months. These were the ghosts that instilled fear and great turmoil in my life. But after two years in this desert experience, God revealed His true purposes for these events. He turned them from being a place of fear, to a place of miracles. He led me to a totally new calling in my life, and He demonstrated to me that He was behind the storm that led to these new discoveries. The events were real. The emotions I went through were real. I had to hold fast to the reality that nothing can touch us without passing through God's sifter. He allows only that which is necessary to touch us. And if it does, it has a purpose. But we may not know it for a while.

Are there some "ghosts" in your midst? Look beyond the appearance and let God turn your ghosts into a miracle.

January 11

Obedience

Ever since I went to Pharaoh to speak in Your name, he has brought trouble upon this people, and You have not rescued Your people at all.   Exodus 5:23

Have you ever felt that the more obedient you are to following God, the more adversity there is? Moses had been instructed to go to Pharaoh and tell him to release the people of Israel. God had said He was going to deliver the people through Moses. The only problem is that God did not tell Moses at what point they actually would be released.

When Moses complained to God, the Lord told Moses that He had to harden Pharaoh's heart in order to perform greater miracles. God was behind hardening Pharaoh's heart. We forget that the king's heart is in God's hand. God had a specific reason for each plague and each delay. God said to Moses,

> *"I have hardened his heart and the hearts of his officials so that I may perform these miraculous signs of Mine among them that you may tell your children and grandchildren how I dealt harshly with the Egyptians and how I performed My signs among them, and that you may know that I am the Lord"* (Exodus 10:1b-2).

God has a reason for everything He does. These delays were designed to bring greater glory to God and were to be a lasting legacy of God's miracle-working power for generations to come.

When the people were freed, God again hardened Pharaoh's heart to go after them. This action of God to harden Pharaoh's heart was to set the stage for an even greater miracle—the parting of the Red Sea. The people were angry with Moses for bringing them to the desert "to die." But God said to Moses, "Why are you crying out to Me? Tell the Israelites to move on" (Ex. 14:15b). There was only one place to go by this time—the Red Sea. God parted the Red Sea, and another greater miracle took place.

Moses learned several lessons that each of us must learn. God's promises are true, but His timing is not the same as ours. God always wants greater glory than what we might be willing to give Him. God puts obstacles and adversity into our lives in order to build perseverance and faith. Why has God put the mountain in your life at this time? To demonstrate His power through your life. To show His glory.

January 12

Wrestling With God

> *The sun rose above him as he passed Peniel, and he was limping because of his hip.*   Genesis 32:31

Jacob was a man who was a controller. He connived and manipulated his way to get what he wanted. It was a generational stronghold passed down through his mother, who encouraged her son to play a trick on his father, Isaac, by pretending to be Esau. This trick led Isaac to give the family blessing to Jacob, which meant Jacob would eventually inherit the land God had promised to Abraham's seed. Jacob also learned control from his uncle Laban who caused Jacob to work for 14 years to take Rachel as his lifelong mate. One must ask which was more ugly in God's sight, the self-centered nature and worldliness of Esau, or the control and manipulation of Jacob?

Control is a problem for men and women. Many women use sex to control their husbands. Many men use power and force to control their wives. Control is at the core of that which is opposite the cross—self-rule. What delivers us from this fleshly nature of control? A crisis. Jacob's crisis came when he was faced with the prospect of meeting a brother who said he would kill him the next time he saw him. Esau had built his own clan and was about to meet Jacob and his clan in the middle of the desert. Jacob was fearful, so he retreated. There he met a messenger from God who wrestled with him. Jacob clung to God and refused to let go of this angel. It is the place where Jacob was given a painful but necessary spiritual heart transplant. From that point on, Jacob would walk with a limp, because God had to dislocate his hip in order to overcome Jacob's strong will.

For businesspeople, God often has to "dislocate our hip" through failure and disappointment. Sometimes it is the only way He can get our attention. Our nature to control and manipulate is so strong that it takes a catastrophic event to wake us up. Yet God did not reject Jacob for these character traits. In fact, God blessed him greatly because He saw something in Jacob that pleased Him. He saw a humble and contrite heart beneath the cold and manipulative exterior of Jacob's life, and it was that trait that God needed to develop. He did this by bringing about the crisis in Jacob's life that led to total consecration. This event was marked by Jacob getting a new name, Israel. For the first time, Jacob had a nature change, not just a habit change. What will God have to do in our lives to gain our complete consecration to His will and purposes?

"Beware of the Christian leader who does not walk with a limp."   Bob Mumford (Used by permission.)

January 13

Finding the Will of God

I desire to do Your will, O my God; Your law is within my heart.
Psalm 40:8

How would you describe the process by which you find and do God's will in your life? For some, finding God's will is like playing bumper cars. We keep going in one direction until we bump into an obstacle, turn, and go in another direction. It is a constant process of elimination, failure, or success. Is this the way God would have us find His will? No. There is much more relationship between hearing God's voice and living within the mystery of His omnipotence in our lives. Perhaps this process is more like water in a streambed. The water is constantly flowing to a final destination. As it presses against the streambed, it gently points the water toward its final destination. There are no abrupt head-on collisions, simply slight modifications of direction. Occasionally, we come to a sharp turn in the contours of our life. For those times, God allows us to stretch our normal response to change. A popular Bible study says that we cannot go with God and stay where we are. Finding and doing God's will always require change. What changes are necessary in your life to join God in what He is already doing?

There is a direct connection between finding and doing God's will and having God's law in our heart. A friend once complained that he did not know what God wanted of him in his life. My immediate response was, "How much time do you spend with God in Bible study, prayer, and meditation on Scripture?" "Only a few minutes a day," he replied. How can we expect to hear and discern God's voice if we don't spend focused time with Him? If you have a spouse, how did you get to know him or her before you were married? You spent time together. You got to know everything about each other. Our walk with God is no different. It isn't enough to have a desire to follow God; we must put our energy into getting to know Him. His will for us flows out of our relationship, it is not an end in itself. Commit yourself to seeking Him more in your life by spending more time with Him. "Call to Me and I will answer you and tell you great and unsearchable things you do not know" (Jer. 33:3).

January 14

Move On!

…"Why are you crying out to Me? Tell the Israelites to move on."
Exodus 14:15

Moses had brought the whole nation of Israel, approximately 600,000, to a dead end in the desert. The only thing between Israel and Pharaoh's pursuing army was the Red Sea. This was after nine plagues God had inflicted on Pharaoh to motivate him to free the Israelites. Finally, Pharaoh had freed Moses and the people, and they left Egypt. They thought they were home free. "Freedom at last," they said. But God did a strange thing. He directed Moses to take a route that led to the Red Sea, instead of the northern route around the Red Sea. God explained that He didn't want them fighting the enemies they would have encountered on this route. But still, there was the issue of the Red Sea.

They finally arrived at the Red Sea, and the people were wondering where they would go from there. News hit the camp: Pharaoh had changed his mind. He was coming after them with his army. Panic set in. The defenseless Israelites cried out, "Was it because there were no graves in Egypt that you brought us to the desert to die?…It would have been better for us to serve the Egyptians than to die in the desert!" (Ex. 14:11b-12)

God sometimes brings each of us to a "Red Sea" in our life. It may be a business problem that can't be solved. It may be a marriage that seems to be failing. It may be a debilitating disease. Whatever your Red Sea, God tells us one thing: "Keep moving." The Red Sea was before them, yet God was angered at Moses and told him to "Keep moving."

"But Lord, the Red Sea is before me." "Keep moving." When we live by sight, we act on what we see. God sets this stage in dramatic fashion. God is into the dramatic. There is no way out without God here. That is just the way He wants it. No one will get glory except God.

A friend once admonished me when I was in the midst of a marriage separation that eventually led to a divorce, "You must not withdraw from being proactive in your faith just because of this trial that you are in. God's hand is on your life. There are too many who are depending on you to fulfill the purposes God has in your life. Keep moving! Keep investing yourself in others." I didn't feel like it. I was in too much pain. But I did it anyway. God met me at the point of my greatest need once I decided simply to be obedient. Getting past myself by investing myself in others helped heal the pain. There is great healing when we look past our own problems and seek to invest ourselves in others for the sake of Christ. This is when our own Red Seas become parted. We begin to walk to freedom. But we will never experience the miracle of the Red Sea in our lives if we don't first "Keep moving."

January 15

Obedience-Based Decisions Versus Skill and Ability

As soon as you hear the sound of marching in the tops of the balsam trees, move out to battle.   1 Chronicles 14:15a

The Philistines were attacking. David wanted to know how to respond. His first inquiry of God revealed that he was to attack the Philistines straightaway and God would give him victory. David followed God's instruction and gained victory. Shortly after, the Philistines mounted another attack. "So David inquired of God again, and God answered him, 'Do not go straight up, but circle around them and attack them in front of the balsam trees' " (1 Chron. 14:14).

David was a well-trained warrior, a strategist. Yet, we find that David's dependence on God to direct his efforts was very great. In fact, after he won the first battle, he went right back to inquire again. This is the most important lesson we can learn from this story. God told David to attack, but only after he heard the marching in the balsam trees.

How many times have you or I operated in the marketplace based only on our skill and ability, without seeking to know the details of God's will in the matter? David could have simply assumed that since he had won the last battle, surely God would give him victory the same way. No. David had learned that communicating with the living God is the only sure way of victory. His skill was not enough. He had to have God's blessing.

How many times have we worked in our business life the same way each time only because it was the way we did it last time? What if God has a better way? What if God has a different plan than ours? "So David inquired of God..." These are the important words that we are to learn from. We must be in such relationship with God that we are constantly inquiring of His mind on every matter. When we do this, we can expect the same results that David achieved—success in our endeavor and recognition by God.

"So David's fame spread throughout every land, and the Lord made all the nations fear him" (1 Chron. 14:17). This is the reward of obedience to God. We don't have to build a name for ourselves. God will see to it that we are honored for our obedience. He wants to make known those servants who are willing to obey Him at all costs.

January 16

God's Tests

..."What have I done? What is my crime? How have I wronged your father, that he is trying to take my life?"*   1 Samuel 20:1

The cost of being one of God's anointed can be great. Those whom God has anointed for service and influence in His Kingdom go through a special preparation. David was anointed to be the next king over Israel. Shortly after this, while still a young boy, he was brought into King Saul's service to play music in Saul's court. While there, the opportunity to stand up against Goliath elevated David for his next stage of development as future king. As his popularity grew so did Saul's jealousy. However, even Saul's jealousy was God's instrument for molding and shaping David.

Saul finally decided he could no longer tolerate David's success and popularity among the people, so he tried to kill David. The confused young shepherd boy spent many years hiding in wilderness caves before he was able to see the hand of God in all of this. No doubt David thought that when he was anointed by Samuel he would be conveniently raised up to be king with all the accompanying benefits of kingship. Not so. God's preparation of David involved much persecution, disloyalty, and hardship. These were the lessons necessary to be a godly king. God brought many tests in David's life, just as He did with Saul. David passed these tests. Saul did not.

When God anoints us, it often is accompanied by some severe tests. These tests are designed to prepare us for the calling God has on our life. Should we fail these tests God cannot elevate us to the next level. For a businessperson, these tests often involve money, relationships, and other issues of the heart.

What if God has chosen you for a specific purpose in His Kingdom? Are you passing the tests He is bringing about in your life? These tests are designed to bring about greater obedience. In most instances it will involve great adversity. The Bible tells us that the King of kings learned obedience through the things that He suffered (see Heb. 5:8). If this is true, why would it be any different for His children? Be aware of the tests God may be bringing before you in order to prepare you for His service.

January 17

Recognizing Our Source

But remember the Lord your God, for it is He who gives you the ability to produce wealth.　　　　　　　　　　　Deuteronomy 8:18a

Pride is the greatest temptation to a successful marketplace minister. When we begin accumulating wealth, managing people, and becoming known for our marketplace expertise, we are most susceptible to falling to the most devious sin in God's eyes—pride. The Bible tells us that God is the reason we are able to produce wealth. It is not of our own making. As soon as we move into the place where we begin to think more highly of ourselves than we ought, God says he will take action.

> *You may say to yourself, "My power and the strength of my hands have produced this wealth for me."....If you ever forget the Lord your God and follow other gods and worship and bow down to them, I testify against you today that you will surely be destroyed. Like the nations the Lord destroyed before you, so you will be destroyed for not obeying the Lord your God* (Deuteronomy 8:17,19-20).

These are strong words from God. It demonstrates His utter impatience for any people who think that what they have accomplished has anything to do with their own power. It is God who gives us the skill, the mind, the resources, the energy, the drive, and the opportunities in life to accomplish anything. When we become prideful in heart, He will begin a process of reproof in our life.

Today is a good day to examine whether we have fallen prey to pride. Are you sharing what God has entrusted to you with God's people, or the needy? Are you being the instrument of blessing that God desires for His people to be? What areas of pride have crept into your life? Ask the Lord to show you this today. And avoid being put on the shelf. Nothing is worse than being cast aside because of our own pride.

January 18

Standing in the Gap

> *I looked for a man among them who would build up the wall and stand before Me in the gap on behalf of the land so I would not have to destroy it, but I found none.*   Ezekiel 22:30

The people of Israel fell into sin when they worshiped the golden calf. It would not be the last time God's people would fall into idol worship. They had forgotten the great things God had done for them. This angered God so much that He was going to destroy the whole nation. Only one thing changed God's mind in the matter—Moses. Psalm 106:23

says, "...had not Moses, His chosen one, stood in the breach before Him to keep His wrath from destroying them." Moses was a man willing to stand in the gap, sacrificially, for those who were not deserving of such sacrifice. This sacrificial love by Moses is called for among His people today.

The prophet Ezekiel described another situation in which God's people fell into sin. God was ready to destroy the nation when He spoke to Ezekiel, asking him if there is a man willing to stand in the gap so that God would not have to destroy His people.

Judah was a man who stood in the gap on behalf of his younger brother Benjamin. Joseph held his brother Simeon hostage as insurance that the other brothers would bring Benjamin to Egypt. Judah had a long history of a me-focused life, but in this instance he came forward to stand in the gap for his younger brother. He responded to the anguish of his father, Jacob, by personally guaranteeing the safe return of both Simeon and Benjamin. Judah's sacrifice was rewarded (see Gen. 42–43).

Just as Christ did, we are to be those who will stand in the gap on behalf of others who are not aware of their own vulnerable condition. It is a proactive sacrificial position. Who is God calling you to stand in the gap for? Perhaps it is a mate; perhaps it is a business associate who has not come to know the Savior; perhaps it is a wayward child. Are you willing to become the sacrificial offering to God to change His plans of judgment because of your willingness to stand in their place? This is a hard teaching. This is what Jesus did for each of us. When we stand in the place of another, God moves because of our willingness to stand on their behalf. If we don't, His plans will go forward because He is a righteous and holy God who will honor His own word, even if it means destruction. Are you willing to stand in the breach of the wall for someone today? Perhaps you are the only person who will stand on someone's behalf.

January 19

The Purpose of Crucibles

The crucible for silver and the furnace for gold, but the Lord tests the heart.   Proverbs 17:3

This proverb describes one of God's strangest mysteries. It is a description of God's formula to refine the human heart in order to bring out its finest qualities. The significant leaders who make the greatest mark for the Kingdom had to experience their own crucible and fire. Without it, the dross can never be removed from the human heart. Without it, the encumbrances weigh us down. God understands the human heart. He understands that for us to become all that He hopes for us, there are seasons of fire. Joseph went through many tests. Succeeding in the test qualified him for greater responsibility. The greater the use in the Kingdom the greater the crucible to prepare the right foundation. Some of God's greatest crucibles are found in the marketplace where we live every day: the employee who betrays our trust, the client who refuses to pay, the vendor who falls short of our expectations.

Each of these is God's tests to find out how we will respond. What tests are being brought your way today? His grace has been provided that we might pass the tests that He brings before us. Should we fail, we need not fear. His grace is sufficient for this as well. Ask God for the grace to walk with Him in whatever tests He has placed before you this day. He is able to accomplish what He wants for you.

January 20

Thirsting After God

...*"Let me inherit a double portion of your spirit"*....
                                                        2 Kings 2:9

The first requirement to move in greater power and authority in God is to hunger for it. Yet even this hunger is born from God. Elisha hungered after God. Elisha saw many miracles as Elijah's servant. But he wanted more. He wanted a double portion of Elijah's spirit. When he asked Elijah for this, the prophet responded, "You have asked a difficult thing." It wasn't because it couldn't be granted. Elijah knew that with great anointing came a great weight of responsibility and difficulty.

Second, humility comes before honor. Elisha was known as the "servant of Elijah." How would you like to be known as "the servant of John"? Your name is not even mentioned. This was the preparation of Elisha. It has been the preparation of many men of God. Consider Joseph, the servant of Pharaoh. Consider David, the servant of Saul.

Third, Elisha committed himself totally to his calling. The Scripture says when Elisha was called to join Elijah, the younger man left his farm business completely. He slaughtered his oxen and had a great feast for the community. It was all or nothing. He could not fall back on his farm trade if his new venture didn't work. This demonstrates Elisha's pioneer spirit in stepping out, not knowing what was ahead.

Do you want greater anointing in God? "You will seek Me and find Me when you seek Me with all your heart. I will be found by you" (Jer. 29:13-14a). Begin thirsting for God's anointing in your heart today. This is the starting place.

January 21

The Skillful Worker

Do you see a man skilled in his work? He will serve before kings; he will not serve before obscure men.   Proverbs 22:29

The Lord has called each of us to be excellent in what we do. Those whom God used in the Kingdom as marketplace ministers were skilled and exemplified excellence in their field. Not only were these men skilled, they were filled with God's Spirit.

Then the Lord said to Moses, "See, I have chosen Bezalel son of Uri, the son of Hur, of the tribe of Judah, and I have filled him with the

Spirit of God, with skill, ability and knowledge in all kinds of crafts—to make artistic designs for work in gold, silver and bronze, to cut and set stones, to work in wood, and to engage in all kinds of craftsmanship" (Exodus 31:1-5).

Consider Huram, the master craftsman of bronze in whom Solomon entrusted much of the temple designs. He was a true master craftsman (see 1 Kings 7:14).

Consider Joseph, whose skill as an administrator was known throughout Egypt and the world. Consider Daniel, who served his king with great skill and integrity. The list could go on—David, Nehemiah, Acquilla and Priscilla.

I recall the first issue of an international publication we began. It was common to hear the comment, "It doesn't even look like a Christian magazine." They were saying the quality and excellence exceeded what they equated to Christian work. What a shame. Has inferior quality become synonymous with Christian work?

May we strive for excellence in all that we do for the Master of the universe.

Whatever you do, work at it with all your heart, as working for the Lord, not for men, since you know that you will receive an inheritance from the Lord as a reward. It is the Lord Christ you are serving (Colossians 3:23-24).

January 22

The Proper Foundation

Unless the Lord builds the house, its builders labor in vain.
Psalm 127:1a

Imagine spending years building an expensive home with the finest materials and craftsmanship. It is a work of art, and the project is almost complete. As the day arrives to move in, a building inspector arrives and hands you a notice that condemns your beautiful home because it doesn't meet code.

Many Christian businesspeople who invest years in their businesses will one day stand before the Lord and realize *they* were building the house, not the *Lord*. God is very picky about motives behind the actions. Before we act, we must ask *why*? Why are we doing what we are doing? Has God called us to this task? Or is the real motive purely financial? Or control. Or prestige.

> *If any man builds on this foundation using gold, silver, costly stones, wood, hay or straw, his work will be shown for what it is, because the Day will bring it to light. It will be revealed with fire, and the fire will test the quality of each man's work* (1 Corinthians 3:12-13).

David learned this principle by the end of his life. Throughout his life he had learned that God always tested him to find out what was in his heart, and what his motive was in his actions. David instructed his son to "...acknowledge the God of your father, and serve Him with wholehearted devotion and with a willing mind, for the Lord searches every heart and understands every motive behind the thoughts" (1 Chron. 28:9a).

January 23

No More Reproach

> ..."Today I have rolled away the reproach of Egypt from you"....
> Joshua 5:9

Joshua and the people had just crossed the Jordan River. They were camped at Gilgal. But before they could proceed they were required to circumcise all the males, because a whole new generation had grown up while living in the desert. This is where Israel, like a worm in a cocoon, was transformed. Circumcision is bloody, personal, and it exposes all that you are. God was saying that before you can become His army, you must roll away the reproach of the Egyptian way of life. You are no longer a slave to the ways of Egypt. It is a time to put aside the old way of life. Many are walking around as goats in sheep's clothes, practicing a form of religion without the true source of truth and power.

Sin in our midst testifies against us. It keeps us in Egypt and never allows us to enter the Promised Land. Our lives must be circumcised in order for us to come out of Egypt into our own Promised Land of spiritual blessing with God. This transformation marks the first time Israel begins to taste the fruit of the Promised Land. No more manna from Heaven. The manna stopped the day after they were circumcised. There was no longer any manna for the Israelites, but that year they ate produce from Canaan.

God is turning our plowshares into weapons of love to usher in a new generation of marketplace warriors. But we will not be effective if we have the reproach of sin in our lives. Ask God to show you what needs to be confessed this day so that no reproach exists. The cross of Jesus takes away all reproaches. Enter the Promised Land with power.

January 24

Seeing a Greater Purpose in Adversity

But Paul shouted, "Don't harm yourself! We are all here!"

Acts 16:28

Paul and Silas had just been thrown into prison. An earthquake erupted and the jail cell was opened. It's Paul and Silas' opportunity. "Deliverance! Praise God!" might be the appropriate response. But this is not what Paul and Silas did. In fact, rather than leave, they sat quietly in their cell area. The guard, in fear of his life, knew that it would be automatic death if prisoners escaped. Paul and Silas did not leave because they saw a higher purpose for which they were in prison. They were not looking at their circumstance; they were much more concerned about the unsaved guard. The story goes on to explain how Paul and

Silas went home with the guard and his family. Not only did the guard get saved, but his entire household as well.

What a lesson this is for us. How often we are so busy looking for deliverance from our circumstance that we miss God completely. God is looking to do miracles in our circumstances if we will only look for them. Sometimes as businesspeople we become so obsessed with our goals we miss the process that God involves us in, which may be where the miracle lies. What if that bill collector who has been hounding you is unsaved and he is there for you to speak to? What if a problem account has arisen due to something God is doing beyond what you might see at this time? Our adverse situations can often be the door of spiritual opportunity for those who need it.

I saw this personally when God allowed me to go through a number of adversities. It took some time, but I saw some great miracles as a result of those adversities. When God said that "all things work together for good for those who are called according to His purposes" (see Rom. 8:28), He meant *all things*. It is up to us to find the "work together for good" part by being faithful to the process. In the next adversity you face, tune your spiritual antennae and ask God for discernment to see the real purpose for the adversity.

January 25

Horizontal Versus Vertical

Glancing this way and that and seeing no one, he killed the Egyptian and hid him in the sand.   Exodus 2:12

Moses saw the pain of his people. He saw the bondage and the injustice. His heart was enraged, and he decided he would do something. He would take matters into his own hands. The result was murder. The motive was right, but the action was wrong. He went *horizontal* instead of *vertical* with God. The action was wrong. Moses fled to the desert, where God prepared the man who would ultimately be the deliverer of a nation. But it took 40 years of preparation before God determined Moses was ready. He was a professional businessman—a sheepherder. It was during the mundane activity of work that God called on him to be a deliverer.

Moses was like a lot of enthusiastic Christian businesspeople who seek to solve a spiritual problem with a fleshly answer. The greatest danger to the Christian businessperson is his greatest strength—his business acumen and expertise to get things done. This self-reliance can become our greatest weakness when it comes to moving in the spiritual realm. We're taught to be problem solvers. But, like Moses, if our enthusiasm and passion are not harnessed by the power of the Holy Spirit, we will fail miserably. Peter had to learn this lesson too. His enthusiasm got him into a lot of trouble. But God was patient, just as He is patient with each of us. Sometimes He must put us in the desert for a time in order to season us so that Christ is allowed to reign supreme in the process.

Before you act, pray and seek the mind of Christ until you know it is God behind the action. Check it out with others. You may save yourself a trip to the desert.

January 26

Passing the Tests

The Lord has torn the kingdom out of your hands and given it to one of your neighbors—to David.   1 Samuel 28:17b

When God anoints a person, a pattern of testing appears to take place at specific times in the leader's life. God often takes each leader through four major tests to determine if that person will achieve God's ultimate call on his or her life. The person's response to these tests is the deciding factor in whether they can advance to the next level of responsibility in God's Kingdom.

Control—Control is one of the first tests. Saul spent most of his time as king trying to prevent others from getting what he had. Saul never got to the place with God in which he was a grateful recipient of God's goodness to him. Saul was a religious controller. This control led to disobedience and ultimately being rejected by God because Saul no longer was a vessel God could use.

Bitterness—Every major character in the Bible was hurt by another person at one time or another. Jesus was hurt deeply when Judas, a trusted follower, betrayed Him. Despite knowing this was going to happen, Jesus responded by washing Judas' feet. Every anointed leader will have a Judas experience at one time or another. God watches us to see how we will respond to this test. Will we take up an offense? Will we retaliate? It is one of the most difficult tests to pass.

Power—Power is the opposite of servanthood. Jesus had all authority in Heaven and earth, so satan tempted Jesus at the top of the mountain to use His power to remove Himself from a difficult circumstance. How will we use the power and influence God has entrusted to us? Do we seek to gain more power? There is a common phrase in the investment community, "He who has the gold rules." Jesus modeled the opposite. He was the ultimate servant leader.

Greed—This is a difficult one. Money has the ability to have great influence for either good or bad. When it is a focus in our life, it becomes a tool of destruction. When it is a by-product, it can become a great blessing. Many leaders started out well—only to be derailed once prosperity became a part of their life. There are thousands who can blossom spiritually in adversity; only a few can thrive spiritually under prosperity.

As leaders, we must be aware when we are being tested. You can be confident that each one of these tests will be thrown your way if God calls you for His purposes. Will you pass these tests? Ask for God's grace today to walk through these tests victoriously.

January 27

Seeing the Works of God

Others went out on the sea in ships; they were merchants on the mighty waters. They saw the works of the Lord....
Psalm 107:23-24a

When you were a child, perhaps you may have gone to the ocean for a vacation. I recall wading out until the waves began crashing on my knees. As long as I could stand firm, the waves were of no concern to me. However, as I moved farther and farther into the ocean, I had less control over my ability to stand. Sometimes the current was so strong it moved me down the beach, and I even lost my bearings at times. But I have never gone so far into the ocean that I was not able to control the situation.

Sometimes God takes us into such deep waters that we lose control of the situation, and we have no choice but to fully trust in His care for us. This is doing business in great waters. It is in these great waters that we see the works of God.

The Scriptures tell us that the disciples testified of what they saw and heard. It was the power behind the gospel, not the words themselves, that changed the world. The power wasn't seen until circumstances got to the point that there were no alternatives but God. Sometimes God has to take us into the deep water in order to give us the privilege to see His works.

Sometimes God takes us into the deep waters of life for an extended time. Joseph was taken into deep waters of adversity for 17 years. Rejection by his brothers, enslavement to Pharaoh, and imprisonment were the deep waters for Joseph. During those deep waters, he experienced dreams, a special anointing of his gifts to administrate, and great wisdom beyond his years. The deep water was preparation for a task that was so great he never could have imagined it. He was to see God's works more clearly than anyone in his generation. God had too much at stake for a 30-year-old to mess it up. So, God took Joseph through the deep waters of preparation to ensure that he would survive what he was about to face. Pride normally engulfs such young servants who have such access to power at such a young age.

If God chooses to take us into deep waters, it is for a reason. The greater the calling, the deeper the water. Trust in His knowledge that your deep waters are preparation to see the works of God in your life.

January 28

Placing Trust in Our Strength

So the Lord sent a plague on Israel, and seventy thousand men of Israel fell dead.   1 Chronicles 21:14

When was the last time your overconfidence cost the lives of 70,000 men? That is exactly what happened to David. David made what might appear to be an innocent request of his general, Joab. But the minute Joab heard the request, he cringed. He knew David was in big trouble for this one. You see, to number the troops was a great sin in Israel because it was against the law. Why? Because it demonstrated that you were placing more trust in numbers than in the living God. David displayed enough pride to cost the lives of 70,000 fighting men. God gave him three choices of punishment for his sin. A plague was the one he chose, and it resulted in the loss of 70,000.

Throughout Israel's history, God set the stage for battles to be won, miracles to take place, and people to exercise faith. The stage was always set so that man could not take credit for what God did. Consider Gideon who was only allowed 300 men to fight an army of 100,000. Consider Jehoshaphat, who had to lead his army with his singers. God defeated the enemy. Consider Joshua, who was told simply to walk around Jericho seven times, and they would get victory. God did things in some very unconventional ways!

How does this relate to you and me as businesspeople? Well, the minute you and I place more trust in our abilities than in God, we are guilty of numbering the troops. How does He punish us? Sometimes it's through letting a deal go sour. Sometimes it's through problems with a client or vendor. Sometimes situations just blow up in our face. Other times, He lets us go on for a long time doing our own thing, but eventually He deals with it.

The lesson here is to learn daily and complete dependence on God. Use your gifts and abilities through the power of the Holy Spirit. Ask Him daily for direction and wisdom. His ways won't always line up with conventional wisdom. When we begin depending on our abilities only, God has a responsibility to make known to us who is the giver of the blessings.

January 29

In the Zone

> *Be strong and very courageous. Be careful to obey all the law my servant Moses gave you; do not turn from it to the right or to the left, that you may be successful wherever you go.*　　　　　Joshua 1:7

In sports, there is a term known as "in the zone." It is a description of a person executing his skills so well that total concentration is taking place, and the athlete is performing flawlessly. It is a wonderful feeling. Performance seems effortless because it comes so easily. For the tennis player, it is hitting every shot right where he wants. For the baseball pitcher, it is throwing to a strike zone that seems big as a house. For the golfer, the fairways are wide, and the hole is big. Everything is flowing just right.

I grew up playing competitive golf. I turned pro out of college for a few years, but later God led me away from playing professionally. When I played competitively, I knew when I was in the zone and when I wasn't. A few years ago, I played in my club championship. It was the opening round, and I was in the zone. I recall the difference was that my mental attitude was focused on executing the swing I wanted to make with little regard to the outcome. I could visualize the swing so well; it was like a movie picture in my mind. Very little thought was given to the outcome of the shot. I knew that if I could make the right swing, the outcome would take care of itself. That day I shot four under par 68. I went on to win the golf tournament. I have had few such days of being "in the zone."

Obedience in the Christian life is being in the zone. When we live a life of obedience, we begin to experience the reality of God like never before. Wisdom grows in our life. Meaning and purpose are accelerated. In the early Church, the Hebrews gained wisdom through obedience. Later, the Greeks were characterized as gaining wisdom through reason and analysis. Today, we live in a very Greek-influenced Church. Many Christians determine if they will obey based on whether the outcome will be beneficial to them. Imagine if the early Church had adopted this philosophy. No walls would have fallen down at Jericho. No Red Sea would have parted. No one would have been healed. No coins would have been found in the mouth of a fish. Reason and analysis would not have led to making the obedient decision. Trust and obey. Leave the outcome to God.

January 30

A Call to Worship

...but they did not listen to him because of their discouragement and cruel bondage.   Exodus 6:9

It is very difficult to lead when those you are leading believe they have been mistreated and have lost all hope. Such was the case when God called Moses to bring the people of Israel out of Egypt. They had lived under many years of oppression and slavery. Yet God heard their cry. He sent someone to bring them out of slavery "so that they might worship God" (see Ex. 8:1). Interesting that God didn't say, "to serve Him." Above all else, God desires our worship. A person cannot enter into true worship of God while still in slavery and bondage.

In Proverbs, the writer tells us that "hope deferred makes the heart sick" (Prov. 13:12a). There is a place in life where life becomes so discouraging and hopeless that we lose all hope, and it can actually make us sick. I have been at this place; it is a scary condition. It brings you to the edge of despair.

The people would not listen to Moses. Yet God did not deliver immediately. In fact, it would be many plagues later before ultimate deliverance would take place. Why does God withhold deliverance at times? It is in order to bring greater glory from the situation. It isn't because He doesn't care. It is because His plan for mankind is resting in these events. It is a finely tuned plan that involves many people and situations—all operating at the same time. It can seem cruel at times. But God knows that His children cannot worship Him if they are in bondage and lose all hope. He won't allow us to be tempted beyond what we can bear. So He has a plan of deliverance for each of us. This plan is not always the kind of deliverance we might think is best. It sometimes has pain surrounding the deliverance. When a mother gives birth, that child is delivered into this world through much pain. But with that pain comes great joy on the other side. Every mother will say the pain was worth it because of the exceeding joy that child brought in the midst of the pain.

What are you in bondage to today? What keeps you from entering true worship? Work can keep us in bondage if we fail to enter into freedom in Christ during our workday. Today, ask God to show you the areas of bondage that you are living in so that you may worship Him.

January 31

Sacrificing at What Cost

> ..."I will not sacrifice to the Lord my God burnt offerings that cost me nothing." 2 Samuel 24:24

One day I was having lunch with a man who had a certain amount of notoriety in his life. After a time of getting to know each other, he said, "How can I help you?" Those words surprised me coming from a man who obviously already had many requirements on his time. My first thought was that I was impressed with the individual. My next thought was to wonder whether it was a genuine offer or just an effort to impress me with his humility and Christian piety. I have since discovered he was sincere.

This encounter reminded me that each of us must be willing to give to others without a motive to get anything in return. It is simply an act of serving others. Jesus said that we must consider others more important than ourselves. When is the last time you did something for another without a motive of getting anything in return?

When King David came to offer a sacrifice and pray for the removal of a plague on Israel, he was given the opportunity to make the sacrifice without the cost of purchasing the sacrificial animals.

> *But the king replied to Araunah, "No, I insist on paying you for it. I will not sacrifice to the Lord my God burnt offerings that cost me nothing." So David bought the threshing floor and the oxen and paid fifty shekels of silver for them. David built an altar to the Lord there and sacrificed burnt offerings and fellowship offerings. Then the Lord answered prayer in behalf of the land, and the plague on Israel was stopped* (2 Samuel 24:24-25).

David, understanding the principle of giving, said he could not offer anything to God that did not cost him something. Otherwise, it was not a sacrificial gift.

When is the last time you sacrificed for another that it cost you something with no expectation of getting anything in return? We can all give something to others, such as our time, our money, or our expertise. This is real Christianity that models the Spirit of Christ. The next time you meet with someone, why not consider how you might be a blessing to that person. Why not ask, "How can I help you?"

February 1

A Talking Donkey

The donkey said to Balaam, "Am I not your own donkey, which you have always ridden, to this day?...." Numbers 22:30

Most businesspeople I know tend to be task-oriented, motivated visionaries. And they will do just about anything to make their projects successful. This great strength can, if not properly bridled by the Holy Spirit, be a great weakness in their ability to fulfill God's will in their life.

Sometimes we want something to succeed so much that we fail to listen to that little voice inside trying to warn us by directing us on a different path. Such was the case of Balaam. He started out as a man of God, but then took the path of a "prophet-for-hire." God was not pleased with Balaam's decision to respond to a pagan king's request that he curse Israel. As Balaam rode his donkey to keep his appointment with the king, God sent the angel of the Lord to stand in the way and oppose Balaam. Although Balaam did not see the angel, his donkey did. Three times the donkey turned from the path and three times Balaam beat the animal in anger. Finally, the donkey turned around, and to Balaam's shock and amazement, began to speak to him, admonishing his master for beating him. Imagine a donkey talking to you! He warned Balaam of the angel of death who was standing in the road with a sword drawn, ready to kill Balaam if he continued.

There are times when pushing harder, trying to manipulate the circumstance, or pressing those around you is not the response to have to the roadblock. God may be trying to have you reconsider your ways. God may be doing one of four things when you are faced with an obstacle: 1) He's blocking it to protect you. 2) His timing to complete this stage is not the same as yours, and He may need you to go through a process of character refinement. 3) He may want other players to get in place, and the circumstances are not yet ready for them to enter. 4) He may be using the process to develop patience in you. Relying on the Holy Spirit to know which one applies to your situation is the key to moving in God's timing.

February 2

Giving Him the Key

Here I am! I stand at the door and knock. If anyone hears My voice
and opens the door, I will come in and eat with him, and he with Me.
Revelation 3:20

A friend of mine tells the story of an encounter he had with a very important government official—the head of state for a country. In the course of some meetings with my friend, the official came up to him and said, "I perceive that there is a difference between you and me. Is it because I come from a different denomination?" My friend began to explain why there was a difference.

"If you were to come to my home, I would invite you in as an honored guest. As my guest, you would enjoy everything I had in my home. However, you would still be a guest. You would not have the keys to the home, and your authority in that home would be merely as a guest. However, if I said to you that I am turning over my home to you and you now have the keys to my home, I would be your servant with the responsibility to run the home through your counsel and direction." My friend continued, "This is the difference between you and me. I have given Jesus the keys to my home [heart]. You have merely invited Him in to yours as an honored guest."

"How can I do this too?" the man replied.

"All you have to do is invite Him in as the new owner."

The man did this and is now allowing Jesus to rule and reign in every detail of his life.

So often many of us enter a relationship with God that brings us salvation. This is the gospel of salvation. But what God really desires for us is to experience the gospel of the Kingdom. He wants us to experience His power and presence every day of our lives and to see His hand at work in us. This only happens when we give Him the key to our life; He must be more than an honored guest.

Where are you today? Has your life with God been more like an honored-guest relationship, or does He have the key to your life?

February 3

Empty Mangers

Where there are no oxen, the manger is empty, but from the strength of an ox comes an abundant harvest.   Proverbs 14:4

When Jesus came into this world, He chose to be born in a most unusual place—a manger. It was no more than a livery stable with goats, oxen, and other livestock animals. There is a distinctive characteristic about a place like this. It is filled with odors and dung from the animals. God seems to work best among the unpleasantness of circumstances. In fact, "where there are no oxen, the manger is empty." What is this really saying? I believe it is saying that in order for Jesus to be present, we must invite those things that bring with them "messes to clean up." God works among the messy things in our lives. And from these messes come an abundant harvest. This is what He did with all His highly used servants in the Bible. God is filled with paradoxes. Why can't life be seamless and smooth? Because God likes to show Himself in the midst of the messes of life. This is what brings us into the harvests. So often the bigger the mess, the bigger the harvest.

When a major road-construction project takes place in a crowded city street, it appears to be absolute chaos. It is inconvenient, slow-moving and tends to get us irritated because it appears we are moving much slower than we would like. It is ugly, and so much of what we see is torn up. But when we look at that same area a few months or years later, we see why the construction was necessary. There was meaning to the mess. It actually made life so much better for those who would use the road.

It has been through the messiest of times in my business and personal life that God has revealed His power and strength in my life. It was when these "oxen" of hardship have walked into my manger that the greatest harvest was manifest. However, when I have sought to remove the "oxen" and rid myself of the odor and the mess, I have fought the ultimate work of God.

God works in mangers.

February 4

Obedience With a Cost

Ever since I went to Pharaoh to speak in Your name, he has brought trouble upon this people, and You have not rescued Your people at all. Exodus 5:23

Have you ever felt like you have been obedient to the Lord for something He called you to do and all you get are more roadblocks? This is the way Moses felt. When Moses went to tell Pharaoh to release the people because God said so, Pharaoh simply got angry and made the people make bricks without straw. Moses caught the blame for this from the people. Moses was just learning what obedience really means in God's Kingdom. You see, Moses had not even begun to release plagues upon Egypt. He hadn't even gotten started yet in his calling, and he was complaining about his circumstances. There were many more encounters with Pharaoh to come, and many more plagues with no deliverances in sight. Why would God tell Moses that He is going to deliver them and not do it?

It was all in timing. God never said *when* He was going to deliver. He just said He would. In the next chapter, we find Moses arguing with God about not being capable of the job God had called him to:

But Moses said to the Lord, "If the Israelites will not listen to me, why would Pharaoh listen to me, since I speak with faltering lips?" Now the Lord spoke to Moses and Aaron about the Israelites and Pharaoh king of Egypt, and He commanded them to bring the Israelites out of Egypt (Exodus 6:12-13).

Do you get the feeling God was losing His patience?

God had a good reason for His delays. He said, "And the Egyptians will know that I am the Lord when I stretch out My hand against Egypt and bring the Israelites out of it" (Ex. 7:5). God not only wanted the people of Israel but also the Egyptians to know Him. It would be the greatest show of God's power on earth.

God often causes delays in our lives that we cannot understand. Sometimes it seems our obedience is not getting rewarded. Jesus said He learned obedience through the things He suffered (see Heb. 5:8). Imagine that—Jesus having to learn obedience. What does that say for you and me? Sometimes God's delays are simply because He wants more glory in the situation, more recognition, more Christ-likeness in you and me through greater patience and obedience. Faint not, for the promise may yet come.

February 5

Understanding Your Gift

Now about spiritual gifts, brothers, I do not want you to be ignorant.
1 Corinthians 12:1

In First Corinthians 12 and Romans 12, the apostle Paul is teaching us about the role of spiritual gifts in the Church. He correlates these gifts to a human body, telling us that each person's gift helps the whole Body of the Church. This is such an important principle for us to learn. I must say I learned this principle regarding my own spiritual gift the hard way.

"God will never speak as strongly to you as to someone else," said my mentor to me one day. The statement shocked me. "What in the world do you mean by that?" I argued with him.

"Your spiritual gift of administration/leading is one of the most dangerous gifts in the whole Body of Christ. The reason is that you can see the big picture better than anyone else, and you're so task-oriented that you will run people into the ground getting your project completed because you think you see it so clearly. That is why the best friend you could ever have is someone with a prophetic gift to discern whether the big picture you see is actually the picture God is directing. It is the one gift that can almost stand alone better than any other—at least that is the opinion of the one with that gift."

Oh, how I have learned this lesson the hard way! He was so right. There have been many a church staff destroyed by a person with the gift of administration. During my years as an ad agency owner, I saw how I stressed out my staff because of the tremendous load I put on them with multiple projects. It was so easy for me because the more balls I had juggling, the better I felt. I was oblivious to how my multi-task personality impacted those around me.

Today, I have some special relationships with intercessors and prophetic people whom I depend on for confirmation of direction. I have learned their spiritual gifts of discernment are of great value in determining strategic direction. I have learned that God has placed within each person a spiritual gift that is designed to make the Body of Christ function better for His purposes. When we discover the spiritual gifts God has placed in those around us, we are better able to see the Body function as a real body—totally dependent on one another. Some of us are more sensitive to God's voice because God has gifted us in that way. Others of us are less sensitive because God wants us to depend on others in the Body for their gifts. Find out whom God has placed around you today and discover a new dimension of spiritual productivity.

February 6

The Black Hole

> …*"My grace is sufficient for you…."*   2 Corinthians 12:9

If you are older than 35, you may recall the early days of the space program. I remember the early spacecraft launch with John Glenn. One of the most exciting and tense moments of his return to earth was his reentry to the earth's atmosphere. I recall the diagram on television of the heat shield on the capsule that had to withstand incredible temperatures to avoid complete destruction. There was a blackout period for several minutes in which mission control had no radio contact. He was in the "black hole." It was a tense time. Either he would make it through, or the spacecraft would burn up in the atmosphere. There were several minutes of silence that seemed like an eternity. Then, mission control shouted with joy when they reestablished contact with the spacecraft. It was a time of rejoicing.

Have you ever had a time when you were in a spiritual black hole in your life? I have. The pressure was unbearable. No sense of God's presence. No sense of anything going on around me. God was about as far away as the man in the moon—at least from my perspective. I think every Christian who is called to make a significant difference in his world experiences times like these. These are the times when we question the reality of God, the love of God, the personal care of God. And He demonstrates to us that He was there all the time. These are "faith experiences" that God does in every person who is called to a higher level of relationship with Him. These times are needful in order to know that we have the "heat shield" that can withstand the incredible heat that comes when we follow Him with a whole heart—a heart that is radical in a commitment to fully follow His ways. Elisha had that spirit. He slaughtered his 12 oxen and burned his plowing equipment so that he would not have the opportunity to return to anything if God didn't come through (see 1 Kings 19:21).

The apostle Paul asked God to remove the heat from his own life one time. God's answer was not what he wanted to hear.

> But He said to me, My grace (My favor and loving-kindness and mercy) is enough for you [sufficient against any danger and enables you to bear the trouble manfully]; for My strength and power are made perfect (fulfilled and completed) and show themselves most effective in [your] weakness. Therefore, I will all the more gladly glory in my weaknesses and infirmities, that the strength and power of Christ (the Messiah) may rest (yes, may pitch a tent over and dwell) upon me! (2 Corinthians 12:9 AMP)

How's your heat shield today? Can it withstand the heat that would want to burn up everything in your life not based in Him? Christ said, "My grace is sufficient." Is that really true in your life? Let His grace be your shield today.

February 7

Decision-Making

Trust in the Lord with all your heart and lean not on your own understanding. Proverbs 3:5

This is one of the most quoted verses in the Bible related to gaining wisdom and direction from God. Yet I have never heard one teaching on this passage that teaches what I believe the psalmist is really saying. The first part is pretty easy; we are to trust with all our heart. But the next part is not so clear. We are not to lean on our own understanding. If we are not to lean on our own understanding, on whose understanding are we to lean? God's!

Throughout the Old Testament we find that God set up structures by which those in authority made decisions. God has always set a principle whereby we are to seek Him in all our decisions, that He might truly make our decisions. In the Old Testament, the priest made decisions based on which way the Urim and Thummim fell inside his breastplate. The casting of lots was another means of allowing a decision to be left with God. Proverbs says, "The lot is cast into the lap, but its every decision is from the Lord" (Prov. 16:33). Another means of making a decision was through the agreement of two or three. No one could be guilty of any crime without the witness of two or three. This was a biblical way of confirming a matter. Still another means of making a decision is through a multitude of counselors.

Given all these scenarios, what are we to gain from these examples? We are told in Jeremiah 17:9a, "The heart is deceitful above all things and beyond cure." So what really protects each of us from the deceit of our own heart? I believe it is the combination of all the above. When we get to a place with God that our decisions are accountable to others, whether that be a wife, a board, or a few close friends who are committed to the same godly ideals, this is when we are protected from the deceit of our own heart. This is one of the hardest things to yield to God—the right to make our own decisions. Yet, it is the most elementary principle God requires of us to receive His blessing in our lives.

This principle took a long time for me to appropriate. However, today I can tell you I would never make a major decision without the counsel of others who are close to me. Relational accountability has become lost in our culture due to our hunger for independence. I have experienced too often the hardship that results from making decisions that God isn't behind. Walking in obedience is the only real freedom in Christ.

February 8

"You Want Me to Do What?"

... *"Throw your net on the right side of the boat and you will find some."* John 21:6a

The disciples were fishing. It was after Jesus had been crucified. Peter had gone through his most agonizing moment in which he had denied Jesus three times. He had lost a friend. No doubt he probably wondered whether the last three years were a dream. What now?

Peter had been prepared three years, but he was not going out to preach; he was going fishing. He had returned to his trade of days gone by. He had a level of experience with Jesus that no other human on earth can boast. This was the third encounter he was about to have with Jesus after His resurrection. Jesus looked to Peter and John in their boat and made a suggestion.

"Friends, haven't you any fish?"

"No," they answered.

He said, "Throw your net on the right side of the boat and you will find some" (Jn. 21:6a).

Now, if you are as seasoned in your fishing as these guys were, wouldn't you be a bit irritated if a stranger suggested that you simply put your nets over the other side to catch some fish? Yet we find that they took this stranger's advice. Once they were obedient, the Lord revealed Himself.

When they followed Jesus' advice, the catch was enormous—153 fish in total. In most cases such a haul would have broken the net. Jesus invited them to have breakfast with Him—fish and bread; He had already started the fire. I can only imagine that this scene would resemble some buddies going out and camping together.

There is so much that we are to learn in this passage about God's ways. As a businessperson, we must understand that after we have spent years with Jesus, this does not always mean we must leave our professions in order to fully follow Jesus. Peter went back to his profession—fishing. It was here that Jesus asked him a simple question: Do you love Me and will you feed My sheep? He didn't say to Peter, "Fishing is a waste of time for you now, Peter." This recommissioning was in the area of his original calling—his work. We need not feel that we must go to the "mission field" to please Jesus. Our work is our mission field. We must, however, make a paradigm shift in our thinking about our place in the business world. We must have an overriding sense of mission and ministry that comes out of that business. This is what is meant when we say that we must all be circumcised before we can enter the Promised Land. When this happens, we can expect to see God fill the nets with His blessings. He wants to do this because He now owns the net, and He can trust us to manage it.

February 9

Sowing in Tears

Those who sow in tears will reap with songs of joy.   Psalm 126:5

Psalm 126 describes an interesting process that goes against our natural tendencies when we are taken into a difficult period in our lives. Whenever we are hurled into a crisis that brings tears, our tendency is to retreat or recoil in fear and hurt. However, there is a better way that God tells us to handle such times of travail.

Those who sow in tears will reap with songs of joy. "He who goes out weeping, carrying seed to sow, will return with songs of joy, carrying sheaves with him" (Ps. 126:5-6). God is telling us that if we will do what is unnatural for us in these circumstances, He will make sure that what we sow in tears *will* return in joy. This is one of the most important lessons I have learned when faced with difficult circumstances. Rather than sit back and allow self-pity and discouragement to consume us, we should plant seed during this time. Reach out to a person who needs a friend. Invest in the life of another. See where you can be a blessing to someone. Give of yourself.

The psalmist acknowledges that we are doing this while we are in our pain. However, during this time we are to sow seed. That seed will return to us in another form. Here is what will happen when we do this. "He who goes out weeping, carrying seed to sow, will return with songs of joy, carrying sheaves with him." We will receive joy and fruit from the seed that we plant during this time. Sheaves represent the fruit of a harvest. We will actually get a harvest from this seed.

"You must not let the circumstances destroy you! Too many in the Kingdom are counting on you to come through this because of the calling on your life!" Those were the words spoken to me by a friend one time when I was in the midst of a very difficult business and personal circumstance that was threatening to destroy me emotionally. This person saw what God was doing and the fruit that God wanted to bring from these circumstances. Sometimes we need others around us to push us through the difficult times. If you find yourself in a difficult place today, see where you can sow some seed. Soon you will be reaping songs of joy.

February 10

Precious Deaths

Precious in the sight of the Lord is the death of His saints.
                                                                Psalm 116:15

The Bible often speaks of death as a requirement of living a life in Christ. This death is not a physical death, but a spiritual death. It is a death of the old so the new can be raised. It is the life of Christ that is raised in us. However, this death can be painful if we do not choose to willingly allow this "circumcision of heart" to have its way. If we are not circumcised of heart, we do not enter into God's promises. Moses was called to deliver a people from slavery. But when he was about to return to Egypt to begin what God called Him to do, God almost killed him. He had failed to take care of the details of obedience. In this case, it was that all the males in his family were to be circumcised. This oversight on Moses' part almost cost him his life. Imagine that—God prepared a man 40 years, and yet, he was almost disqualified because of an oversight. "At a lodging place on the way, the Lord met Moses and was about to kill him. But Zipporah took a flint knife, cut off her son's foreskin and touched Moses' feet with it..." (Ex. 4:24).

None of us will ever enter the Promised Land of full blessing with God unless we have this same circumcision of heart. The psalmist above accurately describes the process of circumcising the heart.

Precious in the sight of the Lord is the death of His saints. O Lord, truly I am Your servant; I am Your servant, the son of Your maid-servant; You have freed me from my chains (Psalm 116:15-16).

We cannot be free to be God's servant until this death takes place in each of us. When this death takes place, we become free—free from the chains of sin that held us back from becoming completely His. Oh, what freedom there is when this death takes place. No longer are we held to the sin of materialism, fear, self-effort, or anxiety; for we are dead to these things.

The Bible speaks of the seed that must die in order for it to spring up and give new life.

I tell you the truth, unless a kernel of wheat falls to the ground and dies, it remains only a single seed. But if it dies, it produces many seeds. The man who loves his life will lose it, while the man who hates his life in this world will keep it for eternal life (John 12:24-25).

Each of us must ask the Lord if our seed has died. Is it in the ground now, yielding the fruit of brokenness before Him? This is the great paradox of a life in Christ—the circumcision of heart and the death process. Ask God to free you to become all that He wants you to be today.

February 11

Becoming a Fool

The fear of the Lord is the beginning of knowledge, but fools despise wisdom and discipline.   Proverbs 1:7

Marvin Wilson, author of *Our Father Abraham*, has written incisively about the various meanings for our word *fool*:

In Biblical wisdom literature, the pupils of the sages and mentors are the unwise, often termed "fools" (Prov. 1:7) or "simple one" (1:22). In wisdom literature, the different levels of fools—both young and old—are the raw material on which the sages had to work, and they represent the varying degrees of rawness. Perhaps as much as anything else, the term fool is descriptive of an attitude, bent of mind, or direction in life, which needs correcting. The various Hebrew words for fool occur more than a hundred times in the book of Proverbs. [Marvin Wilson, *Our Father Abraham* (Grand Rapids, Michigan: Wm. B. Eerdmans Publishing Company, 1989), 284-286.]

The reference to someone being a fool was not necessarily a negative term. A simple fool, or *peti*, was a person who made mistakes but quickly righted them and was restored to fellowship with God and with others. King David was a simple fool, one who made mistakes, but kept a repentant heart toward God. This is why God did not turn away from him for his many sins.

The hardened fool, *kesil* and *ewil*, makes mistakes, but never learns from them and will not listen to others. Such people can expect God's reproof to continue and will eat the fruit of their own way (see Prov. 1:31-32). The hardened fool "returns to his own vomit." King Saul was a hardened fool, one who made mistakes and continued in them even after realizing he was wrong. We're going to err in our ways. The question is, once we know we have made a mistake before God, do we make the necessary adjustments that will allow Him to intervene on our behalf? And will we avoid the same course of action in the future? God says that if we do, He will pour out His Spirit on us (see Prov. 1:23). He will make known His words to us.

The third level of fool mentioned in Proverbs is the mocking fool or *letz*. The mocking fool mocks the things of God. This word means "scoffer" or "scorner." When you encounter cynical people who disregard the things of God, you know these people are "mocking fools."

The fourth level of fool is the God-denying fool or *nabal*. This term relates to the morally wicked person who ignores the disgrace he brings on his family and who despises holiness (see Prov. 17:21). This person says, "There is no God." By failing to acknowledge God for who He is, the nabal declares himself to be a "God-denying" fool.

I have found that it is helpful to try to understand if people are teachable. Are they simple fools, those who make mistakes but seek to learn from them? I can work with those people. But if I sense I am working with a hardened fool, I know I should not spend much time on that person. Jesus did not spend much time trying to convince the rich young ruler. He presented truth, and let him make his decision. Some people must get broken before they can become simple fools. Sometimes it is simply better to let satan chew on people until the ground is fertile enough to present truth to them.

February 12

Worthless Idols

> *Those who cling to worthless idols forfeit the grace that could be theirs.*   Jonah 2:8

Have you ever exercised your will over the will of God? Have you ever been so willful that you were going to go your own way no matter what God said? If so, you have been at the same place as the prophet Jonah. God called Jonah to deliver a message to God's people as a warning. Jonah flatly refused. It was Jonah's will over God's. Guess who won?

Talk about willpower; Jonah had it! In fact, he was so rebellious toward God's will that he got on a ship to go the opposite direction. But he couldn't go far enough. The omnipotence of God caught up with Jonah, and he was hurled overboard when the seas became rough and the ship's crew figured Jonah was the source of their problems. Overboard he went and into the belly of that big fish.

God has a way of getting us to rethink our decisions, to reconsider our position. In fact, we see the extent of Jonah's willfulness by the amount of time he was willing to hang out in the belly of that fish—three full days. Then, Jonah decides enough is enough! Obedience is better than this fish belly and seaweed.

From inside the fish, Jonah prayed to the Lord his God.

He said: "In my distress I called to the Lord, and He answered me. From the depths of the grave I called for help, and You listened to my cry. You hurled me into the deep, into the very heart of the seas, and the currents swirled about me; all Your waves and breakers swept over me. I said, 'I have been banished from Your sight; yet I will look again toward Your holy temple.' The engulfing waters threatened me, the deep surrounded me; seaweed was wrapped around my head. To the roots of the mountains I sank down; the earth beneath barred me in forever. But You brought my life up from the pit, O Lord my God. When my life was ebbing away, I remembered You, Lord, and my prayer rose to You, to Your holy temple. Those who cling to worthless idols forfeit the grace that could be theirs. But I, with a song of thanksgiving, will sacrifice to You. What I have vowed I will make good. Salvation comes from the Lord." And the Lord commanded the fish, and it vomited Jonah onto dry land. Then the word of the Lord came to Jonah a second time: "Go to the great city of Nineveh and proclaim to it the message I give you." Jonah obeyed the word of the Lord and went to Nineveh (Jonah 2:2–3:3a).

In the midst of realizing his own calamity, Jonah made a seemingly out-of-context statement: "Those who cling to worthless idols forfeit the grace that could be theirs." Jonah was thinking of the sailors who threw him overboard and how they prayed to worthless idols. In the business world, we rub shoulders with those who cling to worthless idols every day. How tragic.

But this story's primary message is for every believer. And I can identify with Jonah. There's been many a man placed in the "belly of the fish" to encourage him to fulfill the purposes of God for which He called him. Jonah's situation changed immediately upon his obedience. Obedience is a mysterious thing. Jesus had to learn it through the things He suffered (see Heb. 5:8). If Jesus had to learn obedience through suffering, what does that mean for you and me? Sometimes willing obedience requires encouragement.

February 13

Time to Hear

He who loves Me will be loved by My Father, and I too will love him and show Myself to him.   John 14:21b

We live in a day of 12-step programs for this, four points to success for that, and all forms of programmed means of becoming successful. Have you ever wondered how you can guarantee a greater revelation of Jesus in your life? Jesus tells us how this can be done. It is all tied to obedience. In John, He tells us the following: "Whoever has My commands and obeys them, he is the one who loves Me. He who loves Me will be loved by My Father, and I too will love him and show Myself to him" (Jn. 14:21). The key here is in the last three words. He will show Himself to us because of our loving Him through our obedience. The more obedient we become, the more revelation of His presence we will feel in our life. Jeremiah tells us, "Call to Me and I will answer you and tell you great and unsearchable things you do not know" (Jer. 33:3).

Many Christians wonder why they cannot hear or sense God's presence in their life. It is because they do not seek Him with a whole heart, and they are not obedient to the things He has asked. God does not show us the next move until we are obedient to the first thing He has spoken to us. It is a progressive process. He entrusts the small things to us first, then moves us to the larger. I was like many today who are so focused on seeking the activity of God rather than seeking God Himself. Hebrews tells us that God rewards those who diligently seek Him. In the Old Testament we are told, "But if from there you seek the Lord your God, you will find Him if you look for Him with all your heart and with all your soul" (Deut. 4:29).

I realized if I was going to hear God's voice, I had to make time to seek Him and hear Him. I had to spend focused time alone reading, studying, and seeking His face only. Jesus set the model for this when He often left the crowds to be alone and seek His heavenly Father. I also had to tune my "radio" to His frequency. Static comes into that frequency when I am disobedient. My level of seeking determines the power of my "radio" to reach Him. The more I seek Him, the more I hear Him. Seek the Lord today so that you may be empowered by His presence.

February 14

Having Eyes for One

Then they were willing to take Him into the boat, and immediately the boat reached the shore where they were heading.   John 6:21

The disciples were traveling across the lake to Capernaum when a strong wind arose and the waters grew rough. Suddenly they saw a figure on the water, and they were terrified until Jesus called out to them and identified Himself.

Isn't that the first thing we do when unexpected calamities or even something that we have never experienced before comes into our life? We panic until we can see that God is behind these events in our lives. In Romans, Paul tells us that, "from Him and through Him and to Him are all things. To Him be the glory forever! Amen" (Rom. 11:36). God has an eternal filter in which nothing can touch us unless He permits it. Even satan must have permission to touch us. And God may even use satan for His own ends, as in the case of Job.

God shows us a second principle in this story. The Scriptures say when the disciples were willing to take Jesus into the boat, they reached the shore where they were heading. Recently, I was faced with some very difficult circumstances in my business. I had no income for some time, and I saw no immediate remedy to the situation. The circumstances created fear in my heart. The anxiety began to grow until, one day after my evening prayer walk, the Lord said, "How long do you want to keep your eyes on the circumstances instead of Me? Do you think I have brought you this far to throw you into the water?" The truth was that I was halfway in already because my eyes were looking at the "big waves" surrounding my boat. One night, in a support group for divorced men, the leader asked each of us to keep our eyes on two men who were going to walk from the room. One man represented Jesus, the other, our circumstances. "Now, I want you to keep your eyes on both people," he said. The men stood up and began walking across the room in opposite directions. It was impossible to keep looking at each of them at the same time. So we had to choose which we would focus on.

The lesson was clear. We could not keep our eyes on Jesus and our circumstance at the same time.

February 15

A Joseph Calling

And he sent a man before them—Joseph, sold as a slave.

Psalm 105:17

God is doing a unique work around the world today. He is raising up Josephs throughout the world. Some are still in the "pit" stage of their pilgrimage, while others are heading toward fruitfulness. What does it take for a man to become a true Joseph? It takes years of preparation and testing to be a true Joseph. It takes what the psalmist says in Psalm 105:

He called down famine on the land and destroyed all their supplies of food; and he sent a man before them—Joseph, sold as a slave. They bruised his feet with shackles, his neck was put in irons, till what he foretold came to pass, till the word of the Lord proved him true. The king sent and released him, the ruler of peoples set him free (Psalm 105:16-20).

A true Joseph is one who is a provider both spiritually and materially for those in the Body of Christ. It is a person who understands that he is simply a manager of all that God has entrusted to him. It is a person who has humility and a broken and contrite heart before God. But how does God prepare modern-day Josephs?

Modern-day Josephs are prepared through their own versions of bruised feet, with shackles and necks put in irons. It is often through the adversity of failed finances, failed marriages, failed relationships, and broken dreams. These are the things that try men the most. These are the things God uses to allow the Josephs of our day to be proven by the Word of the Lord. Once proven, God brings them out of their prisons and uses them mightily for His purposes. Joseph went through his own trials—not because of any failure, but because of an incredible calling: to save and provide for an entire nation. God had to prepare this man with 13 years of broken dreams and humble circumstances in order to break every ounce of pride and self-will. God could not afford to have a 30-year-old steeped in arrogance and pride running an entire nation.

When I attended a world conference on global evangelization in South Africa, I was privileged to sit among 45 other men from different parts of the world who had a Joseph calling on their lives. These men of means had humility of heart and a spirit unlike any others I have met in my country. Each one had his own Joseph story. It was an incredible scene that changed my life and my own view of business. This allowed me to see firsthand this phenomenon that is going on throughout the world. Many believe God is raising up these servants to prepare for a worldwide economic earthquake and to fund a global harvest of souls. Even since this conference, one nation is being dramatically affected because of a Joseph who has stepped forward to fulfill his calling for that nation. It is an awesome demonstration of God's power working today.

Are you willing to allow God to do whatever it takes for you to become a true Joseph? Ask the Lord today to do whatever is necessary to fully use your gifts and talents for His eternal Kingdom.

February 16

Spiritual Strongholds

The weapons we fight with are not the weapons of the world. On the contrary, they have divine power to demolish strongholds.
2 Corinthians 10:4

One of the great discoveries I made in later years in my walk with God has to do with living in victory over generational strongholds. The Bible speaks of punishing the children for the sins of the fathers to the third and fourth generations. (See Exodus 20:5.) The only way out of living under the curses of generational strongholds is to acknowledge them before the Father and repent of their reign in our lives. This breaks the curse's future effects.

A stronghold is a fortress of thoughts that controls and influences our attitudes. They color how we view certain situations, circumstances, or people. When these thoughts and activities become habitual, we allow a spiritual fortress to be built around us. We become so used to responding to the "voice" of that spirit, that its abode in us is secure. All of this happens on a subconscious level.

As a businessman, I discovered that I had been influenced by a generational stronghold of insecurity and fear that was manifested in control. This subconscious fear motivated me to become a workaholic, to seek recognition through activities, to control others' behavior to avoid failure, and to have a relationship with God that was activity-based instead of relationally-based. One day God brought about a number of catastrophic events that forced me to look at what was behind these events. I found that the influence of these strongholds was at the core of these symptoms. The Bible speaks of this war on our souls.

For though we live in the world, we do not wage war as the world does. We demolish arguments and every pretension that sets itself up against the knowledge of God, and we take captive every thought to make it obedient to Christ. And we will be ready to punish every act of disobedience, once your obedience is complete (2 Corinthians 10:3,5-6).

The steps to freedom for me came when someone shared that these were sins that I was harboring, and in order to walk free of their influence,

I needed to repent of them. It was through the power of the cross that I no longer needed to be subjugated by their presence. Once I took this step, I began to walk free of their influences. Besides salvation, this became the most important discovery in my entire Christian walk. My relationship to Christ changed immediately. I began to hear God's voice. I began to trust Christ in areas I never thought possible. I could truly experience the love of Christ for the first time.

This knowledge helped me in business as well. One day I was in the middle of a contract negotiation with another Christian business-man. A lawyer had jumped in the middle of the negotiation. My friend began to surface many old feelings that were a source of pain from his past. When I perceived that a stronghold of insecurity and fear was at the core of his response, I interrupted his argumentative discussion with me and said with a very forceful tone, "I am no longer going to listen to the spirit of insecurity that is speaking through you right now! If you don't refrain from this, I am going to leave!" My friend was taken back. He looked at me quite startled. After a few moments, he agreed with my diagnosis. We talked through what he was feeling and completed our negotiation without further incident.

What are the true motivations of your heart? Have you ever looked deeply at these motivations? You might find that these subconscious motivations may be preventing you from experiencing the fullness of Christ in your life. Ask Him to reveal these and then repent of their influences.

February 17

Unexplainable Power

> *I tell you the truth, we speak of what we know, and we testify to what we have seen, but still you people do not accept our testimony.*
> John 3:11

When is the last time God did something in your business life that can only be explained as God? Was it yesterday? Was it just last week?

February 17—Day 48

A month ago? A year ago? The answer to this question may mean several things. If it has been some time since you saw God's activity in such a way that you know it was His hand, you may not be trusting to a level that requires faith. You may not be risking enough for God to show Himself. The converts in the early Church changed the world they lived in because of what they saw and heard. It was the power of the gospel that changed lives, not what they learned from mere teaching. This power drew people to Christ. Things happened that could not be explained as anything other than the activity of God. Is that the kind of faith you are experiencing in your life? Many of us live a wholesome, moral life, but this activity is not seen by those we associate with as anything that cannot also be achieved by themselves. That is why many are not drawn to our lives. God's power is not evident. The Lord has been challenging me to trust Him at levels I have never trusted before. This level of trust has placed me in a vulnerable position. However, the blessing of this relationship is that I see the activity of God as never before, and those close to me see it as well. It builds their faith and draws others to investigate.

Sometimes the activity of God comes in unusual ways. God often sets up scenes that appear to be negative on the front end, but God has orchestrated these events for His glory.

- Without Pharaoh's pursuit of Israel at the Red Sea, there is no miraculous deliverance.
- Without Lazarus's death, there is no raising to life.
- Without Goliath, there is no underdog story.
- Without Peter stepping out of the boat, there is no miracle on the water.
- Without Judas' betrayal, there is no resurrection.

God wants to show Himself in ways you and I cannot imagine. Let God demonstrate His power in your marketplace today. Then, you will see "all men drawn unto Me."

February 18

Weapons of Warfare

Beat your plowshares into swords and your pruning hooks into spears.   Joel 3:10a

In this third chapter of Joel, we hear the prophet describe a time yet to come. It will be a time of great harvest on the earth, and this verse describes the catalyst. A plowshare is an agricultural instrument used to till the soil. At this point in history, it was a tool that spoke of one's vocation. However, the prophet was speaking of a time yet to come. The prophet described the plowshare as an instrument that will be turned into a sword. The sword is often used in the Bible to describe God's Word. The only way a plowshare can be turned into a sword is for it to go through extreme heat, and then the blacksmith must beat that plowshare into shape. Heat and punishment of the metal turns that plowshare into an instrument of battle. God must do this in each of our lives in order for us to be useable as a worthy sword. We are all in a battle—a spiritual battle. Paul describes our battle as one against the principalities of the unseen world. I believe God is going to raise up many in the marketplace to use their plowshare as a weapon of righteousness in these last days. That weapon won't be used for destruction, but as a weapon of love. That weapon of love will yield a great harvest in our lifetime. But this is only part of the story.

God is also going to turn our pruning hooks into spears. A pruning hook is used in two ways. First, it is used to prune a tree for greater growth and productivity. It is also used to cut the fruit from taller trees in which one cannot reach the fruit. This fruit from our vocation is going to be cast forth like a spear, but even more as seed planted to bring the harvest of which Joel speaks. Fruit from our business life is often the financial rewards generated. God wants to use our finances and everything else for His purposes. We must use our vocations and the fruit that comes from them as seed to bring the great harvest that God is planning.

How are you using your plowshare and your pruning hook for God's glory today? Ask God to show you how He wants to use your skills, resources, and relationships to prepare for the great harvest He has planned.

February 19

Saved From Such Men

> *O Lord, by Your hand save me from such men, from men of this world whose reward is in this life....* Psalm 17:14

Whenever I travel over the ocean, I am always reminded of the seemingly insignificant time we have on this earth. I often imagine dropping a glass of water out the window of the jet into the huge body of water below. The Lord then reminds me that this is how my life is compared to eternity—a mere drop in the ocean.

Yet, every day millions of people will go to work seeking to gain that elusive thing called success. The rewards of this life continue to provide the incentive for 60-hour weeks or the extra weekend away from the family. Sometimes we get entrenched in the message of the world. This message is an appealing, seductive call to sell out eternity for the temporal.

As a Christian businessman, I fell for this for many years until the Lord allowed me to wake up. It took some severe wake-up calls, but they did their job. I'm so grateful the Lord cares enough to give us these wake-up calls. He knows what real life is about. We think we know what it is, only to learn once again that real life is only in what is built on eternity. How does this verse line up with where you are today? Are you building around a world whose reward is in this lifetime, or an eternal one? Do those with whom you associate live in such a way that they demonstrate their reward is not concerning this life? Jesus said to seek first His Kingdom and all these things will be added. Amen.

February 20

Seeing Through God's Eyes

They mourned and wept and fasted till evening for Saul and his son Jonathan, and for the army of the Lord and the house of Israel, because they had fallen by the sword. 2 Samuel 1:12

How would you respond if you heard something bad happened to someone who had been trying to cut off your head for several years? King Saul had been seeking to kill David for many years before Saul was thrust into battle against the Amalekites. In this final battle, a sword killed Saul. When the news reached David, instead of rejoicing that his enemy was no longer a problem for him, he responded in a totally different manner. He mourned. Imagine that; he mourned for the one who sought to kill him.

This is a sign of one who can look past an individual who is the source of pain and consider how God views him. God looks on that individual and sees his needs and knows why he responds the way he does. When we begin to see people as God does, we'll no longer look at them as enemies, but as souls in need of grace. This is how Jesus could give of His life for us. He saw our great need, not what we did to Him. When someone wrongs you, do you seek to retaliate, or do you pray to understand the need behind the offender's actions? For several years a person was a source of constant pain and retaliation toward me. There was nothing I could do to change it. God allowed me to go beyond the person's actions to understand what was the source of his need. When I gained that understanding, God gave me a picture of this person inside a prison cell and in bondage. This bondage made him respond to life in this way. I was able to pray for him and genuinely love him in spite of the fact that he persecuted me. This is the kind of love Jesus wants us to have when He tells us to love our enemies and pray for those who spitefully use us.

I believe God does a special work of grace in those who go beyond the realm of normal response to persecution. He brings us to a level of grace we never thought possible. Describing how God worked in Joseph's life, Francis Frangipane reveals what happens when we tap into this grace:

God made him fruitful in the very things that afflicted him. In the land of your affliction, in your battle, is the place where God will make you fruitful. Consider, even now, the area of greatest affliction in your life. In that area, God will make you fruitful in such a way that your heart will be fully satisfied, and God's heart fully glorified. God has not promised to keep us from valleys and sufferings, but to make us fruitful in them. [Francis Frangipane, *Place of Immunity* (Cedar Rapids, Iowa: Arrow Publications, 1996), 93]

February 21

Loose Your Donkey

…"Go to the village ahead of you, and at once you will find a donkey tied there, with her colt by her. Untie them and bring them to Me. If anyone says anything to you, tell him that the Lord needs them…."   Matthew 21:2-3

A donkey was an animal of commerce in Jesus' day. It was used to carry great burdens of goods from place to place and he was known as the "beast of the burden." This donkey no doubt was owned by a village businessperson. But Jesus told His disciples to fetch the donkey for "He had need of it." This donkey played an important part in Jesus' triumphal entry into Jerusalem. It was a day that was the culmination of three years of ministry. Jesus chose to use a vehicle of commerce to bring Him into His most important public display.

We are entering a time in our own history in which God is saying to businesspeople, "Loose your donkey for My purposes. I have need of it." God is preparing His Church to be a vessel for ushering in a great harvest of souls. He is preparing His remnant of businesspeople, who are like a tribe within the Church, to be a major force in this great harvest.

"He will tether his donkey to a vine, his colt to the choicest branch; he will wash his garments in wine, his robes in the blood of grapes. His eyes will be darker than wine, his teeth whiter than milk" (Gen. 49:11-12). Is your donkey tied to the living Vine, the choicest branch of Jesus Himself? When we are tied to the living Vine, designed for His use, we will be useful in God's Kingdom. Jesus wants to free us from the bondage of business slavery; He wants us to walk in freedom so that others may see God's grace flowing through us and our place in the business world. Is your donkey available for His use?

Today, ask Jesus to allow the Vine to flow through you in every area of your life.

February 22

Paneled Houses

> *"Is it a time for you yourselves to be living in your paneled houses, while this house remains a ruin?"* Haggai 1:4

There is a crisis of grand proportions in the spiritual house of God today. The moral fiber of our world has eroded. Greed, idolatry, and pleasure are the gods of our day. And it is no different in the Body of Christ.

The prophet Haggai wrote about a people who had lost concern for the need to build God's house because they were so focused on their own worldly needs. It is a dangerous place to get with God. When our world begins to focus around increasing our pleasure, building bigger and better homes, and failing to make what is important to God important in our own lives, this should be a warning to us.

> *Jesus entered the temple area and drove out all who were buying and selling there. He overturned the tables of the money changers and the benches of those selling doves. "It is written," He said to them, " 'My house will be called a house of prayer,' but you are making it a 'den of robbers' "* (Matthew. 21:12-13).

Jesus came into Jerusalem and found the businesspeople buying and selling in the temple. As far as they knew, this was an acceptable practice in their day. Their fathers did it, and now they were doing it. It was business as usual. Jesus got angry, turned over the tables, and said that His house was a house of prayer. He found the businesspeople of the day seeing His house as a place for profit, not prayer. They had stepped into a place of complacency that was not acceptable to the Lord. When we begin to blend in with the moral condition of an ungodly world, we begin losing God's perspective on life.

It is easy to begin blending in with our culture and to accept what is being modeled by the ungodly. God called us to be salt in a world that needs much salt. "You are the salt of the earth. But if the salt loses its saltiness, how can it be made salty again? It is no longer good for anything, except to be thrown out and trampled by men" (Mt. 5:13). Each of us must ask ourselves if we have lost our salt. Are we having an impact on our world? Or is our world having an impact on us? Ask God to give you a vision for how you can be salt to your world today.

February 23

A Man Who Has God's Favor

> *"…Let us go with you, because we have heard that God is with you."*
> Zechariah 8:23

Few men of God have become extraordinary people of faith without the influence of mentors. A mentor is one who takes responsibility for the spiritual and, sometimes, physical care of another. It requires a commitment from the teacher and the student.

Elijah mentored Elisha. Elisha became one of the greatest prophets in all the Bible. One of the primary reasons for this was Elisha's hunger. Elisha wanted a double portion of Elijah's spirit. It was this hunger that drove Elisha to be sold out to God's purposes for his life.

I have been privileged to have had many mentors throughout my spiritual life. In each stage of my maturity, God brought new mentors who had unique gifts that the previous mentor did not have. God has given me the hunger to desire a double portion of those positive attributes of my mentors. This desire is sorely missing among many today. I fail to see the hunger among many who could be used greatly in the Kingdom. Instead, they get distracted by the cares of this world. It is an attitude of a la carte versus an attitude of pressing in to the full measure of what God might have for them.

Who are the people of God He has placed in your life? Are you learning from them? Are you seeking a double portion of their anointing? What prevents you from gaining from their wisdom and experience? God may have brought them into your life to prepare you to be a man or woman of God with great anointing. However, there is a time of training and waiting to prove out your own faith. Ask God today if there is someone He would have you mentor or be mentored by.

February 24

Godly Rewards

You have said, "It is futile to serve God. What did we gain by carrying out His requirements and going about like mourners before the Lord Almighty? But now we call the arrogant blessed. Certainly the evildoers prosper, and even those who challenge God escape."
Malachi 3:14-15

Have you ever felt that serving God had little reward and the ungodly seemed actually to be more blessed than you? This is what the people of God felt. God heard their cry and responded through the prophet Malachi to explain God's view on this matter.

Then those who feared the Lord talked with each other, and the Lord listened and heard. A scroll of remembrance was written in His presence concerning those who feared the Lord and honored His name. "They will be Mine," says the Lord Almighty, "in the day when I make up My treasured possession. I will spare them, just as in compassion a man spares his son who serves him. And you will again see the distinction between the righteous and the wicked, between those who serve God and those who do not" (Malachi 3:16-18).

Notice that after the people complained about this, they began to talk to each other, and the Lord listened and heard. God had been taking note of those who were serving Him and honoring Him. There is a day coming in which God will honor His "treasured possessions." We will see that there is a distinction between the righteous and the wicked on that day when "the sun of righteousness will rise with healing in its wings. And you will go out and leap like calves released from the stall" (Mal. 4:2). What a beautiful picture of what we will feel like on that day.

Faithful obedience is rewarded by God. It often requires patience, suffering, and perseverance. Be of good cheer; He will reward you if you faint not.

February 25

Fruitful Suffering

> ..."*It is because God has made me fruitful in the land of my suffering.*" Genesis 41:52

Joseph named his second son Ephraim. Ephraim was given to him after he had been delivered from his suffering of 13 years. Joseph said that he named him this because God had made him fruitful in the land of his suffering. Ephraim means "twice fruitful."

Joseph was fruitful in two instances. He was fruitful during his time of adversity and in his prosperity. When God brings us into a time of suffering, it can be a fruitful time. It's rare for us to see the fruit during the suffering period. But know that the roots are going deep into the spiritual soil of our soul because of our pressing in to God during our time of suffering. This is producing a work in our character that cannot be seen until it finishes the process. Such was the case for Joseph.

It was not until several years after such a time of suffering that I began to see the fruit of the trials that the Lord allowed me to experience.

How grateful I am to understand some of the "why" that has led to a new life in Him that I would never have had without this period.

Samson had great anointing but lacked character. We see many today who have great anointing yet lack character. But God is raising up Josephs who not only have great anointing for these days but also great character. Suffering produces character.

If you find yourself in a time of suffering, now is the time to press into God. Let your roots grow deeper. Whenever there is a famine, tree roots are forced to drive deeper into the soil to find water. These times are designed to create such a deep-rooted faith that our natures will be changed forever.

February 26

Spiritual Warfare

For our struggle is not against flesh and blood.... Ephesians 6:12

Have you ever heard someone say, "I will never do business with another Christian"? I hear this comment quite often in my dealings with Christian businesspeople. This comment represents the battle that rages against us by the enemy of our soul to destroy the witness and effectiveness of Christian businesspeople. We must realize that we are in a war—a war for the souls of men, a war to discredit all that a Christian stands for, a war that is designed to divide Christian against Christian.

Satan's ploy in the life of Christian businesspersons is to do several things to make them ineffective as soldiers in the marketplace. First, he wants to discredit them by allowing them to fail other people in their professional services. This often shows up in failing to perform what they committed to do or performing in an unsatisfactory way. Sometimes, this is a result of a downright failure of the businessperson to perform with excellence. In other cases, it may be a misunderstanding in the midst of the service that causes strife and division instigated by the enemy.

The result in both cases is the same: a division among Christians and even non-Christians, further resulting in a damaged witness for

Christ. The apostle Peter admonishes us to "live such good lives among the pagans that, though they accuse you of doing wrong, they may see your good deeds and glorify God on the day He visits us" (1 Pet. 2:12).

There are times when each of us is thrust into situations out of our control. Sometimes this results in our inability to pay a bill on time, or to deliver a service. Defeating satan in these battles requires extra communication with those with whom we are dealing. If the motive of your heart is to do right, then God will give you favor in order to work through these difficult spots. Ask God today to show you where the enemy is seeking to make you ineffective.

We wage a spiritual war that is not flesh and blood. We must fight this war with spiritual weapons applied to practical daily living.

February 27

Knowing Versus Doing

I want to know Christ and the power of His resurrection....
Philippians 3:10

If I asked you the purpose for which God made you, what might you say? You might give a lot of answers that required some action on your part. However, the simplest answer to that question relates to one primary thing: fellowship. The most important thing God desires from us today is to have a deep and intimate fellowship with each of us.

The apostle Paul said he wanted to know Christ, and by knowing Christ he could experience the power of His resurrection. I find this to be the hardest thing for many of us businesspeople to do. So often it is much easier to be busy with the urgent (or even Christian) activity than spending quiet moments before the Lord. Before we realize it, days have passed since our last quiet time with Jesus.

Jesus understood how important quiet moments were with the Father. "After He had dismissed them, He went up on a mountainside by Himself to pray. When evening came, He was there alone" (Mt. 14:23).

The more mature I become in my relationship with the Lord, the more precious this time becomes to me. It is a time I look forward to almost daily. It offers me a time to reflect, to share my concerns with my Lord, and to hear Him speak. In the last few years I have begun prayer walks, which accomplish three things: fellowship, prayer, and exercise. It has changed my prayer life. I have come to understand that Jesus views us as His friend and He wants to spend time with us. We are depriving Him of His time when we put Him aside for the urgent. An interesting thing happens when we make prayer a priority: Urgent things seems to wane as we focus on Him. He makes all these other things fall into place.

Are you taking the time to get to know Him today?

February 28

Coming Out of Babylon

..."*Come out of her, My people, so that you will not share in her sins, so that you will not receive any of her plagues; for her sins are piled up to heaven, and God has remembered her crimes.*"

Revelation 18:4

There is a day when God is going to judge the system of Babylon around the world. What is Babylon? Babylon is a system of doing business. The stronghold of the marketplace is mammon and pride. Dependence on money and misplaced trust are at the core of a Babylonian philosophy of life. Revelation 18 describes a time when God will judge this Babylonian system. It is the one place that we see a system destroyed in one day, even one hour. I do not believe Babylon is a particular city, but a world system. "Therefore in one day her plagues will overtake her" (Rev. 18:8a). "Woe! Woe, O great city, O Babylon, city of power! In one hour your doom has come!" (Rev. 18:10b).

As Christian businesspeople we are called to acknowledge the signs of the times. When the Soviet Union fell, many knew it was going to happen because they could recognize the signs of the times. God has a way of shaking things up. These shakings force us to determine who and what we will place our trust in. God says that we are to "Love the Lord your God with all your heart and with all your soul and with all your mind" (Mt. 22:37).

Are you still living in Babylon in the way you do business? If so, expect to share in the sins of Babylon when God decides to judge her. Ask God to show you where you might be operating in a "Babylonian" system of work.

March 1

Developing Our Heart for God

> *I will rouse your sons, O Zion, against your sons, O Greece, and make you like a warrior's sword.*   Zechariah 9:13b

In the third and fourth centuries Socrates and other Greek scholars began to influence the Church in ways that were different from the Hebraic roots of the early Church. The Greek influence appeals more to the intellect, whereas the early-Church Hebraic model appealed to the heart. The Greek influence resulted in more emphasis on oratory skills and cognitive knowledge of God. Over the many centuries, this influence has shown itself in a more programmatic approach to the gospel rather than a process of living out our faith. So why is it important for us to understand this?

I realized in my own life that I was a product of this Greek system. My walk with Christ focused more on what I knew than on an intimate and powerful walk with God. Knowledge without power to express the life within is of little value. The more programmatic the focus, the less emphasis we place on building deep and caring relationships that result in changed lives. Our early Church fathers knew there was a cost to living out the Word of God, not simply giving mental assent to it.

Are you walking with God today in an intimate fellowship? Or, are you only involved in programs and activities designed to do good things? Reflect on Proverbs 23:12: "Apply your heart to instruction and your ears to words of knowledge." We must listen and respond with the heart. Whatever service we give to God should be a result of our relationship with our heavenly Father, not an end unto itself.

March 2

Tapping Into Our Secret Weapon

He is always wrestling in prayer for you, that you may stand firm in all the will of God, mature and fully assured.　　Colossians 4:12b

"Good morning. Before we begin our staff business meeting I wish to ask John to give us the intercessors' report regarding the direction of our new business development program."

"Our intercessors have been prayerfully reviewing the action plan I gave them. We believe the Lord is directing us in this way. However, our intercessors believe we may need to adjust our direction on this."

Does this sound like a far-fetched illustration of a modern-day company? If we are truly going to remove the separation of what we perceive as holy versus unholy, then we must make some paradigm shifts in our thinking.

The Lord has called you and me to be ministers of the gospel in and through the workplace. This means we must fight our battles, grow our companies, and minister to our employees and vendors through the power of the Holy Spirit. Intercessory prayer is the secret weapon of Spirit-led activity. Imagine having intercessors who are part of your team, committed to helping you make decisions in your business life "that you may stand firm in all the will of God, mature and fully assured." It is a comforting feeling to know the decisions you and I make during the course of a business day are in the will of God.

Some time ago the Lord showed me that I needed to find intercessors for my business. I needed to use intercessors in the daily decision process for my business. This has transformed the way I conduct business. No major decisions are made without prayerful review with my intercessory team. Intercessors are the front-line warriors raised up to do battle for the saints. Ask God to raise up intercessors who can support you as you go forth in the battlefield of the marketplace.

March 3

Forgiveness Ensures Freedom

See to it that no one misses the grace of God and that no bitter root grows up to cause trouble and defile many.   Hebrews 12:15

In business and life the opportunity to harbor bitterness for a wrong suffered is great. We are given plenty of opportunities to grow bitter from relationships that bring hurt and pain. The writer of the Hebrews passage above admonishes us not to miss the grace of God so that we won't take up bitterness as a response to life's pain. He cautions us against this because he knows that a bitter root grows and grows until it eventually defiles many others through a wake of bitterness. If bitterness is allowed to take root, we become imprisoned to it. God's grace will no longer have as great an effect in our lives. We become ineffective, insensitive, and spiritually dead. We can even become physically ill from it. God does not live in bitterness. He lives in grace. He has provided grace for every person to walk in.

One day I was challenged to deal with an individual who hurt me terribly. I was faced with a decision. Would I choose bitterness, or would I choose grace? Oh, how my natural tendency was to choose bitterness. But God provided the courage to choose grace. With that grace came freedom—a freedom to love and even accept the person who was the source of such pain.

This is the real place where Christ's power is most revealed. We cannot live without His supernatural grace. Are you in need of grace today? It is there for the receiving. It will take courage to accept it and walk in it. This will be your step to freedom.

March 4

Knowledge + Action = Faith

For we also have had the gospel preached to us, just as they did; but the message they heard was of no value to them, because those who heard did not combine it with faith.   Hebrews 4:2

The people of Israel were called out of the bondage of Egyptian slavery. God said they would be brought out of 400 years of slavery so that they might worship Him. God desired to bring them into a place of milk and honey—the Promised Land. Yet that generation never entered into the Promised Land. Why? They never took what they knew in their head and transferred it to their heart. Finally, it never resulted in actions that were based on what they believed.

When I was a new Christian I heard an illustration of what belief and faith looked like when combined. If you were a trapeze artist and were skilled at walking across tightropes over high places, you might even be willing to walk across Niagara Falls. In fact, I would have confidence that you could because I had seen your abilities as a trapeze artist. However, if you asked me if you could push me in a wheelbarrow across Niagara Falls, you would be challenging me to put my beliefs into action. This requires faith, participation, and risk, which, until now, was based only on mental assent.

The writer of Hebrews is telling us that if we believe God but do not enter in to those promises, we are like the man who chooses not to get into the wheelbarrow. If we don't act on our beliefs, then we remain in the desert like the people of Israel who never received God's promises. They did not combine what they knew in their head with a faith that was put into action.

Has God spoken to you about an area in your life that requires a step of faith? Let God provide the courage, as He does the knowledge, to act in faith on what you believe.

March 5

Striving Versus Abiding

> *Unless the Lord builds the house, its builders labor in vain.*
>
> Psalm 127:1a

What does it mean for the Lord to build the house? It almost seems a contradiction when we consider that we might be the builders in this passage. God wants us to allow Him to build the house. He explains further:

> *Unless the Lord builds the house, its builders labor in vain. Unless the Lord watches over the city, the watchmen stand guard in vain. In vain you rise early and stay up late, toiling for food to eat—for He grants sleep to those He loves* (Psalm 127:1-2).

God is telling us there is a way of working without striving. There is a way to conduct business without sweating and toiling for outcome. His warning to each of us is to avoid thinking that outcome is based on our sweat and toil. Outcome is based on obedience. That outcome is sometimes more than we deserve. Sometimes it is less than we hoped for. His desire for each of us is to see Him working in our daily work life. He wants us to avoid looking to our own effort to gain an outcome.

One day Jesus called out to Peter from the shore of the lake and suggested he throw his net on the other side of the boat. It was this simple act of obedience that yielded a tremendous catch that he would not have received unless he obeyed.

We are called to work; He is called to bring forth the fruit. He is the vine. We are the branches. Fruit comes forth naturally from a healthy tree.

Today, ask God to show you when you enter into striving. Ask Him to show you the difference between loving trust and obedience and striving for outcome. It can be challenging for us to balance this in our daily work experience. He wants to help us walk in this freedom and rest.

March 6

The Depth and Width of Your Calling

If we are distressed, it is for your comfort and salvation; if we are comforted, it is for your comfort, which produces in you patient endurance of the same sufferings we suffer. 2 Corinthians 1:6

"God must love you a lot! He doesn't allow someone to go through the kinds of adversity you have experienced unless He has a special calling on your life." Those were the words said to me by two different mentors at two different times within a three-year period. Later I would learn another related truth from a respected man of God—a man who lives in another country, a man whom God uses throughout the globe. "The depth and width of your faith experiences are directly proportional to your calling." What were these men of God saying?

They were describing a process of preparation that God takes each of His leaders through when He plans to use them in significant ways. A "faith experience" is an event or "spiritual marker" in your life about which you can say, "That is where I saw God personally move in my life." It is an unmistakable event in which God showed Himself personally to you. It was the burning bush for Moses; the crossing of the Red Sea or the Jordan River for the nation of Israel; Jacob's encounter with the angel. It was the feeding of the 5,000 for the disciples. It was the time when you saw God face to face in your life.

If God has plans of using you in the lives of many others, you can expect that He is going to allow certain faith experiences to come into your life in order to build a foundation that will be solid. That foundation is what you will be able to look back on to keep you faithful to Him in the times of testing. Each of us must have personal faith experiences in which we experience God personally so that we can move in faith to whatever He may call us. Do you need a personal faith experience right now in your life? Pray that God will reveal Himself to you. He delights in doing that.

March 7

Living for a Cause Greater Than Yourself

I can do everything through Him who gives me strength.
                                                    Philippians 4:13

In the thirteenth century a man named William Wallace became the instrument of freedom from England's tyranny over Scotland. A very wicked king ruled England. A tragedy in the life of William Wallace launched him into living for this cause. Initially his cause was revenge, but soon his cause turned to something bigger than himself—freedom for a nation. When he challenged the commoners to fight for this freedom, they responded that the enemy was too great and that they might die on the battlefield. They also refused to fight for the nobles, the knights and leaders who had a vested interest in gaining more land for themselves versus a pure cause of freedom. Wallace's response: "Yes, we might die. We will all die sooner or later. But we will die for a cause worth dying for. So that our children and their children might live in freedom." This story was popularized in the movie *Brave Heart* (Sherman Oaks, California: Paramount Pictures, 1995).

Today we find many Christian businesspeople living a status quo relationship with God that is more characterized as "business as usual" than a life demonstrating God's power. Our focus is often more concerned with improving our standard of living than improving the Kingdom of God through our circle of influence. While this takes place, millions upon millions die without the saving grace of Christ. Many other Christians die never experiencing the freedom in Christ that His blood paid for. God has called each of us to live for a cause greater than ourselves—a life that is dependent on His grace and power to achieve things we never thought possible through our lives. This is His plan for your life. The apostle Paul prayed that He might experience the power of the resurrection in his life. This power is available to you and me to live for a cause greater than ourselves. Ask God what He wants to achieve through your life today. And consider yourself dead already to the consequences of what that might mean for you.

March 8

Faith Versus Presumption

So she said to Abram, "The Lord has kept me from having children. Go, sleep with my maidservant; perhaps I can build a family through her." Abram agreed to what Sarai said. Genesis 16:2

Presumption is based on our own reasoning. Abraham and Sarah fell into presumption when they got too old to have children. God had promised a son to Abraham and Sarah—a son who would fulfill His promise to birth a nation. But Abraham and Sarah were past the normal age for childbearing. So, they concluded that God needed help to work out His plan.

Many businesspeople make the same mistake every day. We make assumptions about what we believe God is doing and wants us to do. However, before we really have full assurance that God has spoken to us on the matter and revealed His perfect action plan, we move forward with our steps to get it done. How do we protect ourselves from presumption? The Proverbs tell us that there is safety in a multitude of counselors (see Prov. 11:14 KJV). Submitting our decisions to others for confirmation protects each of us from the deceit of our own heart. This process will protect us from presumption and encourage us to move in faith. The next time you believe God is directing you toward a specific action, consult with your spouse first, then some close, spiritual friends who will take the time to prayerfully consider your request. If you don't have consensus, wait until you do before you move forward. God will move through this process to His desired will for the matter.

March 9

Confidence in Numbers

David was conscience-stricken after he had counted the fighting men, and he said to the Lord, "I have sinned greatly in what I have done. Now, O Lord, I beg You, take away the guilt of Your servant. I have done a very foolish thing." 2 Samuel 24:10

It just seems to be human nature. As we grow in wealth and ability, our confidence moves from complete trust in the Lord to trust in our resources. King David decided one day that he needed to know how many fighting men he had in his army. This was a grievous sin in the nation of Israel. God always made it clear to the nation that He, not their army, was their source. It was against the law of God to number the troops. David's general, Joab, knew the serious nature of such an action.

But Joab replied to the king, "May the Lord your God multiply the troops a hundred times over, and may the eyes of my lord the king see it. But why does my lord the king want to do such a thing?" (2 Samuel 24:3)

Joab knew that David was treading in dangerous waters when he brought up the idea to him. But David had it in his mind that this is what he was going to do. And he did. The result: God judged David for this sin by smiting the nation with a plague that resulted in the loss of 70,000 lives.

Recently, I was having lunch with a former stockbroker who lost everything in the 1987 stock crash in the United States. He made an interesting comment. "You cannot know how to fully trust the Lord in the financial area until you really have to. When I lost everything, I was forced to trust Him when I knew I could not pay my next bill unless God provided. This was the time I learned to trust God. I never had to trust God before I lost my money because I had plenty. We don't willingly enter this level of trust with God."

Ask God today to keep you from trusting in your own resources. Ask Him how to balance trust and blessing from Him this day.

March 10

When God Restores What the Locusts Eat

I will repay you for the years the locusts have eaten—the great locust and the young locust, the other locusts and the locust swarm—My great army that I sent among you. Joel 2:25

There are seasons in our lives that involve times of famine and times of restoration. Solomon tells us that He has made everything beautiful in its time and that there is a time for everything, and a season for every activity under Heaven. (See Ecclesiastes 3:1,11.)

God brings about both the good and the bad. The seasons of famine have a divine purpose in our lives. They accomplish things that only these hard places can accomplish. But there is a time when those hard places have accomplished their purpose and He begins to restore. God did this with the nation of Israel after a season of famine and devastation.

Be glad, O people of Zion, rejoice in the Lord your God, for He has given you the autumn rains in righteousness. He sends you abundant showers, both autumn and spring rains, as before. The threshing floors will be filled with grain; the vats will overflow with new wine and oil. "I will repay you for the years the locusts have eaten—the great locust and the young locust, the other locusts and the locust swarm—My great army that I sent among you. You will have plenty to eat, until you are full, and you will praise the name of the Lord your God, who has worked wonders for you; never again will My people be shamed. Then you will know that I am in Israel, that I am the Lord your God, and that there is no other; never again will My people be shamed" (Joel 2:23-27).

God wants each of us to know that there is a time when He will restore in order to demonstrate His gracious hand in our lives. He is a loving Father who tenderly guides His children through the difficult places. If God has taken you through a time of leanness, know that He is the restorer of that which the locusts have eaten. Wait patiently for Him to bring this about in your life. He will do it.

March 11

Suffering for the Salvation of Another

Blessed are you when people insult you, persecute you and falsely say all kinds of evil against you because of Me.   Matthew 5:11

Recently, a friend told a true story about one of his closest friends who experienced great suffering for the soul of his persecutor. This man worked on a cargo ship. His boss was the captain. This friend was a committed Christian who shared his faith with others and was a good worker. One day the friend led the sea captain's girlfriend to Christ. The sea captain already hated and ridiculed the Christian worker because of his faith in Christ. When his girlfriend came to Christ, she stopped sleeping with the captain. The captain blamed the Christian man for the change in his girlfriend. One day he entered the restaurant where the Christian man was having lunch. He walked over to his table and began hurling obscenities and began beating him. The Christian man simply tried to defend himself but did not fight back. The captain kept beating him until eventually the man lay on the floor bleeding.

Two men entered the restaurant and saw what was taking place. They jumped the sea captain and took him outside and began beating him. The sea captain was beaten so badly that he needed immediate medical attention. The Christian worker saw the condition of the sea captain, came to his aid, and began helping him. The sea captain was so moved that this man could do this after he had literally beaten him bloody that he began to weep, not understanding what could move a man to have such love in the face of being beaten. The sea captain accepted Jesus at that moment.

The Bible tells us that while we were yet sinners Christ came and paid our penalty so that we might live eternally. Many in the market-place have never known the love of Christ. You might be the only one they ever meet who can introduce them to this love. Ask God to show you how to love the unlovable in your workplace today.

March 12

Understanding the Source of Anger

A fool gives full vent to his anger, but a wise man keeps himself under control. Proverbs 29:11

The marketplace can be a pressure-packed world. The demands that are often put on us can bring out things that we never knew were there. Sometimes we begin to think that the source of that pressure is to blame for our response to the pressure. It could be an event, a spouse, a boss, a client, a child, or even a driver who cuts us off in traffic.

I recall responding to a close friend one time, "If you had not done that, I would never have responded that way." Later I learned that this response had little truth to it. We all choose to get angry. No one else is to blame for our anger.

"The circumstances of life, the events of life, and the people around me in life, do not make me the way I am, but reveal the way I am" [Dr. Sam Peeples].

This simple quote has had a profound impact on how I view my anger now. Anger only reveals what is inside of me. I can't blame anyone but me for my response to a situation. I have learned that anger is only the symptom of something else that is going on inside of me. This quote now resides on my refrigerator door as a daily reminder of the truth about my response to life's situations.

It has been said that anger is like the warning panel on the dash of your car. It is the light that tells us something is going on under the hood and we need to find out what is the source of the problem. I discovered that the source of anger is often unmet expectations or personal rights. We believe we are entitled to a particular outcome to a situation. When this doesn't happen, it triggers something in us. At the core of this is fear, often a fear of failure or rejection, fear of what others think, fear of the unknown.

If you struggle with anger, ask God to reveal the source of that anger. Ask Him to heal you of any fears that may be the root of your anger. Ask God to help you take responsibility for your response to difficult situations.

March 13

Obeying the Spirit of God

> *Now an angel of the Lord said to Philip, "Go south to the road—the desert road—that goes down from Jerusalem to Gaza."*   Acts 8:26

Philip was conducting what we might today call a revival meeting. God was blessing the meeting, and many were being healed and delivered from demonic influence. Here is the scene:

> *Philip went down to a city in Samaria and proclaimed the Christ there. When the crowds heard Philip and saw the miraculous signs he did, they all paid close attention to what he said. With shrieks, evil spirits came out of many, and many paralytics and cripples were healed. So there was great joy in that city* (Acts 8:5-8).

And yet, in the midst of this great event, the Holy Spirit spoke to Philip and told him to remove himself and go to a completely different area to speak to one individual. Philip was so sensitive to the directive of the Holy Spirit that he left what would be deemed a successful event to go speak to another—an Ethiopian eunuch. The result of his obedience was that Philip led the eunuch to faith in Christ and baptized him. The Lord then took Philip away supernaturally to another region many miles away.

God's ways of determining where we invest our time and energy often have little to do with results. The danger for each of us is to determine that we are in the center of God's will simply by the success or failure of the events we are involved in. Our plumbline for determining success can be only one thing: obedience. Philip responded in obedience to the direction of the Holy Spirit.

Are you listening to the voice of the Holy Spirit? Has God prompted you to speak, go, or come alongside another? Ask God today to help you hear the Holy Spirit's voice so that you might be used mightily in your marketplace.

March 14

The First Requirement of Ministry

The priests are in mourning, those who minister before the Lord.
Joel 1:9b

The first requirement for being used by God in the life of others is to mourn on their behalf. We must identify with their pain and suffering. Each of us must be broken for others first.

In order to be fully used by God in the marketplace, we need to understand what breaks God's heart. When we understand what breaks God's heart, we are able to mourn on behalf of a grieving person, or a nation we are called to serve. What breaks God's heart? When we begin to answer this question, we begin the first step to becoming instruments of change for those things that are important to God. Perhaps it is an overemphasis in our own talent and abilities, or lack of complete trust in Jesus. Perhaps it is the lack of respect for human life that leads to the killing of innocent babies. Perhaps it is the deceit and pride that often rule the marketplace of commerce. Or perhaps it is the strife and divisions among His own Body that grieve Him most. When we begin to mourn over our own sins in these areas, God begins to use us as instruments of righteousness to affect these things. It was only when God let me see my own sins in the marketplace and how they broke His heart that I began to be an instrument for His purposes.

Today, ask God to show you what things in your world are breaking His heart. Then see how He might want you to be the priest to affect for Him. The first step is identification with what breaks God's heart.

March 15

Following Only the Father's Commands

Jesus gave them this answer: "I tell you the truth, the Son can do nothing by Himself; He can do only what He sees His Father doing, because whatever the Father does the Son also does."   John 5:19

Have you ever thought about a typical day in Jesus' life? Perhaps He might have had questions like these, "Who am I going to heal today? Who will I visit today? Which person will I deliver from demons this day?" etc. The demands on Jesus' time were great. Yet we see that Jesus allocated His time very deliberately. We don't get the idea that Jesus was flustered or stressed from the activity He was involved in. He often sought times of prayer and reflection away from the disciples. His life appeared to have a balance of quiet moments and active ministry into the lives He came in contact with.

How do we determine what we will be involved in each day of our lives? What keeps us in sync with the will of our heavenly Father for the daily tasks He calls us to? Jesus tells us that He was only involved in those things the Father was involved in. Nothing more, nothing less. So often we determine our participation in an activity based on whether we have the time to do it or whether we desire to participate. The real question we should ask is, "Does the Father want me to participate in this activity?"

"Lord, should I add this Bible study to my schedule? Should I spend an extra night out on this committee this week? Should I take on new business that will take me away from home more? Should my daughter be involved in music lessons?" These are the daily challenges for the world we now live in. We are an activity-based society that often encourages more and more activity, often in the name of Christian virtue.

Our lives will become less cluttered, less stressful, and more fulfilling when we follow the model Jesus provided. It may not always please everyone. Jesus never sought to please everyone. Ask the Lord each day this week how you and He are to spend your time. Yield your schedule to Him. Let Jesus direct your every activity. You may discover that He desires you to cut back some things in order to spend more time alone with Him. He will be faithful to show you. And you will become more fulfilled because you are centered in His will for you.

March 16

Death and Birth of a Vision

I tell you the truth, unless a kernel of wheat falls to the ground and dies, it remains only a single seed. But if it dies, it produces many seeds. John 12:24

Almost every significant thing God births He allows to die before the vision is fulfilled in His own way.

- Abraham had a vision of being the father of a great nation (birth). Sarah was barren and became too old to have children (death). God gave Abraham and Sarah a son in their old age. He became the father of a great nation (fulfillment).
- Joseph had a vision that he would be a great leader and that many would bow down to him (birth). Joseph's brothers sold him to some merchants and he became a slave. Later he was falsely condemned to spend his years in prison (death). God allowed Joseph to interpret the dreams of the butler and baker and later the king, whereupon, he was made a ruler in the land (fulfillment).
- Moses had a vision of leading his people out of the bondage of Egypt (birth). Pharaoh as well as his own people drove Moses out of Egypt after Moses' first attempt to relieve their bondage (death). God gave Moses signs and wonders to convince Pharaoh to free the people and bring them out of Egypt and into the Promised Land (fulfillment).

- The disciples had a vision of establishing the Kingdom of God with Jesus (birth). The very ones He came to save killed Jesus, and the disciples saw Him buried in a tomb (death). God raised Jesus from the dead, and the disciples performed great miracles until the gospel had spread through all the world (fulfillment).
- A grain of wheat has a "vision" of reproducing itself and many more grains of wheat (birth). The grain dies in the ground (death). A harvest springs up out of the very process of "death" in the ground (fulfillment).

Has God given you a vision that is yet unfulfilled? If that vision is born of God, He will raise it up in His own way. Do not try to raise the vision in your own strength. Like Moses, who tried to fulfill the vision of freeing the Hebrews by killing the Egyptian, it will only fail. But wait on your heavenly Father to fulfill the vision. Then you will know that it was His vision when He fulfills it in the way only He can do.

March 17

A Refiner's Fire

For he will be like a refiner's fire or a launderer's soap.
Malachi 3:2b

The Lord has a specific manner of preparing His people for useful service. God desires to turn His children from rough, hard-edged stones into gems of gold and silver.

He will sit as a refiner and purifier of silver; He will purify the Levites and refine them like gold and silver. Then the Lord will have men who will bring offerings in righteousness, and the offerings of Judah and Jerusalem will be acceptable to the Lord, as in days gone by, as in former years (Malachi 3:3-4).

The refiner's fire can only accomplish its purposes when the heat is turned up to extraordinary temperatures. It breaks down the metal in order for it to become moldable and shapeable. Only when the temperatures reach this level can the work be fully accomplished. So it is in our lives.

Until the Lord completes His refining process, the offerings we make are not made in righteousness and cannot be acceptable. Thank God that Jesus is our righteousness and that there is no righteousness apart from Him. Still, the Lord continues to purge all that is not of His righteousness out of our lives. This comes through trials that bring each of us to the end of ourselves in order that He may only reflect that which is Himself.

When God takes you through the refiner's fire, be encouraged because it is His overriding commitment to turn you from a rough, hard-edged stone to a precious metal. He will do this through certain events in your marketplace, your relationships, and other circumstances in your life. Our job is to avoid trying to blow out the fire.

March 18

Discerning the Work of God

Remember Tobiah and Sanballat, O my God, because of what they have done; remember also the prophetess Noadiah and the rest of the prophets who have been trying to intimidate me.
Nehemiah 6:14

Nehemiah set out to rebuild the wall at Jerusalem that had been destroyed. Nehemiah held a position in the Persian Empire that would be comparable to Chief of Staff in our government. Nehemiah wept over the destruction of the city wall and repented for the sins of his generation and the generations before him that had led to the fall of Jerusalem. Nehemiah responded to the news by seeking approval from his superior to take time off to rebuild the wall. Tobiah and Sanballat met Nehemiah's action with resistance, as did Noadiah the prophetess and other prophets. These were the religious and political leaders of his day. They became distractions to his work and opposed him.

Whenever God does a new work, it is often met with resistance by those in the established religious community, and sometimes among those from whom we would expect support. Jesus met the same resistance when He began His public ministry. This same phenomenon happens today. When God begins a new work that cannot be easily explained based upon prior experiences, many make the mistake of assuming it not to be of God. The very people who should embrace and encourage the work become the source of skepticism and opposition. God tells us that His ways are not our ways. He does things in ways beyond our limited understanding.

Before you are tempted to criticize or oppose something that looks different from your past experience, ask God for wisdom and discernment. Examine why you might be tempted to oppose it. The Lord cannot be put in a box. He delights in doing things in ways that may not fit our former paradigms.

March 19

The Fallacy of Full-Time Christian Work

> *Whatever you do, work at it with all your heart, as working for the Lord, not for men, since you know that you will receive an inheritance from the Lord as a reward. It is the Lord Christ you are serving.* Colossians 3:23-24

"I didn't know you were in full-time Christian work," said my close friend as we were driving. "I didn't realize that," she went on. I responded, "Every person who has followed the will of God in their life is in full-time Christian work." God calls some to the mission field, others to be accountants, and others to be advertising executives, and still others to be construction workers. God never made a distinction between sacred and secular. In fact, the Hebrew word *avodah* is the root word having the same meaning of "work" and "worship." God sees our work as worship.

We have incorrectly elevated the roll of the Christian worker to be more holy and committed than the person who is serving in a more secular environment. Yet the call to the secular marketplace is as important as any other calling. God has to have His people in every sphere of life. Otherwise, many would never come to know Him because they would be separated from society.

I learned this lesson personally when I sought to go into "full-time" service as a pastor in my late twenties, only to have God thrust me back into the business world unwillingly. This turned out to be the best thing He could have done for me, because it was never His will for me to be a pastor. He knew I was more suited for the marketplace.

We are all in missions. Some are called to foreign lands. Some are called to the jungles of the marketplace. Wherever you are called, serve the Lord in that place. Let Him demonstrate His power through your life so that others might experience Him through you today and see your vocation as worship to His glory.

March 20

The Anguish of Faith

Do not hide Your face from me or I will be like those who go down to the pit. Psalm 143:7b

Of all the biblical characters, David gives us a glimpse of a man who walked with God with great emotion in victory and in defeat. David never lost a battle throughout his many years of serving as king of Israel. In many of the Psalms, David often lamented about the difficult places where God had placed him. He talked of his enemies and the need for God to deliver Him. He talked of God's everlasting love for him. How do you suppose David came to this understanding after years of being sought after by King Saul who wanted to take his life? His years of turmoil within his family gave him many reasons to lose all hope in a loving God.

David often began his Psalms in a place of discouragement and loss of hope. But He never ended one Psalm in defeat. He always came to a place of victory in God by the end of the Psalm. David always placed his life in God's hands, knowing He would care for him.

> *Let the morning bring me word of Your unfailing love, for I have put my trust in You. Show me the way I should go, for to You I lift up my soul. Rescue me from my enemies, O Lord, for I hide myself in You. Teach me to do Your will, for You are my God; may Your good Spirit lead me on level ground* (Psalm 143:8-10).

It is okay to feel discouragement. It is part of the process of grieving and working through those times of pain. But God wants each of us to allow Him to walk with us in these places. If you find yourself in one of these places, do what David did. Ask God to show you the way and let Him bring the word of His unfailing love to you.

March 21

The Training Ground of God

> *Praise be to the Lord my Rock, who trains my hands for war, my fingers for battle.*   Psalm 144:1

David was a man skilled in war. From his days as a shepherd boy to the days of serving in Saul's army to leading his own army, David learned to be a skillful warrior. How does one become a skillful warrior?

The only way one can become a skillful warrior is to be trained and placed in the middle of the battle. It is only when we are placed in the furnace of battle that we truly learn to fight the real battles. Practice doesn't make you battle ready. War games won't prepare you for facing your real enemy in the battlefield. The stark reality of being in the midst of the battle makes us effective warriors.

Simply reading your Bible will not make you a warrior for the Kingdom. Knowledge without experience is mere folly. Only when you are placed in situations where there is nothing or no one who can save you but God will you learn the lessons of warrior faith. This is the training ground of God, which will make you into a soldier for Christ in the marketplace. Consider it to be suicidal faith—faith that says I want to be dead to anything that keeps me from fulfilling God's purposes for my life. It is when your efforts can do nothing to change your circumstance and you are at the mercy of God. These are the real training grounds of God. Do not shrink back from the battle that God may be leading you to today. It may be a training ground that is necessary for the calling He has on your life.

If you can trust Him in these times, you'll know that you have gained a faith that will move mountains and will sustain you in the most difficult of circumstances. "Praise be to the Lord my Rock, who trains my hands for war, my fingers for battle."

March 22

David's Source of Direction

Let the morning bring me word of Your unfailing love, for I have put my trust in You. Show me the way I should go, for to You I lift up my soul. Psalm 143:8

David is the only person in the Bible whom God describes as a man after His own heart. Despite David's many setbacks he continually sought to know and do God's will in his life. Like many of us, his will got in the way of a sinless life.

In the morning hour, David sought to hear from God. I can imagine David sitting on the open deck of his palace looking over the hills of Jerusalem, listening to God. There, in his morning watch, he felt God's unfailing love. He reaffirmed his trust in God. He also understood that the key to knowing God's will lay in spending such moments alone to reflect on what God had done and was doing in his life.

Teach me to do Your will, for You are my God; may Your good Spirit lead me on level ground (Psalm 143:10).

Sometimes we fall prey to believing that God is not concerned, and that He does not lead us in our work life. We are tempted to think that He leads us in other areas, but not in our daily workplace. The truth is that God is in every aspect of life and desires to direct us.

Do you need direction in your life today? If so, David provides the best example of gaining direction. Set aside the morning hour to draw close to His presence. There, you will sense His unfailing love for you. His direction for your life will be a natural by-product of this time of communion with Him. Ask God to lead you by His Spirit today.

March 23

No Confidence in the Flesh

If anyone else thinks he has reasons to put confidence in the flesh, I have more.   Philippians 3:4b

The apostle Paul surely could relate to the business executive. Paul reached the height of his profession only to have it completely stripped and torn from him. What he thought mattered in life became rubbish compared to what God did in his heart as He destroyed what seemed valuable at the time. It took a dramatic event to bring Paul into this revelation. It took a bright light—blindness, and the most fearful experience a human could have—being addressed personally by God, who was questioning why Paul was persecuting His people.

It would not be too long after his conversion that Paul would learn one of the greatest lessons every child of God must learn. That lesson is to avoid putting confidence in the flesh. In business we are rewarded for achievement. It is a "measurable" life. We work. We see results. We get certain feelings of accomplishment from these activities.

It was not until I was placed in a situation to experience utter failure that I could identify with the words of Paul. I have met other businesspeople as well who achieved great success in their business life only to experience dramatic failure. That personal handshake with failure leads to a realization that:

Whatever was to my profit I now consider loss for the sake of Christ. What is more, I consider everything a loss compared to the surpassing greatness of knowing Christ Jesus my Lord, for whose sake I have lost all things. I consider them rubbish, that I may gain Christ and be found in Him... (Phillipians 3:7-9).

Sometimes God lets us experience great pain to learn the lessons of greatest importance. Knowing Christ intimately is the most important lesson we will learn. Take stock in what you find your greatest pleasure in today. Avoid placing your confidence in things that are but rubbish so that you might know Him more intimately.

March 24

Peace—A Weapon Against Satan

Yea, though I walk through the valley of the shadow of death, I will fear no evil: for Thou art with me.　　　　Psalm 23:4a KJV

In the battles of the marketplace, your peace is actually a weapon. The marketplace creates many opportunities to rob us of our peace. Cash flow concerns, deadlines, relationships—all create stress on us. Your confidence in the God of peace declares that you are not falling for the lies of the devil. You see, the first step toward having spiritual authority over the adversary is having peace in spite of our circumstances. When Jesus confronted the devil, he did not confront satan with His emotions or in fear. Knowing that the devil was a liar, He simply refused to be influenced by any voice other than God's. His peace overwhelmed satan; His authority then shattered the lie, which sent demons fleeing.

There is a place of walking with God where you simply fear no evil. David faced a lion, a bear, and a giant. In this Psalm he stood in the "shadow of death" itself, yet he "feared no evil." David's trust was in the Lord. He said, "...for Thou art with me." Because God is with you, every adversity you face will unfold in victory as you maintain your faith in God! David continued, "You prepare a table before me in the presence of my enemies" (Ps. 23:5a). The battle you are in will soon become a meal for you, an experience that will nourish and build you up spiritually. Only God's peace will quell your fleshly reactions in battle. The source of God's peace is God Himself. If fear has been knocking at your door, begin to face that fear with God's peace. It is God's secret weapon to destroy fear.

March 25

Making Adjustments

> ..."*Throw your net on the right side of the boat and you will find some.*" John 21:6

A former client of mine was the marketing director of a large food brokerage company and told me a story about one of their client grocery stores located in the upper Midwest. It seems that the store could not understand why at a certain time every winter sales plummeted. They studied their product line and interviewed customers. They did everything possible to uncover the mystery. Finally, someone made a remarkable discovery that changed everything.

It seemed that whenever it was really cold outside, the manager raised the temperature in the store. When customers came into the store it was too warm for them, so they removed their coats and placed them in their shopping carts. This meant less room for food and resulted in reduced sales overall. They lowered the temperature of the store, and as a result, the sales climbed back to the levels they were accustomed to. Their adjustment resulted in restoring sales levels.

Jesus stood on the shoreline and watched Peter and a few of the disciples fish. Jesus yelled from the shoreline asking if they had caught anything. They had not. He then suggested they cast their line on the other side of the boat. Without knowing the person who was addressing them, they took His advice. They began catching so many fish they could not bring them in.

Adjusting our lives to God is the first thing that has to happen in order to begin experiencing Him in our daily lives. For some, it is simply following the advice of those above us. For others, it may require a major change in our job situation. Still, for others it could mean making changes in relationships. Whatever the case, you can be sure that until we adjust our lives to God we will not receive His full blessing. Ask Him today where you need to adjust to Him.

March 26

Living a Life of Conviction

For we know, brothers loved by God, that He has chosen you, because our gospel came to you not simply with words, but also with power, with the Holy Spirit and with deep conviction.

1 Thessalonians 1:4-5a

Everyone lives a life of conviction. Whatever we give our greatest time, our greatest energies, and our greatest resources to is a good indication of where our convictions lie. Some live a life of conviction about sports. Some live a life of conviction around pleasure. Still others live a life of conviction about very little that matters at all.

Whenever God chooses to do a deep work in a life, a strong conviction is born of the Holy Spirit. Conversions in the early Church resulted in changed lives that held to a deep, life-transforming conviction regarding what they believed and how they lived out that belief. Paul explains that the gospel they received came not just in words, but also in power, with the Holy Spirit and with deep conviction.

In order to impact the marketplace for Jesus Christ, each of us must be reflecting a faith that is demonstrated through deeply held convictions.

March 26—Day 85

Are you living a life of deep conviction that spurs you on to reflect the power of Christ in your life and the lives of others? Paul was willing to suffer great persecution for his faith in a living God. God calls each of us to a life that is supernatural, not simply a good, moral life. The early Church understood the role the Holy Spirit played in demonstrating this power of the gospel. It was this deep work that resulted in living the gospel with great conviction. If you are not living the gospel with great conviction, ask the Holy Spirit to so fill your life today that the power of His Spirit is truly reflected in your life so that you may impact others in your marketplace.

March 27

Treasures in Darkness

I will give you the treasures of darkness, riches stored in secret places, so that you may know that I am the Lord, the God of Israel, who summons you by name.   Isaiah 45:3

"I have never been in this place before. It is new ground for me, and I find I am way out of my comfort zone. I am scared to death to trust Him at this level. I had to confess to the Lord I have not been able to accept or believe His love for me in this area." Those were the words I expressed to a friend when I was in a difficult place in my life. That day when I confessed those words, God led me to this passage of Scripture.

What we perceive as dark periods in our lives are designed to be treasures from God. They are actually riches stored in secret places. We cannot see those times in this light because of the often-accompanying pain or fear that prevents us from accepting these times as treasures. They have a particular purpose from God's viewpoint: "...so that you may know that I am the Lord...who summons you by name."

You see, unless we are cast into times in which we are completely at God's mercy for breakthroughs in our lives, we will never experience God's faithfulness in those areas. We will never know how personal He is, or that He can be trusted to meet the deepest needs in our lives. God wants each of us to know that we are "summoned by name." Every hair of our head is numbered. He knows every activity we are involved in. His love for you and me knows no bounds, and He will take every opportunity to demonstrate this to us.

Has God brought you into a place of darkness? Trust Him today to reveal that hidden treasure that can be found in this darkness. Let Him summon you by name.

March 28

Resolving the Ownership Issue

The earth is the Lord's, and everything in it, the world, and all who live in it; for He founded it upon the seas and established it upon the waters.   Psalm 24:1-2

As Christian businesspeople, God calls us to view Him as the owner of everything. We are to be stewards of all that He entrusts to us. This is one of the hardest of all commandments to follow for the Christian businessperson because, if we work hard at business, we receive all the benefits of that work. It appears as though all that we have achieved was through our hand. Yet God says that it is by His hand that we are able to make wealth (see Deut. 8). He is the source of that ability. As soon as we become owners and not managers, we fall into trouble with God.

Joseph understood that he was a steward of all the resources of Egypt. God promoted him to affect an entire region of the world. Joseph had more power, prestige, and wealth than any 30-year-old who ever lived before him. The temptation for him in this newfound role in life must have been great. Many a man has not been able to handle material success. Many of God's choicest servants began well in their calling and service to God only to fail at the end. Consider Hezekiah, the great king who achieved many great things but failed to acknowledge God's blessing at the end of his reign. His reign was cut short due to pride. Gideon's fate was similar. Success can lead to pride if we are not careful.

"Not every man can carry a full cup. Sudden elevation frequently leads to pride and a fall. The most exacting test of all to survive is prosperity" [Oswald Chambers].

Ask the Lord today if you are living as a steward or an owner. Put whatever skills and resources you possess on His altar. Then you can expect God to do great things through you.

March 29

Understanding Our Own Calling

…"If I want him to remain alive until I return, what is that to you? You must follow Me." John 21:22

Jesus was talking to Peter after he had just had a very important encounter with Him—one of the last meetings the two would have. This was the third time Jesus had shown Himself to the disciples after His resurrection. It is the famous dialogue between Jesus and Peter in which Jesus asked Peter three times if he loved Him. Jesus followed by commanding, "Feed My sheep." Jesus went on to foretell of Peter's future death. As they were walking together, John was with Peter and Jesus. Peter asked Jesus about John and whether he would die also. Jesus reacted sharply to Peter's comment, telling him not to worry about what John's role or purpose was in life. All Peter had to do was worry about fulfilling his own purpose.

As businesspeople we tend to measure our success on whether we have achieved a certain position or stature in life. Even as Christians the temptation to believe that someone is blessed if they have achieved prominence is always confronting us. In His discussion with Peter, Jesus was getting at the very heart of the matter of a person's calling. Peter was worried about whether his friend John was going to get the same lot in life as he was. Jesus told him it should not be his concern. He was to concern himself only with one thing: his own calling before God.

Are you tempted to compare yourself with where others are in their life? Are you dissatisfied with where God has you right now? Be of good cheer—"[be] confident of this, that He who began a good work in you will carry it on to completion until the day of Christ Jesus" (Phil. 1:6).

March 30

Embracing the Lean Times

But blessed is the man who trusts in the Lord, whose confidence is in Him.   Jeremiah 17:7

Have you ever considered at what point a test becomes so difficult that you decide you can no longer trust in God and you must take over to solve the problem? The prophet Jeremiah describes a situation in which the temptation to solve a financial problem can become so great that we trust in man's way to solve it.

This is what the Lord says: "Cursed is the one who trusts in man, who depends on flesh for his strength and whose heart turns away from the Lord. He will be like a bush in the wastelands; he will not see prosperity when it comes. He will dwell in the parched places of the desert, in a salt land where no one lives. But blessed is the man who trusts in the Lord, whose confidence is in Him. He will be like a tree planted by the water that sends out its roots by the stream. It does not fear when heat comes; its leaves are always green. It has no worries in a year of drought and never fails to bear fruit" (Jeremiah 17:5-8).

Jeremiah drew a sharp comparison between the man who trusts in his own effort to solve his problem and the man who trusts in God when he cannot see the outcome. The man who trusts in God bears fruit despite the circumstances in his life. He does not shrivel when the heat comes; in fact, his roots go deeper into God's grace. He continues to bear fruit in spite of his circumstances.

Recently, a friend from South Africa explained to me that whenever a plant lives in an arid climate, the roots drive deeper and deeper into the soil to get the water they need. This forces the plant to develop a root system that is far beyond the normal plant because it is forced to go deeper to gain the water it needs. Sometimes God forces us to go deeper into the grace of His love in order to build a greater foundation in our own lives. These lean times are designed to accomplish this in us. If you find yourself in this condition, ask the Lord who provides the water for our soul for the grace you need today to continue to bear fruit in the desert.

March 31

An Eternal View of Circumstances

> *Now I want you to know, brothers, that what has happened to me has really served to advance the gospel.* Philippians 1:12

Are your life circumstances advancing the gospel? Can you see the Lord's hand in your life in such a way that all of your life experiences, joys, sorrows, hardships, and training have resulted in advancing the gospel?

Paul was a tentmaker by trade. But he had an overall ministry objective in his business life. That objective left him imprisoned and persecuted at times. But Paul saw these events not as roadblocks to his mission. Rather, they were catalysts to advancing the cause of Christ. Paul's revelation of this kept him from despairing about his circumstances.

One day a little-known pastor who lived in the small African nation of Benin began to pray for his Marxist president. For two years he prayed. Then the Lord told the pastor to go to meet this president and share the gospel with him. The president rejected the gospel, but after another such occasion, the president accepted the gospel and became a

Christian. He was removed from power but was discipled by this pastor. Sometime later this same president was elected again. Today that president is now a Christian leader of a nation committed to spreading the gospel throughout his nation. One man—but millions have been affected by his obedience. This modern-day story is retold in countless lives of those willing to live for a cause greater than themselves.

Are your business and life experiences serving to advance the gospel? What experiences has God allowed in your life that are part of His plan to advance the gospel? Ask Him to help you see your life the way He sees it. Seeing our life the way God sees it will help us avoid discouragement in those times when life appears to be a mystery to us.

April 1

Opening Our Spiritual Eyes

> *And Elisha prayed, "O Lord, open his eyes so he may see." Then the Lord opened the servant's eyes, and he looked and saw the hills full of horses and chariots of fire all around Elisha.*   2 Kings 6:17

Elisha was counseling the nation of Israel against the impending attack of the king of Aram. The Lord supernaturally gave Elisha the plans that the king was implementing, and in turn, Elisha warned Israel of each intended attack. The king could not understand why his plans were continually foiled. It seemed there was a secret informer in his midst. He was furious when he was told it was the God of Israel who was to blame for this inside information. The king decided the only way to resolve the situation was to get rid of the problem—kill Elisha.

The king's forces arrived and surrounded Elisha and his servant. Elisha's servant became upset and fearful when Elisha was not upset. Elisha immediately prayed that his servant's eyes might be opened to see that there was no need to be afraid, because the angels were protecting them.

> *And Elisha prayed, "O Lord, open his eyes so he may see." Then the Lord opened the servant's eyes, and he looked and saw the hills full*

of horses and chariots of fire all around Elisha. As the enemy came down toward him, Elisha prayed to the Lord, "Strike these people with blindness." So He struck them with blindness, as Elisha had asked (2 Kings 6:17-18).

Who is the Elisha in your life? Do you have a mentor friend who can see the activity of God in your life when you cannot see it? We all need to have somebody we can trust to help us see the activity of God. It is often difficult for us to see what God is really doing because we are so consumed by the circumstances of the moment. Ask God today to help open your spiritual eyes that you might see Him in your circumstances.

April 2

Spiritual Contracts

In the first year of his reign, I, Daniel, understood from the Scriptures, according to the word of the Lord given to Jeremiah the prophet, that the desolation of Jerusalem would last seventy years.
Daniel 9:2

When you enter a legal contract, it binds the two parties to fulfill the terms of that contract. In Heaven there are legal contracts that, when fulfilled, allow the spiritual to impact the physical.

Israel had been in captivity to Babylon for 70 years. Daniel, when he investigated the history of his nation, found the prophecy of Jeremiah that revealed there would be 70 years of captivity. He recognized that in order to release his nation from this captivity, there had to be a confession of sin on the part of the nation. Daniel took that responsibility. Although he could not personally repent for his nation, he could acknowledge their sin and repent himself. When Daniel acknowledged this sin before God, something took place in Heaven. God heard this prayer and responded by sending His angel Gabriel to Daniel's side.

We know from history that this was the time when Judah's return from exile began. Daniel's prayer of confession was the spiritual key to the physical manifestation of releasing the nation from captivity to Babylon.

Whenever you want to confront spiritual forces that have dominion over a situation, you must find the source of the problem. Once you find the source of the problem, you must take the necessary steps in the spiritual realm to release God's power into that situation. For Daniel, it meant taking responsibility for the sin of the nation by confessing its sins and asking forgiveness on behalf of the entire nation. This allowed God to begin the process of releasing the nation.

Ask God to show you the source of the problems that may exist in your city, your business, or people you want to see freed to fulfill God's purposes for their lives.

April 3

Is Anything Too Hard for God?

So Sarah laughed to herself as she thought, "After I am worn out and my master is old, will I now have this pleasure?" Genesis 18:12

God had promised Abraham and Sarah a son who would be the seed of a whole nation. Sarah was now beyond childbearing years. So when some angels from God paid Abraham and Sarah a visit to inform them that Sarah was going to have a child, she happened to be listening outside the tent and erupted with laughter. The thought seemed preposterous to her. The angels reminded her that nothing is impossible with God. "Is anything too hard for the Lord? I will return to you at the appointed time next year and Sarah will have a son" (Gen. 18:14). Sarah gave birth to Isaac as foretold.

Recently, I was considering putting on another marketplace-leader summit for ministry leaders who minister to those in the workplace. I had been involved in such an event a year earlier. My friend Gunnar Olson, who is the founder of the International Christian Chamber of Commerce of Sweden, had been involved with me in putting on the first event, so I inquired whether he would be willing to participate in the second event. He wrote me an e-mail letter informing me that an international gathering of Christian marketplace leaders would be taking place on the island of Cyprus in March and asked if I could postpone my event and instead participate in an event in Cyprus and invite other leaders. My initial response was laughter due to my current financial condition. In fact, I had to go to a map to see just where this place was.

The following day I received a call from a man I had met only 30 days earlier. We had not discussed this event in March. "What are you doing tomorrow? I would like you to go to the airport with me to pick up a missionary whom I want you to meet. We'd like to propose an idea to you. Can you come?"

"Sure," I said.

The next day he picked me up and informed me that we were picking up a missionary who was flying in from Cyprus. "We are planning to take 25 businesspeople to Cyprus for an event that Gunnar Olson is involved in and would like you to come and teach your Esau-to-Joseph workshop the day before. We will cover your expenses. Would you be interested in doing this?" Again, I had to laugh as I saw the hand of God orchestrate in such a miraculous way and in such a timely manner to assure me of His involvement in the new directions in my life.

Jesus looked at them and said, "With man this is impossible, but not with God; all things are possible with God" (Mark 10:27).

Are there things that make you laugh when you think of the miracle that would be required for it to take place? Ask God for the miracle you need today.

April 4

The Dangers of Overcontrol

For rebellion is like the sin of divination, and arrogance like the evil of idolatry. Because you have rejected the word of the Lord, He has rejected you as king.   1 Samuel 15:23

A friend of mine who is a jet pilot once told me that whenever a jet goes out of control and begins to spin, the only thing to do is totally take your hands off the controls and the plane will right itself. This goes against our natural inclination to control and manipulate in order to bring things back under control. It is scary to be out of control. Or is it?

Saul was a man out of control. He was losing control of his kingdom to David. He was losing the favor of God and the people. It began as compromises. Eventually he was given a final test to obey the voice of God fully. He was instructed to kill the Amalekites completely; but he failed to follow through. The prophet Samuel delivered a hard word to King Saul, "Because you have rejected the word of the Lord, He has rejected you as king" (see 1 Sam. 15:26). Saul obeyed partially, but not fully. It was partial obedience that led to his removal as king of Israel and his calling from God. But why did Saul do such a thing? "I was afraid of the people and so I gave in to them" (1 Sam. 15:24b). Saul's fear and insecurity made him more afraid of the people and what they thought than of God. At the core of Saul's disobedience was fear of losing control. That fear of losing control led to partial obedience and the loss of his reign as king.

How many of us are in danger of losing God's blessing due to partial obedience? How many of us have such a need to control people and circumstances that we fail to fully walk in obedience to God's voice in our lives? Saul provides a great lesson for us as businesspeople. The need to overcontrol things around us can prevent us from receiving all that God has for us. Today, take an inventory of your control quotient.

Ask God if you are being fully obedient to what He has called you to do this day, and avoid being put on the shelf for disobedience. "To obey is better than sacrifice, and to heed is better than the fat of rams" (1 Sam. 15:22b).

April 5

The Famine That Leads to Freedom

Go down there and buy some for us, so that we may live and not die.
Genesis 42:2b

April 5—Day 95

F. B. Meyer in his book, *The Life of Joseph*, describes a time in the life of the 12 sons of Jacob in which they were driven from their lives of self-satisfaction to an unlikely place to save their lives. Many years earlier they had thrown their youngest brother into a pit, then sold him into slavery. Thirteen years later he became the second most powerful person in Egypt. Now the world was experiencing a famine, and Joseph controlled all the stored grain of Egypt.

As long as the hills were green and the pastures clothed with flocks, as long as the valleys were covered over with corn and rang with the songs of reapers, Reuben, Simeon, and the rest of them would have been unconcerned and content. But when the mighty famine came, the hearts of these men were opened to conviction. Their carnal security was shattered. They were being prepared for certain spiritual experiences they would never have dreamed. And they were being prepared for the meeting with Joseph. This is how God deals with us; He breaks up our nest, He loosens our roots, He sends a mighty famine that cuts away the whole staff of bread. Then, at such times, weary, worn, and sad, we are prepared to confess our sins and receive the words of Christ when He says, "Come to Me, all you who are weary and burdened, and I will give you rest" (Mt. 11:28).

A missionary once said, "There is a place where we will all be obedient." Joseph was a type of Christ in the Old Testament. The famine was an event designed to bring the brothers to repentance and a saving knowledge, physically and spiritually. It created the circumstances that led to freedom for these men. For they had been in bondage to a wicked crime against their brother for many years. It was the forgiveness from Joseph that led to that freedom.

Is your life passing through a time of famine? Are your supplies limited? Is God leading you into directions that you would not normally seek? Perhaps this is God's hand creating circumstances for His purposes. Now is the time to look attentively as He directs you to unlikely sources.

April 6

A New Breed of Businesspeople

Speak to Zerubbabel son of Shealtiel, governor of Judah, to Joshua son of Jehozadak, the high priest, and to the remnant of the people....
Haggai 2:2

Zerubbabel was the governor of Judah 60 years after the great temple built by Solomon had been destroyed. The temple lay in ruins, and the Lord spoke to the prophet Haggai, "Is it a time for you yourselves to be living in your paneled houses, while this house remains a ruin?" (Hag. 1:4) God was calling for a remnant of His people to come out of their comfort zones and restore the glory of God's house.

God is doing this same thing today among Christian businesspeople throughout the world. He is raising up a remnant of businesspeople who are being handpicked to use their resources, skills, and experience to affect nations that have not heard the message of Jesus Christ. The only way they can hear is by commerce being brought into their nation through Christian businesspeople, because these are closed regions to normal missionary efforts.

"But now be strong, O Zerubbabel," declares the Lord. "Be strong, O Joshua son of Jehozadak, the high priest. Be strong, all you people of the land," declares the Lord, "and work. For I am with you," declares the Lord Almighty. "This is what I covenanted with you when you came out of Egypt. And My Spirit remains among you. Do not fear" (Haggai 2:4-5).

The remnant of businesspeople God is calling today understand that they have to come out of Egypt from their past business life. Egypt signifies the way of the world. It represents sweat and toil. It is the flesh. This new way is exemplified by a pioneer spirit. God knows we need to have courage in order to move in this realm. Also, God assures us that His Spirit is with anyone who seeks to live in the realm of supernatural faith.

Are you one of these remnants He has handpicked in these days? Has He called you out of Egypt in order to do extraordinary things in your life for His Kingdom? Ask God to show you how He wants to use you in the marketplace this year. Then act and "be strong, all you people of the land."

April 7

Faith Experiences

These have come so that your faith—of greater worth than gold, which perishes even though refined by fire—may be proved genuine and may result in praise, glory and honor when Jesus Christ is revealed.   1 Peter 1:7

One of the great tragedies of the Christian life is that if we fail to enter into a relationship with God that is born of the Holy Spirit, we are left with a religion, not a relationship. Many a person today lives with an intellectual belief in God, but without a relationship that is based on two-way communication. This is the greatest tragedy of all. It's like having a brand-new car but never having the gas to run it. It can't move you anywhere. It only looks pretty, but one cannot enjoy the ride or smell the newness inside.

Peter tells us that until our faith is proved genuine, we will never be able to give praise, glory, and honor to Jesus, because until such testing He will not be revealed in our lives. Peter describes this in the verse before: "In this you greatly rejoice, though now for a little while you may have had to suffer grief in all kinds of trials" (1 Pet. 1:6). Trials are designed to bring us to a level of trust and experience with God that we would never know otherwise. These "faith experiences" with God allow us to know firsthand the faithfulness of God, the love of God, and the personal nature of God. If you cannot recount several instances when God has met you personally, then chances are your faith has not been born of the Holy Spirit into a living relationship with God. It is easy to fall prey to a relationship to God that never experiences His real presence; rather, it is based on knowledge only. This is a tragic place to be.

If this is where you have been in your Christian experience, ask God today to make Himself real to you. Ask Him to show you His personal nature and love. He desires to do this. Those whom He has called know His voice. He will show Himself to those who are His. "He who loves Me will be loved by My Father, and I too will love him and show Myself to him" (Jn. 14:21b).

April 8

Friendship in the Pit

A friend loves at all times, and a brother is born for adversity.
Proverbs 17:17

"I am in there again," I told my friend. "The pit." A time when no one can cheer you up and you wonder if there ever was or is a God. Have you ever had such times? Discouragement can be devastating even to the best of saints. It can bring us so low. The writer of Proverbs phrased it well when he said, "Hope deferred makes the heart sick" (Prov. 13:12). When we get so low that we despair of our belief, we can identify with the prophet Elijah who wanted to die after being so discouraged with life.

"I'm coming over," my friend said.

"Aw, you don't have to do that," I said.

"I'm coming over. We're going to pray."

About 30 minutes later my friend walked in the door. We sat down on the living room floor and simply lay on our backs as my friend began to pray. I didn't feel like praying. I was too deep in the pit. All I could do was listen. After awhile my friend was quiet. We both sat quietly for ten to fifteen minutes, praying quietly to ourselves. Suddenly my friend said, "First Thessalonians 5:24!"

"What verse is that?" I asked.

"I don't know," she said. "That is the verse He spoke to me."

I grabbed my Bible and looked up the verse. "The one who calls you is faithful and He will do it."

We laughed. Can He be so personal? Can He care that much? That night I grew more in my love of my two friends, not to mention being brought out of the pit.

Do you have a friend who is there when you need somebody at any hour of the day? Are you there for your friend? Ask the Lord how you can be a better friend to someone today.

April 9

The Jezebel Spirit

Nevertheless, I have this against you: You tolerate that woman Jezebel, who calls herself a prophetess. By her teaching she misleads my servants into sexual immorality and the eating of food sacrificed to idols.   Revelation 2:20

One of the major ruling spirits opposing the Kingdom of God today is the spirit of Jezebel. It has dominion over many aspects of society including the marketplace and the entertainment industry. It predominantly lives in females, but is not always gender specific.

The spirit of Jezebel seeks to destroy true worship, the family, morality, and the God-ordained role of male leadership. It misleads and corrupts the Church and seeks to neutralize the lives of prophets, pastors, and other male leadership.

The spirit of Jezebel is best seen in the story of Naboth's garden in First Kings 21. In this story King Ahab desires to purchase some land next to the king's palace. Naboth refuses to sell. When Jezebel hears of this, she embarrasses Ahab, telling him he should be ashamed because he is the king and has every right to the land. She promptly plots against Naboth to get the land for the king. This leads to Naboth's murder. Ahab does not know of this plot by his wife, but when the king shows up to claim the land, the prophet Elijah shows up too and pronounces judgment on Ahab and his wife. In this passage we see that God held Ahab ultimately responsible for the death of Naboth.

Jezebel's ultimate goal is always control, especially over men. Jezebels cause fear, flight, and discouragement. They are often natural leaders. Often subtle and deceptive, they are proud, independent, and rebellious. Jezebels cannot live without Ahabs who allow them to be effective and operate unchallenged. Ahabs fail to operate as godly, loving leaders. Rather, they give in to pressure from the Jezebels, often due to their own insecurities and sexual needs.

The answer to defeating the Jezebel spirit for the person who is influenced by it is true repentance, humility, and brokenness before God. The person who is "Jezebeled" must firmly stand against the sexual exploitation of this spirit.

If you find yourself confronting this spirit, ask the Lord to give you discernment and wisdom. You will need fasting and prayer to win this battle. And it is not a license for men to lord over women, but an understanding that this spirit opposes God's design of the two equal but distinct roles for men and women.

April 10

Planning for Success

I know, O Lord, that a man's life is not his own; it is not for man to direct his steps.   Jeremiah 10:23

In business I hear a lot about planning. Every January I hear businesspeople establishing their planning for the year. Corporations establish plans that cover anywhere from one to five years. Individuals establish personal life plans. There is only one problem that I see with most planning done by well-meaning believers. If God is not the originator and director of the plan, then that plan is doomed for failure. So often, Christian businesspeople set out to plan something that seems good in their own mind. The merits of what is being planned can look great, and it can even be a worthy endeavor. However, that is not the point. When Jesus said He came only to do the will of the Father, He could not consider doing anything that was not what the Father wanted, no matter how good or righteous it might appear to be.

"In his heart a man plans his course, but the Lord determines his steps" (Prov. 16:9). God must give us the vision for what He calls us to do. After we have the vision, we must ask Him if He wants us to take action on that vision and what the action steps entail. The Lord wants to direct each step of the planning process. David learned this lesson when he went to battle against his enemy, the Philistines. One day he inquired of God as to whether he was to go up against the Philistines, and the Lord said, "Yes, but only when you hear the marching in the balsam trees." It is a mistake to reason and analyze in order to come to a decision on a matter. The Lord already knows the answer. It is our responsibility to seek Him to find out His mind on the matter. Our planning must be established in Him. Only when we remain so connected to the Source can we be assured of putting God's plan into place. Also, getting that plan confirmed through others will assure that we are not following the deceit of our own heart.

When you begin to plan next time, ask God for His wisdom for establishing the vision and action steps. You will be surprised how well He can plan.

April 11

The Gospel of the Kingdom

This is how we know we are in Him: Whoever claims to live in Him must walk as Jesus did. 1 John 2:5b-6

When Christ came to earth, He came to bring to mankind the gospel of the Kingdom. Over the centuries, the Church has tended to emphasize only a portion of the gospel. That portion is the gospel of salvation. However, Jesus came that we might have more than just salvation. He came to give us a whole new life that was accompanied by signs, wonders, and His Spirit living in us and revealing Himself to us daily. He came so that we might walk on this earth as He did. If our lives are not reflecting the same things as Jesus' did, we must ask why?

I have noticed three distinct types of businesspeople throughout my 24 years of walking with Christ. First, many of us come to Christ out of a need for salvation. Our hearts have been touched by His call on our lives. We reason and analyze the claims of Christ and make a decision for Him. It is the *convenient* time to accept Him in our lives. This first stage is often characterized by a "Bless me, Lord" attitude toward God. It is the first stage that primarily brings salvation into our lives. Some never really go past this first stage.

The second stage is the *crisis* stage. A crisis takes place in our lives, and we are motivated to seek Christ with a whole heart. However, this motivation is not out of pure love for Christ; rather, it is motivated by the desire to get out of the pain of living. The motivation is to solve the *what* versus the *why* in my life at the time. This stage is best characterized as "Help me, Lord."

In the third stage we begin to experience the gospel of the Kingdom. It is the place where Jesus resided in His walk with His heavenly Father. It is the place of *conviction*. The number of people who live at this level are quite few, but these people are experiencing the reality of a walk with God that is foreign to all others. They are seeing daily occurrences of His involvement in their lives. They are motivated by a deep love for Him. They know Him. These people have an attitude characterized by these thoughts, "Have me, Lord; though He slay me, still will I trust Him."

Where are you today? Have you merely accepted His salvation to simply float along? Or do you seek Him with a whole heart only when a crisis occurs? His desire is for you and me to live a life of conviction, motivated by our love for Him and His love for us. This is where we will experience the gospel of the Kingdom.

April 12

Knowledge That Is Productive

For if you possess these qualities in increasing measure, they will keep you from being ineffective and unproductive in your knowledge of our Lord Jesus Christ.   2 Peter 1:8

Productivity is a term all businesspeople can relate to. It is the by-product of what we desire from our work. Without productivity, we do not make sales, we do not deliver goods, we do not achieve our goals. There are things in our business lives that can creep in making us unproductive. The same is true in our walk with God.

April 12—Day 102

The apostle Peter tells us that we can become knowledgeable of Jesus but fail to be effective and productive in our relationship with Him. We are a society that has great knowledge, but our comparable scale of productivity from that knowledge is extremely weighted to the knowledge side. The apostle Peter tells us there is a solution to this dilemma.

> *For this very reason, make every effort to add to your faith goodness; and to goodness, knowledge; and to knowledge, self-control; and to self-control, perseverance; and to perseverance, godliness; and to godliness, brotherly kindness; and to brotherly kindness, love. For if you possess these qualities in increasing measure, they will keep you from being ineffective and unproductive in your knowledge of our Lord Jesus Christ* (2 Peter 1:5-8).

Is your Christian experience filled with knowledge, but little power? Is there a staleness in your walk with God? Is there an unrest in your soul? It may be due to a need to develop character that only the Holy Spirit can develop out of an obedient heart. Ask the Lord today to add these qualities to your faith so that you can be productive as a soldier of Jesus Christ.

April 13

Your Work

> *I have brought You glory on earth by completing the work You gave Me to do.* John 17:4

The Lord has revealed to us that the number one thing we are to do is love the Lord our God with all our heart and to love our neighbor as ourselves. His desire is for us to know Him and the power of His resurrection. These mandates deal with our relationship with Him. The fruit of this relationship must then result in our glorifying Him by completing the work He has given each of us to do. It will become a by-product of this relationship, not an end in itself.

What is the work God has called you to do? Jesus never did anything the Father had not instructed Him to do. He lived in such communion with the Father that He knew when to turn left and when to turn to the right. Is it possible to have such a relationship with our heavenly Father? I think that if it weren't, He would not have given us such an example.

"Call to Me and I will answer you and tell you great and unsearchable things you do not know" (Jer. 33:3). What has He called you to do? Perhaps you are called to be the best CPA in your city or the best advertising executive or the best office worker or assembly-line person in your company. Whatever work He has called you to do, He will use you as His instrument to accomplish something that He has uniquely prepared you to do.

When our life is complete, what a glorious day it will be if we can each say, "I have completed the work You gave me to do." This will have brought great glory to Him.

April 14

Using Satan for God's Purposes

> *Hand this man over to satan, so that the sinful nature may be destroyed and his spirit saved on the day of the Lord.*
>
> 1 Corinthians. 5:5

Paul encountered a believer who was involved in an incestuous relationship in the Corinthian church. This man was deluded by satan and was controlled by immorality. The man was unwilling to change his behavior, so Paul recommended to the church that tough actions be taken. He spiritually handed this man over to satan for the destruction of his flesh for the benefit of his soul. The idea is that the person will wallow in the pit of sin so long until it becomes detestable to him and he cries out for God's grace. We know this man was a Christian because only a Christian can be subjected to church discipline.

Have you ever known someone who was walking in disobedience and no matter how much you prayed, he seemed oblivious to his sin? God has given one weapon to counter satan's schemes against those who fall prey to satan. That is, let satan have access to them fully so that their lives become so miserable they cry out to God for mercy. Probably few of us have ever had to pray this prayer. However, you should not be fearful of this prayer for any believer who is willingly walking in disobedience. This is love—tough love. There is a time and place for tough love. I have seen this principle work. God restores His children when His Body takes a stand against sin. It is not comfortable for those who take this action.

Do you know someone who needs tough love in his or her life right now? Ask God if it is time to pray the prayer that Paul prayed. "So that his spirit might be saved on the day of the Lord."

April 15

Four Attributes of a Life God Blesses

So this is what the Sovereign Lord says: "See, I lay a stone in Zion, a tested stone, a precious cornerstone for a sure foundation; the one who trusts will never be dismayed." Isaiah 28:16

Whenever God calls us into a consecrated life, it is made up of four distinct stages. Christ often compared this process to building a house. First, we must prepare to build by laying a foundation. That foundation is none other than Jesus Christ Himself. Any foundation other than Christ will not stand.

Second, as we enter a walk of faith with God, He allows each of us to experience trials, testings, miracles, and challenges in life that are designed to provide "faith experiences" that demonstrate tangible evidences of His work in our life: Moses' burning-bush experience, Peter's walk on the water, Joshua's parting of the Jordan River. These experiences built the faith of these people. The depth and width of our calling is directly proportional to the faith experiences He allows in each of our lives. If God plans an international ministry with you, chances are you will experience a higher degree of faith experiences compared to another. The reason is, you will need to look on these to ensure your calling and provide testimony to His work in your life.

The third stage deals with motives. "All a man's ways seem innocent to him, but motives are weighed by the Lord" (Prov. 16:2). What is the motive behind my actions? Is it only financial accumulation? Is it to gain control? Is it to create independence? The primary motive must be God's leading you to take such an action—it must be obedience. These other factors must be by-products of the decision.

Finally, we are prepared to take action. Here we must ask, "Do we have the skill, quality, and ability to enter into this activity?" So often we have not trained ourselves adequately to be successful in our endeavor. You would never want someone working on your teeth who had not been trained and certified as a dentist.

Before you begin your next project, ask yourself these four questions. What is the foundation this project is based on? What experiences has God demonstrated in my life that indicate His involvement? What is my motive for entering this activity? Do I have the skill, quality, and ability to accomplish the task? Answering these questions will tell you whether God will bless your activity.

April 16

The Graduate-Level Test: Self-defense

He will make your righteousness shine like the dawn, the justice of your cause like the noonday sun.   Psalm 37:6

As a believer grows in trusting obedience and love, God often brings a test that seems uncharacteristically cruel. That test is being wrongfully judged by those close to you. It is not for the reactionary. It cannot be passed over by simply gutting it out. Supernatural grace is the only means of passing this one. It is one of those tests the Savior had to experience Himself when being tried by the court of public opinion, the religious community, and the government of His day. His response to the government was silence. His response to the religious establishment was silence at the final judgment. To the rest of His accusers He remained quiet and left vindication to the Father. He lived the commandment He gave to the disciples:

> *"But love your enemies, do good to them, and lend to them without expecting to get anything back. Then your reward will be great, and you will be sons of the Most High, because He is kind to the ungrateful and wicked"* (Luke 6:35).

How do you react when you are accused or mistreated for no reason? Do you listen quietly, or do you justify each and every action? Most of us take pride in doing what is right and expect the same from others, especially our brothers and sisters in the faith. Jesus knew that if you were to be a true follower of His, you would enter this test eventually. It is part of the program. The marketplace gives ample opportunity to be wronged, misunderstood, and maligned. When God brings a measured assault against one of His children, it is to find out if he truly believes in the cross. The cross is where each of us is given the opportunity to die to our pride, our reputations, and our ego. When He allows a measured assault upon us, it is to find out if the cross is sufficient. He wants to see if we will seek to rescue ourselves. Jesus said if we die with Him, we will be raised with Him. When God allows satan to bring the measured assault, ask God for the grace to cling to the cross. Let the pride and arrogance that Jesus wants to remove from our lives be crucified. Thank God for the opportunity to be crucified with Christ. Then your righteousness will shine like the noonday sun and the justice of your cause will be in His hands.

April 17

The Interests of Others

> *Each of you should look not only to your own interests, but also to the interests of others.* Philippians 2:4

One of the walls of Christianity that has existed for centuries is the attitude of many "full-time" Christian workers and businesspeople. Often pastors, missionaries, and other "full timers" (I put this in quotes since all of us should consider ourselves full time) see businesspeople as a dollar sign. They see them as the instrument to fund their next project or provide the support they need. This wrong view toward businesspeople encourages them to harden their hearts toward legitimate projects. It creates a vicious cycle in which satan robs both servants of God of the blessing of each other's gifts and talents.

I once attended an international conference in which businesspeople acknowledged having this attitude toward Christian workers. Christian workers asked for forgiveness for viewing those in business as objects for funding. There was a time of repentance and tears for the selfish attitude and callousness of both groups. Christian businesspeople have more to offer the Kingdom than their dollars, but this is often overlooked.

Paul admonishes us to:

Do nothing out of selfish ambition or vain conceit, but in humility consider others better than yourselves. Each of you should look not only to your own interests, but also to the interests of others. Your attitude should be the same as that of Christ Jesus (Philippians 2:3-5).

If the God of the universe came as a humble servant, we in business must maintain our humble servant attitude toward those who have lesser means and are seeking to serve the Lord. God has entrusted many of us in business with greater resources. The test is to examine whether we are operating in vanity or Christ-like servanthood, looking out for the interests of others.

Ask the Lord to provide the grace to consider each request that comes to you for assistance and to avoid becoming callous to these requests. This is one test from God that He brings to determine whether you will serve others before yourself. The true test of giving is when it has no benefit to yourself.

April 18

Losing Your Life for His Purposes

For whoever wants to save his life will lose it, but whoever loses his life for Me will save it.   Luke 9:24

When the time came for God to fulfill Joseph's dreams, Joseph himself had virtually no interest at all in it. Jesus said, "For whoever wants to save his life will lose it, but whoever loses his life for Me will save it" (Lk. 9:24). God wants to teach us a different set of values so that the kind of thing we start out wanting becomes secondary. God has something in mind for us that is far greater than the interest we began with.

Joseph's day of exaltation had arrived. Yet, through it all, a very real humiliation had to take place. We know about the humiliation Joseph had experienced for 13 years after being sold by his brothers into slavery, then taken to Egypt. We know how he was falsely accused and cast into prison.

Then came a different situation. Joseph had had a triumph and was given an exaltation, but the kind he really never asked for. He did not appear to be all that interested in what was about to happen. He watched as the Pharaoh took his ring off his finger and put it on Joseph's finger. Joseph never asked for that. All he wanted was to go home. He longed to go back to Canaan, to see his father, and to have his dreams fulfilled.

Therefore, here we find an extraordinary incongruity: a humiliation in the heart of vindication. A triumph that was the opposite of everything he, himself, could have envisaged. Joseph wanted to go home, but a one-way ticket to Canaan wasn't available. Before he knew it, he had Egypt in his hip pocket. He had never prayed for that. But God wanted Egypt. What God wanted is what Joseph got.

Joseph was given something that he could be trusted with because it didn't mean that much to him. [R.T. Kendall, *A Treasury of Wisdom Journal* (Uhrichsville, Ohio: Barbour and Company, 1996), January 16 day reading, email books<barbour@tusco.net>].

April 19

Possessions of the Kingdom

But I will punish the nation they serve as slaves, and afterward they will come out with great possessions.   Genesis 15:14

Whenever God brings you through a time of great adversity, you can expect to come out of that experience with great possessions, if you have been faithful through the trial. This is a universal truth. Wisdom comes from obedience, not knowledge. When we have been tested and proven, the reality of our faith results in possessions from God that we would never receive if we had not gone through those trials. These are precious in His sight and should be valued greatly. Those who know you will be amazed at the wisdom that comes from your mouth. It is one of those mysteries of the gospel that only those who experience incredible testing and hardship can explain.

God kept the people of Israel enslaved 400 years, but when the time came to free them from the bondage of slavery, they came out with great possessions. These physical possessions symbolize the spiritual possessions we receive when we come out of being enslaved to those things that have hindered us all our lives. These possessions are to be shared with others so that they also can know how they might become free.

What has God freed you from that allows you to share your possessions with others? Share what God has done in your life with someone you work with today. It may be the possession they need most in their life.

April 20

Unprofitable Anger

Do not be quickly provoked in your spirit, for anger resides in the lap of fools.   Ecclesiastes 7:9

April 20—Day 110

Every day of our lives we are placed in situations that engage us with other people, whether it is in the office, our homes, or in public places. Do you recall the last time someone cut you off in traffic, or you were forced to wait in line because someone up front got held up? Perhaps your employer did something that was downright unfair. Anger can result from many circumstances.

A friend once told me that anger is like warning lights on the front of your car dashboard. They signal that there is something going on under the hood, and we should take a look to examine the source of the problem. Anger can be traced to a few sources. First, when we lose control of a circumstance that we have placed certain expectations on and those expectations do not result in our desired outcome, we are tempted to get angry. The source of this type of anger is both fear and protection of personal rights. You see, when we believe we have a right to something, we have not given the Lord permission to allow an outcome different from what we want. If an outcome is different from our expectations, this may stimulate fear.

For instance, if a vendor failed to deliver an important job on time due to something out of his control, you may respond out of anger. Please know that the source of your anger is the fear of what might happen to you or what this might say about your abilities to manage a project. You no longer are in control of the circumstance and this creates fear in you.

The next time you get angry ask the Lord what is the source of that anger? Did the Lord allow that failure to let you see what is "under your hood"? God has not given us a spirit of fear, but of love, power, and a sound mind (see 2 Tim. 1:7). Give up your rights to expectations that God never gave you. You will find a new freedom in Christ you never knew you could have.

April 21

Mustard Seed Faith in Business

He replied, "Because you have so little faith. I tell you the truth, if you have faith as small as a mustard seed, you can say to this mountain, 'Move from here to there' and it will move. Nothing will be impossible for you."   Matthew 17:20

Does God do miracles in business? Is He concerned about the mountains we face in our work life? Does He want us to bring the everyday problems we face in the workplace to His attention? The answer to every one of these questions is yes. God wants to be involved in every aspect of our lives.

Gunnar Olson, the Swedish founder of the International Christian Chamber of Commerce, tells a story about God performing a miracle in his own business a few years ago. He owns a plastics company in Sweden. They make huge plastic bags that are used to cover bales of hay in the farmlands across Europe. It was the harvest season and they were getting ready to ship thousands of pallets of these bags to their customers. More than 1,000 pallets were ready to ship when an alarming discovery was made. Every bag on the warehouse floor had sealed shut from top to bottom. Scientists declared the entire stock as worthless trash. Nothing could be done. The company would go out of business.

Gunnar, his wife, and children sought the Lord in prayer about this catastrophe. The Holy Spirit spoke through various family members. The wife said, "If God can turn water into wine, what are plastics?" The daughter said, "I don't believe this is from the Lord. We should stand against it." Gunnar sensed they were to trust God for a miracle in this situation. They began to pray. They took authority over this mountain of a problem based on Matthew 17, which gave them the authority to cast a mountain into the sea if faith only the size of a mustard seed could be exercised. The following Monday they went to the warehouse and laid hands on every pallet asking the Lord to restore the bags to their original condition. It took several hours. Later, the employees began to inspect the bags. As they inspected the bags, they discovered that every single bag had been restored to its original condition! An incredible miracle had taken place.

What obstacles have been placed in your life that need a miracle today? Could God be setting the stage in your life for you to trust Him at new levels you've never trusted before? God sets the stage to allow His power to be revealed for those willing to exercise the faith of a mustard seed. All things are possible with God.

April 22

Hearing His Voice

He who belongs to God hears what God says. The reason you do not hear is that you do not belong to God.　　　　　　　　John 8:47

Jesus said that the key to being able to hear God's voice is first to be one of His children. One of the great mysteries of the universe to my logical mind is how God can communicate with six billion people on the earth at the same time. It is one of those mysteries I must let go of because my "hard drive" would crash if I had to explain and understand this before I believed and trusted in Him. It is as though God places a computer chip in each human being, and when we place our faith and trust in Him, it becomes activated. We begin to communicate with Him. Jesus says that if we are a child of God, we can hear God's voice. He further explains this relationship in the following parable:

I tell you the truth, the man who does not enter the sheep pen by the gate, but climbs in by some other way, is a thief and a robber. The man who enters by the gate is the shepherd of his sheep. The watchman opens the gate for him, and the sheep listen to his voice. He calls his own sheep by name and leads them out. When he has brought out all his own, he goes on ahead of them, and his sheep follow him because they know his voice. But they will never follow a stranger; in fact, they will run away from him because they do not recognize a stranger's voice (John 10:1-5).

The Shepherd is always representative of Christ. Sheep are representative of God's children. This passage tells us that the Shepherd communicates with His children. We are called by name and we can listen to our Shepherd's voice. There is another comforting aspect to this relationship. The Shepherd goes before the sheep to prepare the way. Jesus has already gone before us today to prepare our way.

Knowing the Shepherd and His voice allows us to have the assurance that we will not be fooled by another shepherd's voice. The sheep know His voice. It is only when we are dull of hearing that we mistakenly hear another's voice and follow it. Sin can create a poor frequency in our communication with the Shepherd. Make sure your frequency is free of static (sin) today so that the Shepherd can lead you and go before you.

Finally, distractions can also keep us from hearing our Shepherd's voice. When the sheep get entangled in the fence or wander off, they get too far away to hear the Shepherd's voice. We must stay in close proximity to the Shepherd to hear His voice. Stay close to the Shepherd today. Listen and follow. He wants to lead you.

April 23

Understanding the Roadblock

And Joshua said, "Ah, Sovereign Lord, why did You ever bring this people across the Jordan to deliver us into the hands of the Amorites to destroy us? If only we had been content to stay on the other side of the Jordan!"   Joshua 7:7

Have you ever felt like you were doing what God wanted you to do, but your plans were totally frustrated? This was how Joshua felt.

The Lord had been with the people of Israel as they entered the Promised Land. They defeated every enemy because of God's blessing and protection. They had just taken the city of Jericho. The next battle was the city of Ai. They scouted the enemy and determined it would require only 3,000 men to defeat them. They attacked, and soon the reports came back that they were being routed. Joshua could not understand this. He cried out to God asking why this was happening.

> *The Lord said to Joshua, "Stand up! What are you doing down on your face? Israel has sinned; they have violated My covenant, which I commanded them to keep. They have taken some of the devoted things; they have stolen, they have lied, they have put them with their own possessions. That is why the Israelites cannot stand against their enemies; they turn their backs and run because they have been made liable to destruction. I will not be with you anymore unless you destroy whatever among you is devoted to destruction"* (Joshua 7:10-12).

Whenever we open ourselves up to sin, we become liable. God removes His protective shield from our lives in order for the sin in our lives to be purged out. He often uses the enemy of our souls to accomplish the task. If you feel you are being thwarted in some way, examine your life to see if there is any sin that is the cause of the problem. Adversity is not always due to sin, but it can be. Ask Him. He will show you. As with Joshua, God immediately answered this prayer when Joshua asked. He desires for His children to live in a right relationship with Him.

April 24

Healing Before Ministry

> *And after the whole nation had been circumcised, they remained where they were in camp until they were healed.*   Joshua 5:8

Before the nation of Israel could go into the Promised Land they had to be circumcised. Circumcision is painful, bloody, and personal. God requires each of us to be circumcised in heart before we are allowed to enter and receive the blessings that await each believer in the Promised Land.

This circumcision can often be very painful. Circumcision requires losing our old way of life. The process of spiritual circumcision may mean a loss in areas that have been a part of our lives in order to draw us to the Savior. God understands this. Consequently, like the people of Israel, we must wait until we are healed before we begin to be effective in our calling. If we launch out too early, we will be ineffective and may risk infection and disease and will not be at our full capacity. God wants each of us to walk in His healing grace.

The people of Israel fought only two battles when they were coming out of Egypt. In the Promised Land they fought 39 battles. Each of us must be prepared to enjoy the benefits of living in the Promised Land. However, we must also be prepared to wage war against the enemy of our souls. Make sure the Lord has provided the needed healing to your circumcision experience before you enter the Promised Land.

April 25

Sweating Outcomes

In vain you rise early and stay up late, toiling for food to eat—for He grants sleep to those He loves.   Psalm 127:2

Coming into the Promised Land in business will change the way you and I view our work. No longer will we see getting up early and staying up late as God's way. Living in the Promised Land in business means we know that God is the source of our provision and that our work is an act of worship to Him. Provision is a by-product, not an end in itself. Work is no longer something that must be sweated and toiled upon to make ends meet. "Could this really be true?" you might be saying. God has made it clear that obedience is the assurance of provision. Whenever we go beyond the normal workday due to fear of non-provision, we are operating in unbelief. We are saying that it is up to us to make things happen. Sure, there are times when we work longer hours due to a deadline, but we must be sure the motive is not out of fear of loss or fear of non-provision. If we are obedient to what God has called us to, He will provide our every need. This can be a hard lesson for goal-oriented businesspeople.

I recall coming into this understanding. I had been a workaholic. Long hours were common. Then God shook up my world and I was challenged by a friend to examine my motives for working long hours. I realized the source of those long hours was fear. Once I came into this understanding, I refused to work long hours even though the natural man would tell me I'd never make things happen if I worked a normal work week. Again, this reasoning is based on a lack of faith. If we are obedient to what God has called each of us to, we will not lack. At times it may be less than what we might like; at other times it may be more than we deserve. These are God's ways.

The Bible tells us to come out of Babylon. Babylon is a system of work and philosophy that is contrary to God's ways. Are you operating in any aspect of work from a Babylonian value system? Ask the Lord to reveal this to you. Begin to walk in the freedom He has given us in our work life.

April 26

Fears That Keep Us From His Presence

> *Then all the people of the region of the Gerasenes asked Jesus to leave them, because they were overcome with fear. So He got into the boat and left.* Luke 8:37

Jesus did many miracles when He lived on earth. One of those miracles involved the deliverance of a demon-possessed man. The people of the community witnessed this awesome demonstration of God's power when Jesus commanded the demon spirit to come out of the man and go into the herd of nearby pigs. The man was healed and sat at Jesus' feet.

You would expect the people who witnessed this to embrace Jesus as one performing good deeds and to honor Him. The opposite was true. Instead, they were overcome with fear. Why? Many of us respond the same way to Jesus when He does an out-of-the-ordinary act among His people. We are fearful because we have never personally experienced this before. So, we draw wrong judgments. The result is that Jesus removes Himself from us.

The Lord is able to do far exceeding above what we think. Jesus does not remain in the places where there is fear of His goodness. It is often subconscious fears that prevent us from going to a deeper level with Him. The people in Gerasenes could not benefit from Jesus' presence because of their fears.

Have you feared Jesus because of what He might require of you? Have you feared that He might ask of you something you are not prepared to give? Do not let your fears drive Him from your presence. His motive is always love for His children. You can trust Him.

April 27

Unrighteous Acts

…"Shouldn't you walk in the fear of our God to avoid the reproach of our Gentile enemies?"   Nehemiah 5:9

Nehemiah was the cupbearer to King Artaxerxes in Babylon. Jerusalem's walls had been destroyed and word had come to Nehemiah that the remnant of his people left in Jerusalem were distressed over the plight of the wall.

Nehemiah was grieved over this situation. He appealed to his king for permission to rebuild the wall. When he got to the city, he found many problems among his own people due to an economic crisis in the region. Among the classes affected by the economic crisis were (1) the landless, who were short of food; (2) the landowners, who were compelled to mortgage their properties; (3) those forced to borrow money at exorbitant rates and sell their children into slavery. It was unlawful for Hebrews to charge interest to other Hebrews.

> *Although we are of the same flesh and blood as our countrymen and though our sons are as good as theirs, yet we have to subject our sons and daughters to slavery. Some of our daughters have already been enslaved, but we are powerless, because our fields and our vineyards belong to others* (Nehemiah 5:5).

Nehemiah stepped forward to admonish his people for this wrongful action on the basis that not only was it wrong, but God would respond to such action by making them susceptible to His judgment through the Gentile enemies.

Nehemiah was modeling to each of us a spiritual principle regarding sin. Whenever we sin, we give God permission to unleash the enemy into our souls to judge that sin. Nehemiah understood this principle and warned the people of what this action would encourage from God. The people repented and returned the money gained through usury.

As Christian businesspeople we must make sure that our practices are righteous in God's sight. If not, we can expect the enemy to be released to judge that sin. Ask the Lord today if there is any unrighteousness in your business practices that makes you vulnerable to judgment.

April 28

Tests of the Heart

> *Remember how the Lord your God led you all the way in the desert these forty years, to humble you and to test you in order to know what was in your heart, whether or not you would keep His commands.* Deuteronomy 8:2

Has God performed a heart test on you lately? There are times in our lives when God leads us into the desert in order to let us find out what is in our heart. These times can be very difficult and humbling. They can test our mettle like no other time. Desert times often mean we are living without those things we are normally accustomed to: water, food, limited supplies—and with few comforts. In modern terms, it may mean a different environment. God is performing a very important work during these times. He wants to know if we can be obedient to Him in these times; or will we be obedient only when times are good?

He humbled you, causing you to hunger and then feeding you with manna, which neither you nor your fathers had known, to teach you that man does not live on bread alone but on every word that comes from the mouth of the Lord. Your clothes did not wear out and your feet did not swell during these forty years. Know then in your heart that as a man disciplines his son, so the Lord your God disciplines you (Deuteronomy 8:3-5).

These desert times may mean experiencing new ways of provision from the Lord. Like manna from Heaven, it may mean seeing miracles we've never seen before. Like clothing that never wears out, it may mean seeing your normal capabilities expanded. Like walking hundreds of miles without pain, desert experiences provide new lessons and new experiences that only these times can teach us.

What desert experience has He brought into your life lately? Perhaps it is a lean time in business. Perhaps it is a new environment. Whatever it is, when God decides to bring new disciplines into our lives by bringing us into the desert, do not fear the heat that is sure to come. He is walking beside you in order to test you and find out what is really in your heart. Ask for His grace to pass the test. He wants to bring all of His children into the Promised Land.

April 29

First Fruits

All the silver and gold and the articles of bronze and iron are sacred to the Lord and must go into His treasury.   Joshua 6:19

One of the earliest examples of the practice of giving God the first fruits of the increase was when Joshua and the people entered the Promised Land for the first time. When they crossed the Jordan River, their first battle was Jericho. God set a precedent with this battle by instructing them not to take any spoils from it. Unlike future battles, the fruits from this victory were to go into the treasury as a remembrance of their first victory in the Promised Land. In addition, the city of Jericho was to be a lasting monument to God's faithfulness. God instructed Joshua never to rebuild this city. If they or anyone in the future attempted to rebuild the city, the life of the firstborn would be required. Years later, Ahab attempted to rebuild this city and his firstborn died as a result. God never forgets to enforce His Word.

Is your work a lasting monument to the faithfulness of God in your life? Is it bringing glory to the Father? Are you giving the first fruits from your increase to God? God has encouraged us through this story to give the first fruits of our work to Him so that He will be glorified through our work. This is a tangible way for us to acknowledge that God is the source of all blessing.

April 30

Avoiding Self-Based Faith

> *We live by faith, not by sight.*   2 Corinthians 5:7

Over the years I have run into many businessmen who make the statement, "Whenever I get things in order in my business, I want to get more involved in ministry." What are these men really saying? They are saying that as soon as they can get the amount of money that creates security, they will trust God. They are saying that what they have been doing to date has not been ministry. This separation of "work and faith" is common among our culture. We fail to understand that life is sacred to God and there is nothing "holy" and nothing "sacred" in itself.

I would love to hear one businessperson say, "I have spent my life in this business. The Lord has blessed me with great resources. However, now I want to see His faithfulness in this stage of my life. That is why I am giving away my wealth and trusting Him to provide for me through new ways." Wouldn't that be a novel concept? That is exactly what C.T. Studd, the great cricket player in the 1800s, did. He was reared in a wealthy home, but his deep conversion experience led him to take actions that forced him to trust God in ways he never had to before. He became one of the great missionaries of all time.

Whenever we seek to plan ways of ministry that depend on our ability to manipulate and plan outcome, this is not faith. The ministry that comes from this will be minuscule. Faith that bears fruit is faith that is born from experience with a living God. It is faith that says, "I don't know where the next check is coming from. All I know is that God told me to do this and trust Him for the next step." That is faith that moves mountains and moves God's heart. God rarely allows His servant to see beyond the next faith step. However, those who are willing to take the first step and leave the outcome to Him see His works.

Others went out on the sea in ships; they were merchants on the mighty waters. They saw the works of the Lord... (Psalm 107:23-24).

May 1

Being Given Over to Death

For we who are alive are always being given over to death for Jesus' sake....So then, death is at work in us, but life is at work in you.
2 Corinthians 4:11-12

It is the great mystery of the gospel of Jesus Christ. Death gives life. Jesus' death on the cross gave life. The death of a vision brings new vision. The death of a seed gives new life. It is the central focus of God's requirement for experiencing Him—death. When Jesus extended us an invitation to experience salvation and a relationship with Him, it came with a great cost, our very lives. Yet what we don't realize is that until we relinquish our total lives, we really aren't living at all. Without this death we will continue to strive, manipulate, and fret over every detail of life. It is when we finally say, "Yes, Lord, I am Yours completely," that we experience real freedom for the first time. This is the only time when Christ is fully seen in and through our lives. Christ describes our lives as vessels—vessels for Him to be revealed in and seen by others.

How is your vessel today? When people look inside, will they see a life that is dead to all things, save the life of Christ revealed? In the marketplace, we are faced with challenges each day that seek to instill fear and control at every turn, but Christ says He wants to live through your life in the marketplace. He wants to reveal Himself to your fellow workers today. However, He can only do this if our vessel is free of ourselves. Ask Jesus what things must die today in order for Him to live completely in and through you.

May 2

Ability Versus Availability

His pleasure is not in the strength of the horse, nor His delight in the legs of a man; the Lord delights in those who fear Him, who put their hope in His unfailing love.   Psalm 147:10-11

Do you ever feel so skilled in what you do that you require little help from others? Perhaps you may feel that you are more skilled than any other in your field. Does God need your skills and abilities in order to accomplish His purposes on this earth? The answer is NO.

One thing God does not need is our skills and abilities. However, He does give us the privilege to exercise our gifts and abilities for His service. That service may be as a computer technician, a secretary, an ironworker, or even a lawyer. God calls each of us to our vocations to work unto Him. To believe that He needs our skills to accomplish His mission on earth would be to lower our understanding of an all-encompassing and all-powerful God. The psalmist tells us that His pleasure is not in our strength and ability, but His pleasure is in the attitude of the heart. It is what we find in the heart that helps determine whether ability is translated into availability. You see, God is looking to and fro throughout the earth for a man or woman who is fully committed to Him. A man or woman who is committed to fearing the Lord and placing his hope in His unfailing love is the person God seeks to support.

"For the eyes of the Lord range throughout the earth to strengthen those whose hearts are fully committed to Him" (2 Chron. 16:9a). When our agenda becomes His agenda, we can expect God to fully support all that we do.

If we want to see our skills and abilities multiplied a hundredfold, then we must make them completely available to His service. Where are the opportunities in which God is calling you to be available to Him? Next time someone asks you to be involved in some activity, before you say yea or nay, make sure you check in with the Master of our decisions to ensure that your gifts and talents are being used as He desires.

May 3

Our Labor in the Lord

> *Therefore, my dear brothers, stand firm. Let nothing move you. Always give yourselves fully to the work of the Lord, because you know that your labor in the Lord is not in vain.*
>
> 1 Corinthians 15:58

There is a paradigm shift going on among a remnant of business-people today. That paradigm shift is a focus on using our business and work life as a platform for ministry versus a platform solely for material success. There is a remnant of businesspeople throughout the world today who understand their birthright in the marketplace is to reflect Christ fully in and through their work. It is reflected by a commitment to use their resources and skills to provide a product of excellence with the overall motive to affect people for Jesus Christ. The difference is that these individuals have an overriding ministry objective to their work.

When the apostle Paul tells us to fully work unto the Lord, he does not mean we must be working as missionaries in "full-time Christian effort." He understands that all of life is holy and sacred to God. If our motive is to serve God where we are, then our labor "in the Lord is not in vain."

As you begin your work today, ask God if you are working with the primary motive of reflecting His life and character through your work on this day. Let nothing move you from this motive being central to your activity. The Lord will reflect His power and leading in and through your life when this becomes your primary motive.

May 4

Impossible Tasks

But He answered, "You give them something to eat."   Mark 6:37a

Has anyone ever asked you to do something that seems totally ridiculous? The very suggestion of their instruction may have brought laughter or even anger for proposing the idea.

I imagine that the disciples may have felt this way when Jesus responded with this comment when they asked him how they were going to feed the 5000 who stayed around to hear him speak. The disciples suggested a logical answer to the problem, "Send the people away so they can go to the surrounding countryside and villages and buy themselves something to eat" (Mk 6:36).

That wasn't the answer Jesus wanted. He saw the need of the people. He had compassion on them. He wanted to solve the problem with a Kingdom response, not logic. He asked them what they had in their hand.

So often what we already have in our hand is what Jesus wants us to use to solve our problems. We must add faith to what we already have in our hand. Then we will see the gospel of the Kingdom manifested to solve problems in a supernatural way. Jesus wanted to meet a need in which God would receive the glory. Sending the people away did not meet the need, nor did it bring glory to the Father.

Do not settle for the gospel of salvation only. Jesus came that we might experience the gospel of the Kingdom in its fullest sense. Our job is to look past our logical reasoning and see how God might want to solve our problem in a supernatural way.

May 5

When God Seems Far Away

Why, O Lord, do You stand far off? Why do You hide Yourself in times of trouble?   Psalm 10:1

One of the great mysteries of God is His ways. Some of His ways almost appear to bring us into the most difficult places, as if He were indifferent to our circumstances. It would appear that He is turning His head from our sorrows. These events in our lives have a particular objective to perform for us. That objective is to bring us to the end of ourselves that we might discover the treasure of darkness. "Yet when I hoped for good, evil came; when I looked for light, then came darkness" (Job 30:26).

When we are taken into these dark periods, we begin to see light that we never knew existed. Our sensitivities become heightened and our ability to see through spiritual eyes is illuminated. Unless we are taken into these times, our souls never develop any depth of character. We do not gain wisdom, only knowledge. Knowledge is gained through understanding; wisdom is gained through the experience of darkness.

After we go through these periods, we discover that God was, in fact, with us throughout the entire time. It does not feel or appear that He is there when we are in the midst of the dark periods. However, He is there walking with us. He has told us countless times that He will never leave us. However, when we are in those dark periods, it does not feel like He is there because He does not rescue us from the circumstances. He does this for our benefit in order that we might become more like Jesus. Jesus learned obedience from the things He suffered (see Heb. 5:8). What does that say about how you and I will learn obedience?

May 5—Day 125

Embrace the dark times and gain the wisdom that God intends for you from these times.

May 6

The Value of Words

And do not swear by your head, for you cannot make even one hair white or black. Simply let your "Yes" be "Yes," and your "No," "No"; anything beyond this comes from the evil one.

Matthew 5:36-37

Imagine for a moment that you are living in Jesus' time. It is before Jesus has begun His public ministry. He is a carpenter in your local town of Nazareth. You have asked Jesus to make a table for you. You're on a deadline and you must have it in a week. You agree on the price of $100 for the table and the date of one week for completion. A week later you arrive to pick up the table. You lay your money down on the table and Jesus says, "Mr. Johnson, I am sorry but the table is not ready. I ran into complications. Also, I can no longer honor the price I gave you. It is now $150 instead of $100."

Two years later you hear about this same Jesus who is preaching to the local townspeople. How are you going to view this Jesus? You probably won't give much credence to His message because of your personal experience. Our lives have an ability to reinforce the message we stand for, or they can violate it and make it totally ineffective. This literally happens all over the world in different settings with Christian businesspeople. Our message becomes ineffective because we have not done what we said.

I know people who, when they tell me they plan to do something, I can expect them to follow through about 50 percent of the time. I am sure you have had the same experience. Words and commitments are made with little meaning behind those words. However, I know others who will follow through almost every time. The only time they don't is when something falls outside their control. I quickly learn whose words have substance behind them.

There are times when we are unable to perform or deliver what we promised due to outside influences. The key to turning these potentially negative circumstances into a witness for Christ is communication. If we are unable to pay a bill on time, we must communicate with those we owe and make a good faith effort to resolve it within our means. In these cases, God's purposes are being performed as well if we seek to do the right thing.

Do your words mean anything to those who hear them? Do you make commitments and fail to follow through on them? What would others say about how you follow through? Ask the Lord today to show you how you are doing in this area. You might even want to ask three people who are the closest to you how you fare in this area.

May 7

Changing Besetting Habits—The $10 Challenge

Jesus replied, "I tell you the truth, everyone who sins is a slave to sin." John 8:34

"I hate being late," my friend lamented. "It has been a problem for me all my life."

"Do you really want to change that?" I asked.

"Yes, I do."

"All right. Every time you are late to work or anywhere else where you have committed to be at a particular time you must give me $25."

"No way!" my friend responded. "I would go broke! But I will do $10."

"All right, $10 it is. It has to be a large enough amount of money for it to hurt your pocketbook."

"Believe me, that will hurt," my friend said. About a month later my friend found great motivation to be on time to every place she had to be. In the first week, I got only $10 from my friend. The next week, $20. The third week, nothing. By the fifth week, my friend had changed a lifelong habit that had hindered her all her life. In order for my friend not to be resentful of me for the money she had to give, we put it in a jar to be given to some other Christian cause. This ensured my motive was only for her best interest.

Some might be reading this now and say it is legalism. For my friend it was freedom. For the first time she had some means of changing a behavior that had caused her problems in relationships and her own work habits. Psychologists tell us that it takes 21 days to form a habit. So, if you need to change some habit, you need to be actively engaged in that new behavior at least 21 days. My friend needed help to change a habit she didn't like about herself. It took another individual to hold her accountable, and it took a potential loss of something to provide the added incentive.

A successful businessman was experiencing a difficult marriage. When counseling the couple over dinner one night, a friend of mine noticed that the man often criticized his wife. After further counsel it was determined the man simply could not love his wife. My friend asked him if he truly wanted to see change in his marriage. When the man said he did, my friend said, "Every time you criticize your wife you must agree to give me $100." This man was well-off and needed substantial incentive to change his behavior. After the man rebelled and retorted, he agreed in front of his wife. A few weeks later a report came back that things were changing. This man did not want to write any checks to my friend. Although it was a competitive game to the man, it was also yielding some positive changes in his marriage. He began to acquire the habit of avoiding criticism of his wife, which was killing her spirit.

What are the habits that keep you from becoming all that God may want you to become? Do you desire change enough to be accountable in a way that it costs you something when you fail? Ask a friend to hold you accountable in an area that needs change. You will find new freedom as you conquer old besetting habits.

May 8

Being Choked by Wealth

> *Whoever loves money never has money enough; whoever loves wealth is never satisfied with his income....*   Ecclessiastes 5:10

Businesspeople are especially susceptible to a trap in their spiritual lives—one to which others may not be so susceptible. That trap is wealth. Scripture tells us that if we are having our basic needs met for food and clothing, we are considered to have riches. Jesus cautioned us against living a lifestyle that required more than our basic necessities. However, it is clear that Jesus was not against wealth, but against a dependence on wealth. Jesus continually taught that a dependence on anything other than God was evil. Whenever Jesus determined that money was an issue for an individual, He addressed it and found that the individual could not let go. This was true for the rich young ruler. When talking about what he must do to inherit the Kingdom, Jesus told him to do the one thing that would be the most difficult—to give away his wealth and follow Him. Jesus was not saying this was what every person must do, only the rich young ruler, because Jesus knew this was his greatest stumbling block. For others of us, it could be something else Jesus would ask us to give up (see Mt. 19:16-30).

In the parable of the sower in which He describes four types of people, Jesus also gave us another example of the problem money creates for any follower of Jesus.

A farmer went out to sow his seed. As he was scattering the seed, some fell along the path, and the birds came and ate it up. Some fell on rocky places, where it did not have much soil. It sprang up quickly, because the soil was shallow. But when the sun came up, the plants were scorched, and they withered because they had no root. Other seed fell among thorns, which grew up and choked the plants. Still other seed fell on good soil, where it produced a crop—a hundred, sixty or thirty times what was sown (Matthew 13:3b-8).

The one who received the seed that fell among the thorns is the man who hears the word, but the worries of this life and the deceitfulness of wealth choke it, making it unfruitful (Matthew 13:22).

Much like the frog in the boiling pot, if we are not careful we gradually begin to acquire and walk the treadmill of material gain. Those around us begin to expect more and more. Soon we begin expanding our lifestyle. Before we know it, we are worrying about how to take care of what we acquire. Our emphasis becomes what we own versus our relationship with Jesus and His Kingdom. One day I woke up and realized I had a cold heart toward God. Apathy toward the things of God became apparent. I was still going through the motions of service toward God, but with no power. We wake up to realize Christ is no longer Lord of our lives, much less of our money. The greater independence money gives us, the less dependence on God we need. Christ talked much about money in the Kingdom because He knew how much of a problem it was. This is why we have so few who are bearing 100, 60, or 30 times what is sown.

Do you have the same hunger for God that you once had? Has financial blessing had an adverse effect on your passion for Jesus Christ? Ask Him today if your heart has grown cold as a result of financial blessing. Ask Him to keep you hungering for more of His presence in your life.

May 9

The Flight of Geese

Also in Judah the hand of God was on the people to give them unity of mind to carry out what the king and his officials had ordered, following the word of the Lord.   2 Chronicles 30:12

A major corporation conducted a study on the flight of geese. In their study they found that geese fly in a "V" formation with one goose in the lead. After a period of time, this goose relinquishes the lead to another goose. During flight they noticed head movements of the leader that seem to give signals to the other geese flying, perhaps to let the others know how he was doing. They estimate that the formation flight pattern reduces wind drag due to the lift the other birds receive and believe it increases their performance by up to 70 percent. Whenever one goose drops out, another goes with it. These two geese do not catch up to the original pack, but join another group later.

Independence is one of the strongholds of the marketplace. The entire system feeds the desire within us to gain recognition from our individual achievements. We wrongly believe financial independence frees us from needing to depend on anyone else. The fact is, dependence on others is a good thing. It can bring us into a unity of spirit that accomplishes much more with less effort while meeting needs for each of us. Christ talked a lot about unity among brothers and sisters. He said that others would know we are Christians by our love for one another and by our unity. We need to depend on others so that we don't go it alone. By walking together we increase our strength. By going it alone we must carry a load we were never intended to carry. God did not create us to go it alone. By joining together we accomplish more for Jesus Christ. Ask the Lord today if there is an independent spirit within you that prevents you from joining others in the mission He has called you to.

May 10

Entitlements

And being found in appearance as a man, He humbled Himself and became obedient to death—even death on a cross!   Philippians 2:8

Society today has duped many of us into believing that the world owes us. It owes us a good living, a loving spouse, good health throughout our whole life, sexual pleasure when we want it, and paid vacations the rest of our lives. The world has told us if we work hard and do right, we are entitled to these things. This is the Esau perspective on life. For a mere meal, he sold his own birthright for a simple pleasure to which he felt entitled.

Society and even the Church is more pleasure-focused than ever before. George Barna, the Christian researcher, cites,

> We are not a society that simply enjoys its time off. Our leisure appetites drive us. It is increasingly common to hear people turning down job offers because the hours or other responsibilities would interfere with their hobbies, fitness regimens and other free time activities. Even our spending habits show that playing has become a major priority. The average household spends more money on entertainment than it does clothing, health care, furniture or gasoline.

Recreational activities have jumped more than 10 percent in the amount of time given to them. [George Barna, *Frog In The Kettle* (Ventura, California: Regal Books, 1990), 82.]

What are the motives for our work life? Is it only to gain increased pleasure and leisure time? Jesus said He came only to do the work of the Father. I am sure that Jesus had times of refreshment in His life that allowed Him to get recharged for the mission God called Him to. However, He understood the balance of maintaining mission and play. When we view life with an attitude of entitlements, we are susceptible to becoming disappointed, resentful, and even bitter when our expectations go unmet. Ask the Lord if you need to relinquish any rights that may be hindering your freedom to experience His love and grace.

May 11

An Encounter With God

So I was left alone, gazing at this great vision; I had no strength left, my face turned deathly pale and I was helpless.　　　　　Daniel 10:8

Daniel received a vision that troubled him greatly. He wanted understanding of this vision. He set himself out to understand the vision by fasting for three weeks. Three days after his three weeks of fasting, a messenger of God appeared to Daniel. The messenger explained that Heaven had heard his prayer from the first day, but the angel was temporarily prevented from coming by the prince of Persia, a demon angel, who sought to thwart God's messenger from coming to Daniel.

There are times in our lives when we must set ourselves to seeking God with all our hearts. It is in these times that we hear from Heaven in ways we may never have experienced before. Daniel's perseverance in prayer was rewarded with a personal encounter with Heaven. However, in order to receive from God, Daniel had to be left alone, his strength removed, and be placed in a helpless condition. When we have no ability in our own strength to move Heaven or the events around us, we are in position to hear from Heaven. It is the acknowledgment of our humanity and our frailness that places us in a position to have a personal encounter with the living God.

Do you need a personal encounter with God today? Do you need God to intervene on your behalf? Seek Him with all your heart. Demonstrate to Him you are serious. Get alone and acknowledge your helpless condition before Him. He will reward you with His presence.

May 12

A Fleeting Shadow

Man is like a breath; his days are like a fleeting shadow.
                                                        Psalm 144:4

Every time I fly over a large body of water, I imagine opening the window of the jet and pouring out my coffee into the immense body of water below. I imagine the time that I spend on this earth compared to eternity is no more than that cup of coffee. The incredible size of the ocean compared to one small cup of coffee is what our life is like compared to eternity. Why then do we invest so much in temporal pursuits when we know that our investment here can have so much impact on our eternity? It is the great paradox of human behavior, especially for Christians.

Does your business life have an overall ministry objective to it? This does not mean we must be constantly involved in "Christian activity." It only means that we should be about what God has called us to do with the motive of being obedient to this mission. Do not let the worries and cares of this life keep you from having an eternal impact on the lives of those you meet each day. Satan has a way of keeping our focus on the problems of today rather than the spiritual opportunities before us. He is master of the urgent, not the important.

Therefore, my dear brothers, stand firm. Let nothing move you. Always give yourselves fully to the work of the Lord, because you know that your labor in the Lord is not in vain (1 Corinthians 15:58).

May 13

The Plans of Tomorrow

You are a mist that appears for a little while and then vanishes.
James 4:14b

A group of businesspeople meet at my office every week for fellowship, study, and prayer. One man attended our group for several years. Jim was well liked and in good health. One Thursday he showed up as usual. The next morning I received a call, "Jim is dead! He died in his easy chair last night!" Jim had no prior problems and there was no indication he was about to go be with the Lord. Naturally, it came as a shock to us all.

Whenever things like this happen close to home, it brings us face to face with our mortality. A friend of mine said he was challenged by someone to do an experiment. He challenged him to live his life for one year as if it were the last year he would live. He responded to the challenge and did as proposed. It changed his life forever. He began to focus on different priorities and people when he viewed life in these terms.

James gives us a perspective on viewing tomorrow.

Now listen, you who say, "Today or tomorrow we will go to this or that city, spend a year there, carry on business and make money." Why, you do not even know what will happen tomorrow. What is your life? You are a mist that appears for a little while and then vanishes. Instead, you ought to say, "If it is the Lord's will, we will live and do this or that" (James 4:13-15).

Life is fragile. Consider where you are investing your time and energies. Someone once said they had never heard anyone on his deathbed say that he wished he had made more money in his lifetime or he wished he had made a certain deal. Usually it is something like, "I wish I had spent more time with my kids." Ask the Lord to give you His priorities for your life.

May 14

A Two-way Relationship

He wakens me morning by morning, wakens my ear to listen like one being taught.   Isaiah 50:4b

The prophet Isaiah describes his relationship to God as a relationship that has two-way communication. Have you ever felt that your communication with God was only one way—you to Him only? Isaiah tells us, "The Sovereign Lord has given me an instructed tongue, to know the word that sustains the weary....The Sovereign Lord has opened my ears, and I have not been rebellious; I have not drawn back" (Is. 50:4-5).

The key to Isaiah's relationship with God lies in four important principles:

1. He had an instructed tongue. Isaiah had given over rule of his life completely to God's purposes.
2. He knew the word of the Lord, which allowed him to sustain and encourage others.
3. He took time to listen.
4. He did not flee from the tough assignments. He didn't shrink back.

If we are to be able to listen to God, we must follow the same principles. Knowing and spending time studying God's Word allows the Holy Spirit to bring to mind His instructions for what He wants for us. Recently, I became very busy in my work and other activities. It wasn't long before I felt distance between God and me. I had to make a conscious decision to carve out more time alone to listen, study, and meditate on His Word. This is the lifeline for the follower of Jesus. When we begin to lose the relationship, we are susceptible to becoming rebellious, going our own way. Invest your life in this relationship so that you may continue to hear His voice and sustain the weary ones around you.

May 15

Overcoming Our Past

Then the Spirit of the Lord came upon Jephthah.   Judges 11:29a

We've all heard stories of individuals who have overcome extreme hardship during their childhood years. Children of alcoholics, orphans who never have parents, loss of parents to a fatal crash, childhood disease—all difficult circumstances to overcome.

Jephthah was a man who overcame his obstacles and refused to allow his circumstances to prevent him from becoming great in God's sight. He was born to Gilead, a result of his father's adulterous encounter with a prostitute. Gilead's wife bore more sons, decided to reject Jephthah, and drove him away from their home saying, "You are not going to get any inheritance in our family because you are the son of another woman." Imagine the rejection this young man felt as he was cast away from his own family.

This experience taught Jephthah to become a hardened warrior. Today he probably would have been part of a street gang. As he got older, his reputation as a warrior became known to those in his country—so much so that when the Ammonites made war on Israel, the elders of Gilead went to Jephthah and asked him to be their commander. Jephthah had to fight off those feelings of rejection from previous years.

"Didn't you hate me and drive me from my father's house?" he responded. He overcame his hurt and pain, and responded to the call God had on his life.

It is said that if we were to help the butterfly remove itself from the cocoon, the butterfly would not be strong enough to survive. It is the struggle that prepares the butterfly to become strong enough to fly. Without the struggle in the cocoon, it could not survive as a butterfly.

The Lord prepares each of us in similar ways. Some of our childhoods seem to have been harsh and born from a seemingly unloving God. However, the Lord knows our struggle and will make our life an instrument in His hand if we will follow Him with an upright heart. He does make all things beautiful in His time if we are willing to be patient.

May 16

Sowing in Tears

Those who sow in tears will reap with songs of joy.   Psalm 126:5

The most difficult place to keep moving in faith is the place of extreme pain. Extreme pain, especially emotional pain, can become immobilizing to the human spirit if it is allowed to overcome us. The psalmist tells us there is only one remedy for overcoming painful circumstances that will result in joy. We are to sow in the midst of these times. You cannot do this if you live by feelings alone. It is an act of the will. This act requires that we go outside ourselves in pure faith.

I learned this principle during one of the deepest periods of my life. I had lost much that was dear to me. A mature man in the faith admonished me to reach out to others in spite of my own pain. "Invest in someone else," he said. I did not realize what a place of healing and comfort that would become.

"He who goes out weeping, carrying seed to sow, will return with songs of joy, carrying sheaves with him" (Ps. 126:6). Pain can become a source of joy if we take the first step by planting seed. There is a harvest that will come if we sow in the midst of tears.

May 17

Being a Person Under Authority

…"I tell you the truth, I have not found anyone in Israel with such great faith."   Matthew 8:10

The centurion came to Jesus and told Him of his servant who was paralyzed and in terrible suffering. He came to Jesus because he believed He could heal him. He told Jesus of the matter, and Jesus was willing to come with the centurion. But the centurion would not have it. He knew that Jesus, being under the authority of Heaven itself, did not have to see the servant to help him. The centurion understood authority. He understood that he himself had certain rights that his position granted him to have power over situations and people. He also was a man under authority. The centurion understood Jesus' position and what power that position held in Heaven—the power to heal his servant if He chose to exercise that authority.

When Jesus saw that the centurion understood this principle of authority and that He did not have to visit the servant to heal him, He acknowledged the centurion's faith. Jesus knew it took great faith to understand authority and whether He had the authority to do what was being asked.

God has placed a system of authority in our world that requires faith to operate under its boundaries: fathers over sons and daughters, employers over employees, government leaders over the people, church leaders over church members. These are authority structures God has placed in our lives to protect and guide us to His will. Some confuse position with worthiness or qualifications of that position. It is the position that God works through. The fact that an authority may not be a Christian may have no bearing on whether God can work through him as your authority. It is only when that authority counsels against a biblical mandate that we should not follow that person's guidance. The hand of the king is in the hand of God.

Today, we find few who understand this system of authority God has ordained. It requires great faith to operate in this realm. Yet Jesus said that when we understand this, we demonstrate the kind of faith that He rarely sees. Be a person of rare faith. See the authorities placed in your life as those God is using to protect you.

May 18

Building a Solid Foundation

*But everyone who hears these words of Mine and does not put them
into practice is like a foolish man who built his house on sand.*
Matthew 7:26

There were two kinds of people in the days of Jesus. Some heard
the words that Jesus spoke and were awed by His wisdom and understanding but did nothing about what they heard. Others heard those
words and acted on them. Jesus said that those who heard the words but
failed to put them into practice were foolish and likened them to building a house on sand. How foolish, indeed, it would be to build a house
on sand.

The person who followed what Jesus taught was a person who
would be sure to weather life's storms.

*Therefore everyone who hears these words of Mine and puts them
into practice is like a wise man who built his house on the rock. The
rain came down, the streams rose, and the winds blew and beat
against that house; yet it did not fall, because it had its foundation
on the rock* (Matthew 7:24-25).

You never know how well your house is built until it is tested by
the elements. Torrential rains reveal the quality of your roof. Wind and
cold reveal how well your home is insulated. Heat and sun reveal the
quality of your paint and siding. All these elements reveal whether a
solid foundation has been laid to make your home a secure and lasting
place to live.

Many of us find that we have given only lip service to God's commands. We are faced with the reality that our foundations are not strong
enough to weather life's storms. How do we react when the trials come?
Do we fret and worry? Do we take life into our hands? Do we respond
inappropriately when we don't get what we want? The Lord uses these
times to help us recognize whether our foundations are sand or rock. Ask
the Lord today if you have built on His rock. If so, you can be comforted
to know that you can weather any storm that may come your way.

May 19

Selling Your Birthright

> *Then Jacob gave Esau some bread and some lentil stew. He ate and drank, and then got up and left. So Esau despised his birthright.*
>
> Genesis 25:34

Esau was brother to Jacob. One day he came back from hunting in the fields. He was hungry and tired. His brother Jacob was preparing some stew and Esau asked Jacob for a bowl. Jacob used this time to negotiate for what seems unimaginable—the family birthright.

Why would Esau take his birthright so lightly? Because he did not understand its value. Every business day countless men and women exchange their birthrights for worldly goods, because they see what the world has to offer as more valuable than what God might offer.

This is not all their fault. Satan has blinded the minds and hearts of men and women for centuries. He does not want them to know the tremendous gold mine that awaits the child of God. Their inheritance is filled with meaning, purpose, and rewards that await them both here and in Heaven. Satan keeps men and women from seeing the real value of their own godly inheritance.

Your role as a marketplace Christian is to be the key that unlocks this prison that keeps so many in captivity. You may be the one to reveal the truth that allows them to enter into the inheritance God desires for them. Pray that God allows you to see each unsaved person you encounter as one who needs the key you hold in your hand. Then you will add to your own inheritance laid up for you in Heaven.

May 20

Becoming a Mighty Man

All those who were in distress or in debt or discontented gathered around him, and he became their leader. About four hundred men were with him.   1 Samuel 22:2

Have you ever felt that you could accomplish a whole lot more if you had more talented people around you? Perhaps you are in an office and think that some of your fellow workers don't quite measure up. Imagine what David must have thought in the years following his anointing by the prophet Samuel as the next king of Israel. He spent the next many years running from King Saul. Now God was beginning to bring men to support David. But what kind of men? The down-and-out. God gave David not the elite or the sophisticated; He gave him those who were in debt and discontented with life. David turned those men into the best fighting men of their day. In fact, David never lost a battle during his entire reign as king of Israel—quite a feat for a bunch of no-name, lowlifes! Some of those men became an elite group known as David's Mighty Men. These were the elite of the elite, the Navy Seals, the Few Good Men, the Green Berets. Whatever you call them, they were exceptional warriors.

Jesus took a few men who weren't exactly the cream of the crop either. He built His life into these men, which resulted in 12 men who turned the world upside down. Are you one of God's mighty men or women? Are you investing your life to build other mighty men or women? David and Jesus set the example of what can be done when we invest in others. God does extraordinary things through men who have an extraordinary God. Ask God to use your life to be a mighty man or woman for a cause greater than yourself. He delights in such prayers.

May 21

Becoming Aware of God

..."*Surely the Lord is in this place, and I was not aware of it.*"
Genesis 28:16

Jacob was forced to flee his family after receiving the blessing of God from his father, Isaac. He ran as a result of his broken relationship with his brother, Esau, who threatened to kill him. He was alone after leaving his family and was sleeping in the wilderness area at Bethel. It is here that Jacob encountered God personally for the very first time. He had a dream in which Heaven was opened up to him. The Lord spoke to him there and gave him a promise to give him the very land on which he was lying.

This encounter with God made him realize that God was in this place, even though he had not been aware of it. God had to remove Jacob from all that was of comfort to him in order to reveal Himself to Jacob. What began as a crisis that forced him to be removed from his family and friends led to an encounter with the living God and a fresh vision of God's purposes for his life.

How often we go about our daily routine and fail to recognize that God is in the place where we are. God had to bring Jacob to a place of separation from his old life and remove all his worldly possessions. He was alone with God at Bethel; nothing else could distract him from an encounter that would change his life.

God often must do radical things in the life of the servant in whom He has special plans: separation from family, removal of physical and emotional resources, an encounter with God. These are often the hallmarks of ownership by God that build a vision into a life.

May 22

God's Preparation for Moving Out

In this way the man grew exceedingly prosperous and came to own large flocks, and maidservants and menservants, and camels and donkeys.   Genesis 30:43

Jacob left his homeland after suffering a broken relationship with Esau for stealing the family blessing. He went to work for his uncle Laban where he stayed for 20 years. It came time for him to leave, but he had no physical assets to show for those years under Laban. Laban had taken advantage of his nephew in every way. (In some ways, Jacob was reaping the seed he had sown his entire life as a manipulator and controller.) Nevertheless, God's hand was on Jacob, and He had plans to prosper him. However, Jacob had one problem—he had no resources of his own. For Jacob to launch out on his own, he would need resources. In those days, resources often meant large flocks of animals. God gave Jacob a dream that resulted in a strategy for creating wealth by multiplying his sheep. Even though Laban sought to thwart Jacob's efforts, God overcame the evil in Laban to allow Jacob to prosper.

There are many important lessons for us in this story. First, when God decides it is time to move you into a larger place of His calling, He has the ability to provide the resources you need to support the call. God gave Jacob a dream that resulted in a strategy never used before to build wealth. It was totally from God's hand. It was creative and new. God called Jacob to move out after he had demonstrated his faithfulness in 20 years of serving Laban. He learned to live under authority and served Laban faithfully, even though he knew he was being taken advantage of.

God will do the same for you and me. However, a word of caution: Be sure the strategy is born from above, and not from self-effort. The difficulty for most of us businesspeople is to learn the difference between the strategy born of God versus the strategy of self-effort.

May 23

Wrestling With God

So Jacob was left alone, and a man wrestled with him till daybreak.
Genesis 32:24

All that Jacob had lived for was coming down to one event—his reunion with Esau. More than 20 years had passed since Jacob had manipulated his father's blessing away from his brother Esau. During these years God had been changing Jacob from a controller and manipulator to a man who was learning to trust God. He was now ready to meet Esau. However, he was fearful that Esau may take revenge on him and his family for his past sin, so he sent a gift ahead, while he retreated and sought mercy from God.

As an angel appeared to Jacob, he realized the only hope he had was in God. Only if God blessed him would he survive this ordeal. In the past, Jacob would have sought to solve his problem his way. Now, he wanted only God's way. He wanted Him so badly that he wouldn't let go of the angel. He was striving with God, but it was the right kind of striving. Jacob was striving to have all God's blessing on his life. He was seeking God with all that he had. "When the man saw that he could not overpower him, he touched the socket of Jacob's hip so that his hip was wrenched as he wrestled with the man" (Gen. 32:25). The only way to overcome the strong will of this man was to physically immobilize him. The angel touched the socket of Jacob's hip. It was painful; it broke him. This was the final stage of removing the old nature from Jacob. It was the place of complete brokenness and surrender. No longer would Jacob walk in his own strength. He would now have to lean on a cane, symbolic of his leaning on God alone.

It was the final act from God in Jacob's life that was celebrated with a new name—Israel. No longer would he strive with God or man. The process was now complete. God could now bless this man abundantly. He gave him favor with Esau and restored their broken relationship.

What does God have to do in our lives to remove the controlling and manipulative nature that so often is part of a businessperson's life? Perhaps it will require a time of immobilizing, loss of a job, loss of income, loss of health, loss of a close relationship. These are His methods of preparation. Your new nature will not be complete until you've stopped striving with God through your own self-efforts. If God is taking you through this process, be encouraged; it is because of the inheritance He has prepared for you. However, the inheritance can only be received when God brings us to total dependence on Him.

May 24

Working Versus Striving

So he said to me, "This is the word of the Lord to Zerubbabel: 'Not by might nor by power, but by My Spirit,' says the Lord Almighty."
Zechariah 4:6

Your greatest obstacle in fulfilling God's purposes in your life is the skills you have acquired to perform well in your business life. One of the great paradoxes in Scripture relates to our need to depend on the Lord; yet at the same time, we're instructed to use the talents and abilities God gives us to accomplish the work He gives us to do. It has been one of the most difficult principles to live out. How do we know that what we achieve is by the power of the Holy Spirit in our life versus our own abilities, and is there a difference? When we reach a level of excellence and performance in our fields, it actually becomes an obstacle to seeing God's power manifest in our work. What we naturally do well becomes the object of our trust. When this happens, God retreats. You see, God allows us to develop skills, but these must be continually yielded to God's Spirit. There will be times when God will use these skills to accomplish His purposes. There will be other times that God will not use any of our skills just to ensure that we know it is by His power that we can do anything.

It is the oxymoron of all oxymorons for Christian businesspeople. Learning not to act until God shows you to act is a sign of maturity in God. "Do not lean on the natural skill which you have been given. Let God manifest Himself in what you are doing," said a mentor who has learned this balance of skill and walking with God. "You must almost restrain from doing those things you know you are prone to do and actually go against them."

I was learning this lesson recently when I was asked to participate in a large event that would give great exposure and much needed financial increase to my ministry. It made all the sense in the world to participate. Then I prayed with a friend and asked the Lord His mind on it. The Lord showed us this was not His plan for me. I declined the invitation.

Ask God to teach you what it means to walk according to the power of the Holy Spirit in your business life. Develop a listening ear to the small voice inside that wants to direct your efforts by His Spirit.

May 25

The Goal of the Christian Life

I tell you the truth, unless a kernel of wheat falls to the ground and dies, it remains only a single seed. But if it dies, it produces many seeds. John 12:24

The goal of the Christian life is death, not success. A popular teaching says that if we follow God, we will prosper materially. God may, in fact, bless His people materially, but few can make this claim among third-world countries. Wealth must never be the goal of a person's life, only a by-product.

A missionary to a Middle-Eastern country has shared a motto among their ministry team: "God does not require success, but radical, immediate obedience." Jesus' obedience gained Him the cross. It did not gain Him popularity among the heathen, the religious or financial success, or a life of pleasure. His obedience resulted in His death on the cross. This is the same goal Christ has for each of us—death of our old nature so that He might live through us. That may not sell well among outcome-based Christian businesspeople, but it will result in an eternal reward that far exceeds any earthly reward. "Behold, I am coming soon! My reward is with Me, and I will give to everyone according to what he has done" (Rev. 22:12).

The Christian life is a paradox—the first will be last, death in return for life, and we are encouraged to offer praise to God to overcome a spirit of heaviness. It requires faith in a God who operates from a different set of values that are sometimes difficult to measure from human standards. Let death work in you a life that only God can raise up.

May 26

Hearing the Father Speak

My sheep listen to My voice; I know them, and they follow Me.
John 10:27

An Englishman tells a true story of his encounter with a Muslim man while walking in the country. The Englishman wanted to share the gospel with this man but knew little of Muslim beliefs. The two men talked as they walked and agreed they would each share their beliefs with one another. The Muslim went first and dominated the time of sharing. The Englishman asked the Holy Spirit how to share his faith with the Muslim man. "Do you consider your god your father who speaks?" asked the Englishman.

"Certainly not," replied the Muslim man.

"That is one of the big differences between your god and my God. I consider my God as my Father who speaks to me personally."

"You cannot prove that," stated the Muslim man.

The Englishman again prayed to himself, "Lord, how do I prove this to this man?" A few moments later the two men began walking toward two young ladies on the other side of the road coming toward them. As they approached, the Englishman spoke to the ladies and made small conversation. He then said to one woman, "I believe you are a nurse, is that correct?"

The woman was startled that a man whom she had never met had just informed her of her occupation. "How would you know that? I have never met you before," she questioned.

He replied, "I asked my Father and He told me." The Muslim had his proof.

Many of us do not hear God's voice because we do not believe He speaks or desires to speak to us. In order to hear, we must listen. In order to listen, we must believe that He speaks. Ask the Lord today for a listening ear so that others might know that you have a heavenly Father who speaks.

May 27

The Greatest Test

I know, my God, that You test the heart and are pleased with integrity.
1 Chronicles 29:17a

God tests His children to know what is in their hearts. God's desire for each of His children is to walk in relationship with Him, to uphold His righteousness and integrity. It is a high calling that we will fail to achieve without complete dependence on Him.

The greatest tests come not in great adversities, but in great prosperity. For it is in prosperity that we begin to lose the sensitivity to sin in our lives. Adversity motivates us to righteousness out of a desire to see our adversity changed. Prosperity fails to provide this motivation for obedience. We fall into a satisfaction and confidence in life that is based on our prosperity rather than on God.

Hezekiah was a great godly king. He was a faithful, God-honoring king most of his life, but toward the end he became proud. God wanted to find out if he would still honor Him and recognize His blessings in his life. He failed the test when God sent an envoy to his palace to inquire about a miracle that God performed on behalf of Hezekiah. The test was designed to find out if Hezekiah would publicly acknowledge the miracle performed on his behalf.

But when envoys were sent by the rulers of Babylon to ask him about the miraculous sign that had occurred in the land, God left him to test him and to know everything that was in his heart (2 Chronicle 32:31).

Hezekiah's failure resulted in his children failing to carry on as rulers of Israel, and the nation would eventually be taken over by Babylon.

The lesson of Hezekiah is clear. If we are to remain faithful to our Lord, we must remain steadfast in our obedience to Him. Prosperity can be our greatest test. Ask the Lord to give you the grace to be a faithful follower during times of prosperity.

May 28

Abraham, Isaac, and Jacob

Then Joseph said to his brothers, "I am about to die. But God will surely come to your aid and take you up out of this land to the land He promised on oath to Abraham, Isaac and Jacob." Genesis 50:24

I was boarding the airplane in Frankfurt, Germany, when a mentor of mine asked me this question, "Would you consider why God referred to Himself as the 'God of Abraham, Isaac and Jacob'? Why didn't He simply say, 'the God of Jacob'?" *What a strange question*, I thought to myself.

For the next hour I racked my brain trying to discover the meaning to this question. I had never read it in a commentary, and the Scriptures do not really say why this is so. It became a good exercise with the Holy Spirit that led to some interesting observations—one from my mentor, one from my own insight.

First, could it be that the Lord has given us a "type of trinity" in Abraham, Isaac, and Jacob? Abraham was considered a father figure to the nation of Israel. Isaac was the son who had to be sacrificed on the altar. Jacob was the man who had to learn to walk according to the Holy Spirit instead of his flesh. Each of these patriarchs had a particular relationship with God to fulfill.

My friend asked about an hour into the flight, "So, what did you discover?"

I told him of my observation.

"Hmm...that is interesting. I believe that what we also see in the patriarchs are examples of three distinct types of personalities. If the Lord had cited only one of the patriarchs, we would tend to seek to model that leader. However, the Lord has given us three distinct personalities in whom He performed His work. Abraham was the pioneer who ventured out into unknown territory and was considered righteous for his faith. Isaac was faithful to follow in his inheritance with few ups and downs in his life. He had the fewest calamities among the three. He was called simply to be faithful to what had been already given. Jacob had extreme conflict in his life. He suffered more pit experiences than either of his predecessors. He had much conflict in relationships that became the source of his inheritance. Each of us can identify with one of these men in how God has related to them."

God works in each person's life uniquely, and He has provided examples of lives for us to identify with from the Scriptures. Who do you identify with most in your Christian pilgrimage? Discover this for yourself. You will find encouragement as you seek to learn from someone who has gone before you.

May 29

One of the Twelve

And He died for all, that those who live should no longer live for themselves but for Him who died for them and was raised again.
2 Corinthians 5:15

It is believed that there were about 5,000 believers during the time of Christ. Among those believers, it was thought there were three types. The largest number of believers were those who came to Jesus for salvation. They served Him little beyond coming to Him to receive salvation. A much smaller number, say 500, actually followed Him and served Him. Then, there were the disciples. These were those who identified with Jesus. They lived the life that Jesus lived. Each of these ultimately died in difficult circumstances. They experienced the hardships, the miracles, and the fellowship with God in human form.

If you had to say which group best represented your life, which one would you fall into—the 5,000 who simply believed, the 500 who followed and sought to implement what they were learning from the Savior, or the 12 who identified completely with the life and mission of the Savior? Jesus has called each of us to identify with Him completely. "This is how we know we are in Him: Whoever claims to live in Him must walk as Jesus did" (1 Jn. 2:5b-6).

Pray that God will allow you to walk as Jesus did. Experience His power and love in your life today so that others will see the hope that lies in you.

May 30

God's Motives

He brought me out into a spacious place; He rescued me because He delighted in me.   2 Samuel 22:20

Questioning someone's motives for their activities can become an overriding response to those to whom we relate. Wrong motives can result in broken relationships, poor business decisions, and falling out of God's will. Sometimes we do not know the motive of another person. It is wrong for us to assume what their motive is until we have confidence that we know their intentions. When we respond or react prematurely, we become judge and jury over them.

God has a motive for every one of His children. His desire is to bring us into a spacious place. He wants us to go beyond our borders of safety and security so that we might experience life at a level that goes beyond ourselves. What do you think of when you think of a "spacious place"? No limitations? A large, grassy field? Open air? These are positive images. Sometimes these spacious places encourage us to step out in faith into areas where we've never ventured. Sometimes we need to be rescued by the Lord. When Peter walked on the water, God was inviting him to a spacious place. He went beyond the borders of his boat and ventured into a whole new world. He didn't have complete success in his venturing out, but it was a process that would lead him to the next victory in his faith walk with Jesus. Sometimes failure is what is needed in order to move us to the next level of faith with God. However, we must be willing to fail and let God rescue us.

The Lord delights in this process. His motive for His children is always love. It is always to bring us to a new level of trust and dependence on Him.

May 31

The Cost of Broken Covenants

During the reign of David, there was a famine for three successive years; so David sought the face of the Lord.　　2 Samuel 21:1a

There was a famine in the land, and David equated that famine to the blessing or lack of blessing from God. He sought God to know why there was a famine. The Lord did not take long to answer: "It is on account of Saul and his blood-stained house; it is because he put the Gibeonites to death" (2 Sam. 21:1b). Many years earlier, when Joshua entered the Promised Land, the Israelites were tricked by the Gibeonites into believing they were travelers when they were actually enemies of Israel. The Gibeonites tricked Israel into making a peace treaty with them. It was one of the first major mistakes Israel made after entering the Promised Land. As a result of the peace treaty, the Gibeonites were kept as slaves to Israel. This was never God's intention for Israel. He had wanted Israel to destroy all their enemies, but they made an error in judgment that required that they honor a covenant with the Gibeonites.

Saul made a decision to disregard this covenant with the Gibeonites and sought to annihilate them. David sensed there was something preventing God's blessing on Israel. As a nation they had violated a covenant made before God. Now they were reaping the consequences.

There are two things we can learn from this story. First, when we make a covenant, God expects us to fulfill it. God is a covenant maker. He made one with Abraham, Isaac, and Jacob. He made one with each of us through Jesus Christ. The Scriptures are numerous regarding the importance of honoring our commitments.

Second, God is a very longsuffering God. He gave Israel many years of grace before He exercised judgment for their sin. However, there always comes a day when God must uphold His standard of righteousness.

Are you failing to walk in God's blessing due to some failed commitment? Calamities can befall us for many reasons; sin can be one of them. In the case of Israel, David had to make things right with the Gibeonites. When he did this, God removed the famine, and Israel again was prosperous. When you feel you lack God's blessing on your life, ask the Lord if there are any past-generation sins that you may need to repent of. He may be waiting on us before He can release His blessing on our lives.

June 1

Preparation for Greatness

He trains my hands for battle; my arms can bend a bow of bronze.
2 Samuel 22:35

David was a mighty warrior, and God described him as a man after His own heart. God took David through a training ground that could be looked on as cruel and unusual punishment by many a person. God chose him at a young age to be the next king, yet King Saul rejected him and hunted him down. David was a fugitive for many years. He had uprisings in his own family, and he had relationship problems. He had a life of extreme ups and downs. He certainly did not have a life free of problems; he made mistakes. He was human like all of us, yet he learned from his mistakes and repented when he failed. This was David's training ground; it made the man. Without these hardships, it is doubtful David would have accomplished what he did.

Toward the end of David's life, he recounted his relationship with God. It is a sermon on God's ways of dealing with a servant leader.

It is God who arms me with strength and makes my way perfect. He makes my feet like the feet of a deer; He enables me to stand on the heights. He trains my hands for battle; my arms can bend a bow of bronze. You give me Your shield of victory; You stoop down to make me great. You broaden the path beneath me, so that my ankles do not turn (2 Samuel 22:33-37).

God was David's source for everything. God gave him the ability to achieve the many extraordinary things in his life. It was a lifelong training ground that moved him from one plateau to another, often dropping into a ravine of despair and hopelessness from time to time. These are God's ways. They drive us deeper and deeper into the heart of Him who has prepared a way for us. Let God take you to the heights or depths He desires for you. He never promised smooth sailing during the trip, but He did promise to be the captain and companion along the way.

June 2

Those in Whom God Delights

His pleasure is not in the strength of the horse, nor His delight in the legs of a man; the Lord delights in those who fear Him, who put their hope in His unfailing love.   Psalm 147:10

Mammon and power are the ruling strongholds of the marketplace. If you possess either of these, you will be courted by those who serve the marketplace in hopes of increasing market share. It is a competitive environment that often gives way to decisions and actions that are dictated by the financial bottom line. A recent newspaper article stated that employers are requiring workers to put more time into their jobs, often requiring weekend work in order to be more competitive. For the Christian worker, this brings pressures on the family and will result in "lost market share" in the spiritual realm.

The Lord has a different measuring stick. The Lord is not impressed with your ability or what you can do for Him. Only one thing delights Him—people who fear Him and put their hope in His unfailing love. What does it mean to fear God and place our hope in His love? It means we acknowledge that God is the source of all that we are. He is the one who gives us the ability to work, plan, and execute. He does not want us to look to our abilities, but to His abilities. Sometimes it is difficult to balance these two perspectives. However, if we ask God to show us how to maintain this balance, He will do it. Put your hope in His unfailing love today. Then you will know that your heavenly Father is looking on you as a proud Father.

June 3

Performing Miracles With Your Staff

But take this staff in your hand so you can perform miraculous signs with it.   Exodus 4:17

What is the staff God has put into your hand? Is it being a builder? Is it being an office worker? Is it being a doctor? Moses' staff represented his vocation as a shepherd. God had something in mind for his vocation— to perform miracles. And awesome miracles He did! God turned the Nile river into blood with the touch of the staff. He turned the staff into a snake. He parted the Red Sea with it. These are just a few of the miracles God did with that staff.

When we yield our talents and abilities to the Lord, God can perform miracles through them. First, Moses had to yield what He had in his hand to God. Only after this took place could God use that staff. As long as Moses held onto it, God could not and would not perform miracles through it.

Until we come to this place with our heavenly Father, we will fail to see miracles performed in our work. He delights in showing His power through us. When we become an open vessel, we can expect to see things happen.

Have you given your staff to the Lord? Offer it to Him and see what He might want to do through it. Your life will never be the same.

June 4

A New Remnant of Priests

Aliens will shepherd your flocks; foreigners will work your fields and vineyards.   Isaiah 61:5

God is calling forth a remnant of businesspeople whom He will use mightily to bring good news to those who have never heard the gospel. The "10/40 Window" is commonly referred to as those areas of the world where no one has heard the name of Jesus Christ. This region represents many of the Muslim nations in the Middle East, India, China, and the former Soviet Republics. If Christian missionaries are not welcome in these countries, how do you suppose God plans to bring His message to these people? Certainly He loves these people just as much as He loves us.

God is mobilizing His businesspeople around the world to be the vessels who will bring the good news to these peoples. These countries welcome commerce, and in most cases this represents the only way to bring the gospel to these nations. In these countries, businesspeople are often viewed as those who have corrupt morals. However, God wants to change this. The "Joshuas and Calebs" are spying out the land. This class of businessperson has a pioneer spirit that is seeking ways of penetrating strongholds of spiritual darkness in these countries. God is raising them up. They see the risks, but they see the awesomeness of God that enables them to accomplish something for His Kingdom by using their resources and talents.

> *And you will be called priests of the Lord, you will be named minis-*
> *ters of our God. You will feed on the wealth of nations, and in their*
> *riches you will boast. Instead of their shame My people will receive a*
> *double portion, and instead of disgrace they will rejoice in their*
> *inheritance; and so they will inherit a double portion in their land,*
> *and everlasting joy will be theirs* (Isaiah 61:6-7).

Businesspeople in these nations will be called priests of the Lord. They will feed on the wealth of these nations. The wealth of these nations are the souls who are precious in God's sight. Salvations will be their true reward as a result of their efforts. No longer will the shame many of these people live under rule their lives. God will set them free.

Has God called you to be such a vessel? Has He called you to be a catalyst in some way? Ask your heavenly Father if He might want you to affect nations for Him.

June 5

Effective Leadership

> *And when the Israelites saw the great power the Lord displayed*
> *against the Egyptians, the people feared the Lord and put their trust*
> *in Him and in Moses His servant.* Exodus 14:31

What makes an effective Christian leader today? Is it charisma? Is it ability? Is it communication and oratory skills? God's view of an effective leader has nothing to do with these qualities. They may be a part of an effective leader. However, the core attribute of a Christian leader is his integrity with God and his obedience to follow Him. When this happens, God manifests His power in and through that leader. Moses was effective because he was willing to obey the commands God gave him. When Moses did this, God manifested His presence in him. The result was that people followed. They followed because they saw God working in and through the man. They saw that this man was worthy of following because God's anointing was on him.

When people see the Lord's power manifested in your life, they will have a healthy fear of the Lord. They will look at you and say, "This person has something I don't have that is worthy of more investigation." Your challenge is to seek the Lord with a whole heart, resulting in God's power being manifested in the daily activities of your life. When this happens, you can expect others to be drawn to what they see in you. The problem with many Christians today is that non-Christians see nothing different about the way they live to motivate the unsaved to desire their faith.

What makes you different from your neighbor? Is your experience with God noticeably different from that of the man next door? If you're not experiencing regular encounters with God, it's time to ask why not. We don't live day-to-day for the next spiritual experience, but we should see by-products of a life centered in God that is reflected in fruit from His presence in our lives.

June 6

Disobedience Rooted in Fear

> *Then Moses said to them, "No one is to keep any of it until morning."*   Exodus 16:19

Have you ever seen God do something really good in your life only to find that you have abused the blessing He gave you? Such was the case of the Israelites as they were traveling through the desert on their way to the Promised Land. God was providing for them in miraculous ways. Manna was provided each day as their bread. God gave Moses specific instructions as to how this manna was to be eaten. God said each one was to gather only what he needed for that day. No one was to keep it until the next morning.

"However, some of them paid no attention to Moses; they kept part of it until morning, but it was full of maggots and began to smell. So Moses was angry with them" (Ex. 16:20). God was teaching the Israelites daily trust in His provision for them. He wanted them to trust Him one day at a time. If they tried to hoard, God put a self-destruct feature in the manna. Yet God also told them to gather two days' worth on the sixth day so that they would have manna to eat on the seventh day. Interestingly, this manna did not stink or have maggots.

For many years I gathered manna in business out of fear of not having enough. One day, the Lord decided that manna should be destroyed in order for me to learn total trust in His provision. When we operate out of fear, we can expect the Lord to lovingly discipline us in order to help us learn to trust Him. There is a danger when we seek to "insure ourselves" against calamity. If your actions are born from fear, you can expect God to demonstrate His loving reproof so that you might not live in fear.

June 7

Your Testimony

I tell you the truth, we speak of what we know, and we testify to what we have seen, but still you people do not accept our testimony.
John 3:11

Over the last several years I have seen two distinct types of Christian businesspeople. One type enthusiastically teaches their Bible knowledge to others. These people, though they may be genuine in their motive, lack one essential ingredient to being effectively used by God— a testimony. The second type of people I have encountered has a genuine testimony of what God is doing and continues to do in their lives. This was the case in the early Church. Men and women were able to give powerful testimony of events and experiences that could only be explained as a work of God.

God desires to build a testimony in each of us. Each of us is one of God's chosen vessels to reflect His power in and through us. When others see this power reflected, they are impacted because they cannot explain that power. God desires to frame your life with experiences designed to reflect the character and nature of Christ. Sometimes these events can be very devastating, but they are designed to reveal His power in and through us.

Every one of us has a testimony. What would others say your testimony is today? Can others see God's work in your life? Is your testimony one of Bible knowledge only? Are things happening in your life that can only be explained as God? These can be problematic questions for each of us. Ask God to build a testimony of His life in and through you today.

June 8

Forgiving Ourselves

> *If we confess our sins, He is faithful and just and will forgive us our sins and purify us from all unrighteousness.*   1 John 1:9

The apostle Peter was one of three disciples who walked with Jesus closer than the other nine. He was the most enthusiastic and the one man who was willing to step into territories where others would not dare. He was the first to step out of the boat and walk on water. He wanted to protect Jesus at times when Jesus rebuked him for having a demon influence him. He cut off the ear of the guard who wanted to arrest Jesus in the garden. As Peter matured, the Holy Spirit harnessed his many extreme emotions.

The greatest trial for Peter was when he denied the Lord just before Jesus was crucified. Three times he denied knowing Jesus. Jesus predicted that the cock would crow after the third time just to reinforce the prophecy to Peter. Peter was crushed when he realized he had failed His Lord so badly.

The Lord forgave Peter for his denial. However, gaining forgiveness from Jesus was not the most difficult part for Peter. The hard part was forgiving himself. As we mature in the faith, we begin moving in victory after victory with our Lord. Then out of nowhere, an event happens that reveals our true sin nature, and we are confronted face to face with this reality. We cannot believe that we are capable of such sin. There is no good thing in us save the grace of Jesus Christ and His blood that cleanses us. When God looks at us, He looks at the blood of Christ that has covered our sin. He does not look at our sin once we confess it.

When we have difficulty forgiving ourselves, this is pride at its deepest level. We are making an assumption that we should never have sinned and that we are too mature to sin. This is a trap from the enemy of our souls. People who cannot forgive do not recognize from what they have been forgiven. That includes us.

June 9

Power of the Tongue

The tongue has the power of life and death, and those who love it will eat its fruit.   Proverbs 18:21

Words have the power to motivate or destroy, energize or deflate, inspire or create despair. Many successful executives can remember the time their father failed to give affirmation to them as a child. The result was either overachievement to prove their worth, or underachievement to prove he was right.

Many a wife has lost her ability to love because of a critical husband. Many a husband has left a marriage because of words of disrespect and ungratefulness. Stories abound regarding the power of words. There are just as many stories of those who have been encouraged, challenged, and comforted with words that made a difference in their lives.

Jesus knew the power of words. He used parables to convey His principles of the Kingdom of God. He used words of forgiveness and mercy. He used words to challenge. He used words to inspire His disciples to miraculous faith.

Do your words give life? Do they inspire and challenge others to greatness? Who does God want you to encourage through your words today? Affirm someone close to you today.

June 10

Are You a Threat?

> *One day the evil spirit answered them, "Jesus I know, and I know about Paul, but who are you?"*　　　　　　　　　　Acts 19:15

Are you a threat to the kingdom of darkness? If satan and his demons had a board meeting and your name came before the board, what would they say? Would they say that you are one of their most feared enemies and they needed to keep many demons harassing and opposing you? Or would they say, "Gentlemen, this person poses no threat to our activities. Leave him alone. He needs no help from us." There are millions of church-going believers sitting in pews Sunday after Sunday who pose little threat to the kingdom of darkness.

If we truly believe that we war against rulers and principalities that cannot be seen, then we must realize that their mandate is to hinder any believer who is seeking to walk in the fullness of God. However, "greater is He that is in you, than he that is in the world" (1 Jn. 4:4b KJV).

If you are seeking to fully follow the Lord, you can expect harassment from the enemy. God permits temptation because it drives us deeper into the soil of God. These times reveal God's power to keep us and walk us through the temptations. Our message becomes fruitful when it is born out of obedience and suffering for His name. Do not consider it strange if you find yourself fighting major battles the more obedient you become to the Master. God desires each of us to become a feared enemy of hell in order to affect satan's domain. When you begin to feel harassed, chances are you are beginning to affect the kingdom of darkness, and satan doesn't like this. So, how many demons do you think are assigned to you?

June 11

Such a Time as This

> *On the third day Esther put on her royal robes and stood in the inner*
> *court of the palace, in front of the king's hall.* Esther 5:1a

Esther was a woman who lived for a cause greater than herself. God used this woman to save the entire Jewish people from extermination. However, before God could use her, she had to come to a place of death in herself. It was not an easy decision. Her uncle Mordecai was the instrument God used to challenge her to measure up to the task.

> *Do not think that because you are in the king's house you alone of all*
> *the Jews will escape. For if you remain silent at this time, relief and*
> *deliverance for the Jews will arise from another place, but you and*
> *your father's family will perish. And who knows but that you have*
> *come to royal position for such a time as this?* (Esther 4:13b-14)

Mordecai was telling it straight. For her to speak up meant great risks if the king did not receive her. It was automatic death if the king did not extend his scepter, which meant acceptance of her approach to the throne. It was also a time to realize that God may have brought her to this place and time for this specific purpose. However, if she did not respond in faith, God would use another instrument to deliver the people. What would she do?

> *Go, gather together all the Jews who are in Susa, and fast for me. Do*
> *not eat or drink for three days, night or day. I and my maids will fast*
> *as you do. When this is done, I will go to the king, even though it is*
> *against the law. And if I perish, I perish* (Esther 4:16).

On the third day of the fast she came and stood in the inner court of the palace, in front of the king's hall. She was like Jesus who stood in the inner court of Heaven on that third, resurrection day. She gave up her life, but God raised it up on that day and delivered an entire people from destruction because of one woman's willingness to give up her life for a greater cause.

God has called each of us to a purpose greater than ourselves. Know that it will require death before life can be given to this purpose. It must be His life that lives, not ours.

June 12

When Planting Yields No Fruit

You have planted much, but have harvested little....   Haggai 1:6

Have you ever worked and worked only to yield very little from your efforts? Such was the case for the businesspeople during the time of the prophet Haggai. Finally, God spoke through the prophet Haggai to inform the people why their efforts were not yielding any fruit. There was a specific reason this was happening.

"You expected much, but see, it turned out to be little. What you brought home, I blew away. Why?" declares the Lord Almighty. "Because of My house, which remains a ruin, while each of you is busy with his own house. Therefore, because of you the heavens have withheld their dew and the earth its crops. I called for a drought on the fields and the mountains, on the grain, the new wine, the oil and whatever the ground produces, on men and cattle, and on the labor of your hands" (Haggai 1:9-11).

God had finally had enough. His priorities were not His people's priorities. So, He withheld in order to get their attention. Zerubbabel was governor of Judah at the time. He was a godly man who sought to do God's will. He listened as the prophet gave these words; then he responded.

Then Zerubbabel son of Shealtiel, Joshua son of Jehozadak, the high priest, and the whole remnant of the people obeyed the voice of the

Lord their God and the message of the prophet Haggai, because the Lord their God had sent him. And the people feared the Lord (Haggai 1:12).

Sometimes God has to stir up the spirit of one man to initiate needed change. Zerubbabel was that man. Scriptures say, "The Lord stirred up the spirit of Zerubbabel" (Hag. 1:14). God is stirring up the spirit of a remnant of businesspeople throughout the world today. They are seeing what breaks God's heart, and they're responding. Has God placed the spirit of Zerubbabel in you? Are you one who will make a difference for the Kingdom, or are you concerned about building bigger and better barns? The Lord is calling forth His people in these last days to make a difference. Ask Him what He wants to do through you.

June 13

Humility in Relationships

All of you, clothe yourselves with humility toward one another, because, "God opposes the proud but gives grace to the humble."
1 Peter 5:5b

I'll never forget the first time I discovered what a feeling was. It was in my early forties. *Surely not!* you may be thinking. Yes, it is true. Since then, I have discovered many men still live in this condition. It took an older mentor to help me understand the difference between information and a feeling. Wives are frustrated because their husbands share information, but not their feelings. They want to know what is going on inside their man. The fact is, most men have not been taught to identify feelings, much less how to share them. It is something that men must learn to do because it is not a natural trait. If they do share their feelings, society often portrays them as weak. No man willingly wants to be portrayed as weak.

In order to become an effective friend and leader, one must learn to be vulnerable with others and develop an ability to share feelings. It is a vital step to becoming a real person with whom others can connect emotionally. This is not easy to do if your parents did not teach you to share your emotional life with others. Emotional vulnerability is especially hard for men. Author Dr. Larry Crabb states,

> Men who as boys felt neglected by their dads often remain distant from their own children. The sins of fathers are passed on to children, often through the dynamic of self-protection. It hurts to be neglected, and it creates questions about our value to others. So to avoid feeling the sting of further rejection, we refuse to give that part of ourselves we fear might once again be received with indifference. When our approach to life revolves around discipline, commitment, and knowledge [which the Greek influence teaches us] but runs from feeling the hurt of unmet longings that come from a lack of deeper relationships, then our efforts to love will be marked more by required action than by liberating passion. We will be known as reliable, but not involved. Honest friends will report that they enjoy being with us, but have trouble feeling close. Even our best friends (including spouses) will feel guarded around us, a little tense and vaguely distant. It's not uncommon for Christian leaders to have no real friends. [Larry Crabb, *Inside Out* (Colorado Springs, Colorado: Navpress, n.d.), 98-99.]

If this describes you, why not begin on a new journey of opening up your life to others in a way that others can see who you really are? It might be scary at first, but as you grow in this area, you will find new freedom in your life. Then, others will more readily connect with you.

June 14

Perception Is Not Reality

> *The lions may roar and growl, yet the teeth of the great lions are broken.*   Job 4:10

In the advertising business we often say that "perception is reality" for the person who views our advertising message. It does not matter whether the audience believes the message to be true, only that they perceive it to be true. Their actions will be the same whether they believe it or only perceive it.

The enemy of our souls is very good at this game. He may bring on us what we perceive to be true when it is a lie. It may appear that there is no way around a situation. He may bring great fear on us. When we buy into his lie, we are believing only what we have chosen to perceive to be true. It usually has no basis of truth. Such was the case when Peter looked on the waters during a night boat journey with the other disciples. At first glance, he and the disciples screamed with fear, thinking that what they saw was a ghost. It was actually Jesus.

Satan's name means "accuser." He travels to and fro to accuse the brethren. He brings an impressive front to all he does, yet behind that front is a weak, toothless lion with a destination that has already been prepared in the great abyss. He knows his destination, but he wants to bring as many with him as possible; so he often has a big roar, but little bite.

The next time some event comes into your life that creates fear and trembling, first determine the source. Look past the emotions and evaluate the situation in light of God's Word. Perception is not always reality.

June 15

When God Speaks

…"The Lord is with you, mighty warrior."   Judges 6:12

Has God ever spoken directly to you in such a way that you knew that it was actually His voice speaking to you specifically? I don't mean just an appropriate verse of Scripture, or a circumstance that seemed probable that it was God. I am talking about a situation that you know that you know it was the God of the universe speaking directly to you.

In the book *Experiencing God*, authors Henry Blackaby and Claude King say that one of seven important steps to experiencing God in everyday life is how God speaks to us. "God speaks by the Holy Spirit through the Bible, prayer, circumstances, and the church to reveal Himself, His purposes, and His ways." [Henry Blackaby and Claude King, *Experiencing God* (Nashville, Tennessee: LifeWay Press, 1990), 225]

You can examine the life of every major character in the Bible and see this principle expressed in the way God worked in each of their lives.

One of the ways God speaks is through others. God often used others to speak to individuals, especially in the Old Testament when God often spoke through the prophets. This is still one of the ways He speaks today.

Several years ago I was in a church on the west coast that I had never been in before. I was in the midst of a tremendous trial. Three people prayed for me, and as they did, they began to describe a picture that was reflective of my life since I was a young Christian. It was a very accurate picture of my life. About a year later a man from Virginia prayed with me in my office. After our prayer time, he began to describe what he had just seen as a picture of my life. It was the same picture that had been described a year earlier. A year after that I was on a trip overseas and a man from England whom I had never met before came to me. He and I had a time of prayer together, and at the end of our prayer time he described a picture he had just seen in his mind while we were praying. Again, it was the same type of picture as the two previous encounters. Only this time, one element was added that was important for me to know related to what God was doing in my life at that time. When God chooses to speak into our lives through others, it can be an incredible blessing. He speaks in many ways. This is just one of them.

God desires to encourage us by speaking to us. He does this in many ways. The next time someone speaks into your life, prayerfully consider whether God is using that person to convey something important He wants you to know.

June 16

Receiving Your Inheritance

> *But the Danites had difficulty taking possession of their territory, so*
> *they went up and attacked Leshem, took it, put it to the sword and*
> *occupied it....*   Joshua 19:47

What is your spiritual inheritance God has reserved for you? When God told the Israelites they were going to receive the Promised Land, it was not given to them on a silver platter. In fact, they would encounter 39 battles in taking the land God promised to them. It took a joint effort between God and the Israelites to engage and battle the enemy that maintained control of the land.

God has given you and me a spiritual inheritance that must be won in the heavenlies. A dear friend and mentor once counseled me after watching my life over a period and said, "The Lord has given you a spiritual inheritance. That inheritance lies in relationships, and because it lies in relationships, that is the place the enemy has attacked you most. The enemy always attacks us in the area where we are to receive our inheritance. You must walk in faithfulness and obedience to His righteousness in how you deal with relationships." These were words of wisdom that have since guided my path. The Lord has proven these words to be true.

What is the spiritual inheritance He has reserved for you? What areas of your inheritance must you take possession of? The enemy of your soul does not want you to take possession. Put on your armor and begin walking in obedience into the areas God has called you to possess.

June 17

Learning To Stand

> *..."Stand firm and you will see the deliverance the Lord will bring*
> *you today...."*   Exodus 14:13

The Israelites had just left 400 years of slavery in Egypt. They had fled to the desert, but they had come to a dead end at the Red Sea. Word reached them that Pharaoh had changed his mind. He was sending his troops to recapture the Israelites. They cried out to their leader Moses, complaining that he had brought them that far only to die in the desert.

Learning when to move and when to stand is the greatest challenge for a businessperson. We are trained for action. We are not trained to sit idly and wait. We are trained to solve problems, not wait for them to resolve themselves. However, God says there are times to wait. We are to wait until He says go. If we go before He says go, we likely will make our situation worse. If the Israelites had attempted to cross the Red Sea before it parted, they would have drowned. If they had fled north to try to avoid the Egyptians, God would not have moved in a miraculous way. God cannot work on our behalf if we continually try to solve our problem when He has instructed us to stand still. Standing still is sometimes the greatest action we can do, although it is the most difficult thing to do in the Christian walk.

Stand still when He says stand and see the deliverance of the Lord.

June 18

Faithfulness in Our Calling

He went out to meet Asa and said to him, "Listen to me, Asa and all Judah and Benjamin. The Lord is with you when you are with Him. If you seek Him, He will be found by you, but if you forsake Him, He will forsake you."   2 Chronicles 15:2

Asa was the king of Judah from 912–872 B.C. He reigned for 41 years and was known as a good king who served the Lord with great zeal. He reformed many things. He broke down idol worship to foreign gods; he put away male prostitutes and even removed his own mother from being queen because she worshiped an idol. The Scriptures say that as long as he sought the Lord, the Lord prospered his reign.

However, Asa was not totally faithful in his calling. There came a time in his life when he made a decision to no longer trust in the God of Israel. He lost his confidence in God as his deliverer. The prophet Hanani came to Asa to inform him that God's blessing was no longer on his life because of an ungodly alliance he had made.

> *Were not the Cushites and Libyans a mighty army with great numbers of chariots and horsemen? Yet when you relied on the Lord, He delivered them into your hand. For the eyes of the Lord range throughout the earth to strengthen those whose hearts are fully committed to Him. You have done a foolish thing, and from now on you will be at war* (2 Chronicles 16:8-9).

There are no guarantees that if we began well we will finish well. The life of Asa tells us this. It is only through God's grace that we can be faithful to our calling. Each of us is capable of falling away from God. Pray that God will keep you faithful to the purposes He has for your life. He strengthens those whose hearts are fully committed to Him.

June 19

The Strength of Brokenness

> *The bows of the warriors are broken, but those who stumbled are armed with strength.* 1 Samuel 2:4

There is an oxymoron throughout the Bible. It says that brokenness is strength. How can this be? How can brokenness be strength? In order to use men and women to their fullest extent, the Lord has to break His servants so that they might have a new kind of strength that is not human in origin. It is strength in spirit that is born only through brokenness.

Paul was broken on the Damascus road. Peter was broken after Jesus was taken prisoner. Jacob was broken at Peniel. David was broken after his sin with Bathsheba. The list could go on of those the Lord had to break in different ways before they could be used in the Kingdom.

June 19—Day 170

When we are broken, we see the frailty of human strength and come to grips with the reality that we can do nothing in our own strength. Then, new strength emerges that God uses mightily. God resists the proud but gives grace to the humble.

Do not fear brokenness. For it may be the missing ingredient to a life that emerges with a new kind of strength and experience not known before. Pray for a broken and contrite heart that God can bless.

June 20

Being Fully Persuaded

> *Being fully persuaded that God had power to do what He had promised.*
> Romans 4:21

Why did God consider Abraham a righteous man? It was because Abraham looked beyond his own limitations of age and strength and considered God as the one who could accomplish His own goals. Abraham came to a place in his life where he realized it had little to do with him and all to do with God. His part was initiating the faith within himself.

> *Against all hope, Abraham in hope believed and so became the father of many nations, just as it had been said to him, "So shall your offspring be." Without weakening in his faith, he faced the fact that his body was as good as dead—since he was about a hundred years old—and that Sarah's womb was also dead. Yet he did not waver through unbelief regarding the promise of God, but was strengthened in his faith and gave glory to God (Romans 4:18-20).*

What are the things in your life that are mere impossibilities? What are the mountains in your life? Are these there in order to build your faith in the one who can enable you to ascend to the peak? Once you know that it is His will for you to pursue, do it with faith. Faith requires action when we know it is He who is leading. It may require risk. Faith is sometimes spelled R-I-S-K. Abraham did not limit God. It is this confidence in God that God honored and rewarded. He wants to do the same with you and me.

June 21

God's Authority

I will not speak with you much longer, for the prince of this world is coming. He has no hold on Me, but the world must learn that I love the Father and that I do exactly what My Father has commanded Me....   John 14:30-31

There is a constant war going on between our flesh and the Spirit. As Christians, the Spirit seeks to move us under the authority of His domain in order for us to fulfill all that we were created for. Every person was designed to be under some form of authority. Jesus modeled this in His own life. He lived under the authority of His heavenly Father. He made no independent decisions. He, unlike us, was sinless and always remained under His Father's authority. He acknowledged that the prince of this world has a hold on many, but did not have a hold on Jesus.

The prince of this world does have his hold on many in our world, even among our brothers and sisters. The one thing most of us want the greatest is the freedom to make our own decisions. It goes all the way back to the Garden of Eden when the decision was made to exercise a personal right: freedom to decide, freedom of choice, freedom from hindrances, freedom from pain. However, Jesus said He had no freedom of choice. He chose only the Father's desire for His life. He was the ultimate model of a man under authority.

Each day we must determine if we'll willingly choose to be under the authority of the Father and the direction of the Holy Spirit. It is a choice each of us must make. It is a choice that actually leads to freedom, not bondage. Choosing to live under the authority of our heavenly Father frees us to gain the greatest fulfillment in life—His mission and the purposes He has for us. It is the little decisions of daily life that reveal whether we truly live under His authority.

June 22

When Fear Keeps Others From Their Destiny

No one else dared join them, even though they were highly regarded by the people.   Acts 5:13

Every business day in thousands of offices across the globe, Christians testify of God's grace in their lives in some way. Sometimes it comes through a subtle performance of their duties with a smile and peace that non-believers cannot understand. In other cases, there might be more visible, unexplainable examples of God's work. This was the defining difference in believers in the early Church. They lived a life that followed with signs and wonders that could not be humanly explained.

The apostles performed many miraculous signs and wonders among the people. And all the believers used to meet together in Solomon's Colonnade. No one else dared join them, even though they were highly regarded by the people. Nevertheless, more and more men and women believed in the Lord and were added to their number (Acts 5:12-14).

How often we have heard non-believers acknowledge their respect for the Christian businessperson, but they dare not join them in their persuasion. It is this fear of the unknown that keeps many a non-believer on the path to hell. Who has God placed in your path today to help detour from a path of eternal torment to a path of freedom and eternal life? The Lord desires that each should come to knowledge of the truth so that they might be saved. As you enter the marketplace today, ask the Lord for a divine appointment that might be the turning point for a lost soul. There's no prayer the Lord will delight in more than this one.

June 23

Divine Appointments

I am sending you out like sheep among wolves. Therefore be as
shrewd as snakes and as innocent as doves.   Matthew 10:16

"Os is now taking over this division. He will be managing all of
these activities from now on. You should know that he has a different
management philosophy than what you may have experienced before.
He has a biblical management philosophy. Os, would you like to explain
what they could expect from you in this regard?"

These were the words spoken to me by a non-Christian CEO
recently when he decided to increase my responsibilities in the company. We had never spoken of spiritual issues before.

Each business day, you and I will have the opportunity to stand
before presidents, marketing directors, secretaries or other coworkers to
create a defining moment. When that happens, there is a good chance
you will be thought of as someone to avoid. You might be considered
"religious" or "fanatic." If so, consider this a great compliment because
it says you are standing apart from the crowd.

> *Be on your guard against men; they will hand you over to the local*
> *councils and flog you in their synagogues. On My account you will*
> *be brought before governors and kings as witnesses to them and to*
> *the Gentiles. But when they arrest you, do not worry about what to*
> *say or how to say it. At that time you will be given what to say, for*
> *it will not be you speaking, but the Spirit of your Father speaking*
> *through you* (Matthew 10:17-20).

You may never be flogged for your faith. However, you may very
well be brought before others to give account for what you believe. It
may be at a water cooler, or it could be during lunch with a coworker. In
whatever situation you find yourself, the Holy Spirit awaits the opportunity to speak through your life to that person who needs to hear. Ask
the Lord whom He wants to speak to today through your life.

June 24

Living an Obedience-Based Life

They trusted in Him and defied the king's command and were will-ing to give up their lives rather than serve or worship any god except their own God.   Daniel 3:28b

Have you ever known someone who lived an outcome-based Chris-tian experience? What I mean by this is that their decisions are made based on the positive or negative outcome, not on absolute obedience.

Shadrach, Meshach, and Abednego were three men who lived an obedience-based life. When King Nebuchadnezzar passed a law that said all were to worship his idol, these young men determined they would not worship anything other than God. You can be sure these men did not make this decision at the time of the decree. Their decision actu-ally had been made years earlier. Their convictions were already in their hearts.

Each of us must come to a place of knowing what our boundaries are in given situations. What will you tolerate from your employer? What situation crosses the line for you? Where are the boundaries for questionable practices in your life? If these are not worked out ahead, you will live a life of situational ethics, determining what decision to make based on the merits of the situation.

Shadrach, Meshach, and Abednego were willing to die for what they believed. In this case, they were delivered from the fiery furnace. God used their faithfulness to impact a king, and they were promoted to higher positions.

Are you an obedienced-based Christian? Or are there situations that can move you based on the outcome? God wants to know that we will stand firm on the issues that are important to Him, no matter what the outcome may be. God is looking for those who are radical in their obedience. Does this describe your commitment to Christ? If not, pray for this kind of conviction. The Lord will honor you for this.

June 25

My God Shall Provide

And my God will meet all your needs according to His glorious riches in Christ Jesus. Philippians 4:19

Have you ever gone through a time of complete dependence on God for your material needs? Perhaps you lost a job and could not generate income on your own. Perhaps you got sick and could not work. There are circumstances in our lives that can put us in this place.

When God brought the people of Israel out of Egypt through the desolate desert, they had no ability to provide for themselves. God met their needs supernaturally each day by providing manna from Heaven. Each day they would awake to one day's portion of what they needed. This was a season in their lives to learn dependence and the faithfulness of God as provider. By and by, they entered the Promised Land. When they did, God's "supernatural provision" was no longer required. "The manna stopped the day after they ate this food from the land; there was no longer any manna for the Israelites, but that year they ate of the produce of Canaan" (Josh. 5:12). In both cases God was the provider of the need.

For most of us, we derive our necessities of life through our work. Like the birds of the fields we are commanded to go out and gather what God has already provided. It is a process of participation in what God has already provided. Sometimes it appears it is all up to us; sometimes it appears it is all up to God. In either case we must realize that the Lord is our provider; the job is only an instrument of His provision. He requires our involvement in either case.

You may say to yourself, "My power and the strength of my hands have produced this wealth for me." But remember the Lord your God, for it is He who gives you the ability to produce wealth, and so confirms His covenant, which He swore to your forefathers, as it is today (Deuteronomy 8:17-18).

Acknowledge the Lord as the provider of every need you have today. He is a faithful provider.

June 26

Remaining Vertical With God

When they hurled their insults at Him, He did not retaliate; when He suffered, He made no threats. Instead, He entrusted Himself to Him who judges justly.   1 Peter 2:23

Have you ever been wrongfully accused? Oh, the need to defend and justify becomes so great. "What will people think if they believe these things are true?" we reason. Imagine what Jesus thought as they hurled insults and threats upon Him. The God of the universe had visited planet earth only to be slandered and accused of blasphemy.

Jesus could have done two things in response. He could have used His power to put the people in their place. He could have responded "horizontally." He could have fixed the problem right then. However, He chose to respond in a different way. He chose to "entrust Himself to Him who judges justly." It requires great faith to entrust ourselves to God in the midst of personal assault. However, if we can do this, we will discover a level of grace and wisdom that will be birthed from this experience that we never thought possible. We will discover a freedom in God we never knew before. Whenever we suffer for righteousness without seeking to protect our reputation and rights, we are placing our total faith in the one who can redeem us. This activates God's grace in our lives and enables us to experience God's presence like never before.

Ask God to give you the grace to stay vertical with Him. Avoid the temptation of responding horizontally each time some event comes into your life that you want to "fix." Entrust yourself to the one who judges justly. It may be a divine appointment for your growth to another level in grace.

June 27

Our Counselor

But the Counselor, the Holy Spirit, whom the Father will send in My name, will teach you all things and will remind you of everything I have said to you. John 14:26

I was driving down the interstate feeling discouraged from an appointment I had just had. A former employee's company was seeking to displace me and my company as their source for our services. It had been one of many difficult events during those months. As I was driving, some words popped into my mind, *No weapon formed against you shall prosper.* I could not tell you where those words came from other than I knew the Holy Spirit was speaking them to me; I knew they were in the Bible. I knew they were in the Old Testament.

When I returned to my office that day, I searched for the key words in my concordance and found the verse. "No weapon forged against you will prevail, and you will refute every tongue that accuses you" (Is. 54:17a).

Jesus said that the Holy Spirit would remind us of the things He desires us to know. There are times in our lives when the Holy Spirit speaks into our spirit words designed to encourage us or give us what we need at the moment. That is just one of the roles of the Holy Spirit in the life of the believer. The more you know God's Word, the more often you'll recall verses the Holy Spirit will bring to mind for a given situation. Study God's Word and allow the Holy Spirit to remind you of the things He desires you to know.

June 28

Pleasing to the Lord

Prepare it with oil on a griddle; bring it well-mixed and present the grain offering broken in pieces as an aroma pleasing to the Lord.

Leviticus 6:21

There is a requirement to be blessed at a deeper spiritual level by God. Christ requires it of each of His servants. He required it of Paul when He struck him down on the Damascus Road. He required it of Joseph when he was left in the pit and then sold into slavery. He required it of Jacob when he left his homeland penniless and needy. He required it of most every major leader that He used significantly—brokenness.

Brokenness cannot be achieved on your own. It is something God does Himself. We cannot determine that we are going to be broken, but we can refuse to become broken. When God begins this deeper work in our lives, we can kick and scream and refuse the process. We can manipulate and strive to stay on top, but this only delays His work.

Pride and mammon are ruling strongholds of the marketplace. Brokenness is considered a weak position in the marketplace. However, God says until we are broken we cannot be an aroma pleasing to the Lord. God wants you to be an aroma in the marketplace. In order for this to happen, you and I must be a broken vessel in His hand. Pray that God would allow you to become a pleasing aroma to Him no matter the cost.

June 29

Settling Disputes

Casting the lot settles disputes and keeps strong opponents apart.

Proverbs 18:18

We prayed about it. We discussed it. My friend had one desire; I had a different one. "Okay, let's settle the issue the way the early Church settled matters when an agreement could not be achieved. Let's flip a coin."

"You must be joking!" my friend lamented.

"No, the early Church cast lots often to determine a course of direction or even select the disciple who would take Judas' place."

"Okay," my friend agreed. We flipped the coin and the matter was quickly settled.

In the Old Testament there are many examples of casting lots for determining a decision. We hear little of this method today. Most of us do not want to release the decision process to this seemingly "flippant" process; yet the Lord says, "The lot is cast into the lap, but its every decision is from the Lord" (Prov. 16:33). Flipping a coin is the equivalent to casting a lot. It removes our own opinions and leaves the final outcome to the Lord. Pray before you take such an action. It will surprise you who is willing to submit a decision to the Lord and who isn't. It removes the element of control from both parties.

I believe the Lord would first have us make decisions through agreement and continued prayer for the decision. However, there are times when this approach can be the quickest and simplest. It removes each person's temptation to lord it over the other. Cast the lot and settle the dispute.

June 30

Seekers of God

God looks down from heaven on the sons of men to see if there are any who understand, any who seek God. Psalm 53:2

Are you a man or woman who is a seeker of God? The Lord delights in seeing those children of His who truly understand the meaning of life and why there is only one thing worth seeking—God Himself.

I can always tell when I have not been seeking God. The cares of this life, the urgent over the important, and the petty irritations—these are the symptoms of a life that has not been in the presence of God. Do we understand, really understand? That is the question God raises to each of us today. If we understand, then why do we spend day after day toiling and fretting over what doesn't matter? Can we set proper boundaries in our lives that don't allow our time with Him to be continually stolen away? It is a challenge in a world that screams "activity, activity!"

Do you have a consistent time of seeking Him in your life? Are you committed to developing that intimacy with your Lord that He so desires? If not, ask Him today to help you. This is the longing of His heart. Ask Him to make it the longing of your heart. Then you will demonstrate to Him that you understand, and you will be a seeker of God.

July 1

Proving the Word of God

They bruised his feet with shackles, his neck was put in irons, till what he foretold came to pass, till the word of the Lord proved him true.   Psalm 105:18-19

God spoke to Joseph as a young boy through a dream and vision regarding his future. He could not understand its complete meaning at the time, but he knew it had great significance. Joseph knew God had a destiny for his life. However, the proving out of that word from God was filled with 13 years of waiting, rejection, pain, sorrow, and no doubt, questioning God's faithfulness.

His life was all but a life of influence and impact as a prisoner and slave. No doubt he wondered whether that dream was simply some vain imagination. David must have felt the same when he was anointed king over Israel as a young man only to spend years of fleeing from King Saul. God's preparation for greatness in His Kingdom is often filled with difficulty. God is more concerned about developing the inner life of his servant. That inner life can only be prepared by removing all *self*-confidence and replacing it with *God*-confidence. God-confidence is only developed in the furnace of life.

Is the Lord proving His word in your life? Perhaps He is using circumstances and events to move you into a place of patient waiting as He puts you in the place He desires for you. This is the place where the foundations of your soul mature. Let Him prove your faith.

July 2

Living for a Greater Cause

I can do everything through Him who gives me strength.
Philippians 4:13

What does it mean for businesspeople to live for a cause greater than themselves in our day and time? Jeremiah Lanphier was a businessman in New York City who asked God to do this in his life in 1857.

> In a small darkened room, in the back of one of New York City's lesser churches, a man prayed alone. His request of God was simple, but earth-shattering: "Lord, what wilt Thou have me to do?" [John Woodbridge, ed., *More Than Conquerors* (Chicago, Illinois: Moody Press, 1992), 337]

He was a man approaching midlife without a wife or family, but he had financial means. He made a decision to reject the "success syndrome" that drove the city's businessmen and bankers. God used this businessman to turn New York City's commercial empire on its head. He began a businessmen's prayer meeting on September 23, 1857. The meetings began slowly, but within a few months 20 noonday meetings were convening daily throughout the city. The *New York Tribune* and the *New York Herald* issued articles of revival. It had become the city's biggest news. Now a full-fledged revival, it moved outside New York. By spring of 1858, 2,000 met daily in Chicago's Metropolitan Theatre, and in Philadelphia the meetings mushroomed into a four-month long tent meeting. Meetings were held in Baltimore, Washington, Cincinnati, Chicago, New Orleans, and Mobile. Thousands met to pray because one man stepped out. *Annus Mirabilis*, the year of national revival, had begun.

This was an extraordinary move of God through one man. It was unique because the movement was lead by businessmen, a group long considered the least prone to any form of evangelical fervor, and it had started on Wall Street, the most unlikely of all places to begin.

Could God do something extraordinary through you? Take a step. Ask God to do mighty things through you.

July 3

Your Epitaph

He will bless those who fear the Lord— small and great alike.
Psalm 115:13

What will be written on your epitaph? How do you want people to remember you? What type of legacy will your life leave behind?

I interviewed a very successful and powerful man one time for a magazine when this question came up. The man ran an international business that is a household name to all. He was a professed Christian, but he had difficulty answering my question. "I always knew someone would ask that question some day. I am not sure I am any more prepared to answer it now either," was the man's answer. He grappled for a few nice words, but it was clear he had not seriously considered his life much beyond his business success.

It is said of George Washington Carver that he got up early in the morning each day to walk alone and pray. He asked God how he was to spend his day and what He wanted to teach him that day. Carver grew up at the close of the Civil War in a one-room shanty on the home of

Moses Carver—the man who owned his mother. The Ku Klux Klan had abducted him and his mother, selling her to new owners. He was later found and returned to his owner, but his mother was never seen again.

Carver grew up at the height of racial discrimination, yet he had overcome all these obstacles to become one of the most influential men in the history of the United States. He made many discoveries with the use of peanuts and sweet potatoes. However, after he recommended farmers to plant peanuts and sweet potatoes instead of cotton, he was led into his greatest trial. The farmers lost even more money due to the lack of market for peanuts and sweet potatoes. Carver cried out to the Lord, "Mr. Creator, why did You make the peanut?" Many years later, he shared that God led him back to his lab and worked with him to discover some 300 marketable products from the peanut. Likewise, he made over 100 discoveries from the sweet potato. These new products created a demand for peanuts and sweet potatoes, and they were major contributors to rejuvenating the Southern economy.

As he made new discoveries, he never became successful monetarily, but he overcame great rejection during his lifetime for being black. He was offered six-figure income opportunities from Henry Ford, and he became friends with presidents of his day, yet he knew what God had called him to do. His epitaph read:

> He could have added fortune to fame, but caring for neither, he found happiness and honor in being helpful to the world. [John Woodbridge, *More Than Conquerors* (Chicago, Illinois: Moody Press, 1992), 312.]

July 4

Play to Your Strength

There are different kinds of gifts, but the same Spirit.
1 Corinthians 12:4

Have you ever tried to do anything that you were not gifted to do? I am not a handy man. If there is a household project, like a plumbing leak or anything mechanical—forget it. God has not given me any "natural" gifts for such things. And I'd prefer not buying anything that requires assembly!

I have a friend who can fix or assemble anything. It comes naturally to him, and he loves to help me. This same person looks at some of my abilities and marvels. We appreciate the gifts God has given to each of us. These differences have created a need for one another. God wants each of us to need one another. The Scriptures describe the Body of Christ in the same way. Each person is a member of His Body with gifts and talents designed to make His Body perform as a multi-talented group, all playing to the same tune. It is when one member is "out of tune" or decides he doesn't like his gifts, or decides to do something he is not designed to do that the orchestra begins to sound off key. Imagine if the parts of the human body decided they didn't want to fulfill their parts any longer. That body would no longer function effectively because one or more of its members were not performing the functions they were designed for.

What has He equipped you for? What role has He called you to play in God's Kingdom? When one link in the chain is weakened, the whole chain is susceptible to breaking. God made it that way so that we could help that weak link. He made it that way so we would be forced to depend on one another. Are you being a strong link in the chain of God's Kingdom? Ask Him if you are fulfilling your role as He designed.

July 5

Death Works in You

We do not want you to be uninformed, brothers, about the hardships we suffered in the province of Asia. We were under great pressure, far beyond our ability to endure, so that we despaired even of life. Indeed, in our hearts we felt the sentence of death. But this happened that we might not rely on ourselves but on God, who raises the dead.
2 Corinthians 1:8-9

Have you ever gone through a very difficult time in your life? These times make us value life. They make us appreciate the simple things that we took for granted before the crisis. When we are restored from such a trial, it is as though we have been given a new beginning. We can place a greater value on what we had before and use it for His purposes. Perhaps for the first time we can identify with others who find themselves in a similar trial.

I recall having an attitude of superiority over those who went through a difficult financial crisis. Because I had never experienced any financial crisis in my life, this pride kept me from identifying with such people. Then the Lord brought such a trial into my life. I learned a great deal during that period. I learned that the world and even Christians often treat such people as lepers. Like me, they didn't know how to relate. Now, I appreciate the little things that I never would have valued without that trial. The experience taught me greater dependence and faith in the provision area of my relationship with God.

When God brings death to one area of life, he resurrects it in a new way. Death works in us to bring new life and new perspectives. These are designed to press us forward in ways that we never would have moved without the experience. God knows how much this is needed in our life to gain the prize He has reserved for each of us. It is His strategic mercy that motivates Him to bring such events into our life. Press into Him, learn of Him, and rely on Him.

July 6

Our Work Versus Our Value

The Lord God took the man and put him in the Garden of Eden to work it and take care of it.				Genesis 2:15

Man was created to have seven basic needs. Each of us has a need for dignity, authority, blessing and provision, security, purpose and meaning, freedom and boundary, intimate love and companionship.

July 6—Day 187

When we go outside God's provision to meet these needs, we get into trouble.

Every man has a need to work and gain satisfaction in caring and seeing something come from his efforts. Many of our basic needs are derived from our work; it was one of the first acts God did for man in the Garden of Eden. He gave him responsibility to care for and work the Garden. God knew man needed to be productive. He needed to gain satisfaction from his work.

The danger of this is when we allow our work to be our complete source of purpose and meaning in life. This leads to a performance-based life. A performance-based life says, "As long as I perform in my work, I am acceptable to myself and others." This is a subtle trap for all of us. It can lead us to become workaholics if we are seeking acceptance through what we do. Sometimes this can be on a subconscious basis.

Our value must be centered in Christ, not in what we do. If we lose our job or our business, this should not devastate us if we are centered in Him. It will certainly create difficulties, but God is the orchestrator of all the events in our lives for His purposes. Even difficult times have purposes.

Today, ask the Lord if you have a proper balance in your work life. Is Christ the central focus? If you work long hours, ask yourself why. You might discover that God may not be the central focus.

July 7

The Consequence of Faith

We were therefore buried with Him through baptism into death in order that, just as Christ was raised from the dead through the glory of the Father, we too may live a new life. Romans 6:4

If you commit yourself to live for Christ in and through your business life, there will be a consequence of faith. You could avoid much hardship and take a much easier road in life if you do not choose to live an obedient life of faith in Christ. This is a spiritual law. None of us is excluded from identification with the cross.

When we commit ourselves to fully follow Christ, He begins a "circumcision" process in each of us designed to rid all that is of the world system from our lives. This circumcision is required of every believer. Moses had much preparation from God for His calling to free the people of Israel from Egypt. He spent years in training as a young boy in the family of Pharaoh. He tried to free the people through the flesh by killing an Egyptian. That cost him 40 years in the desert of loneliness and toil before God said he was prepared to free the people from their suffering. God invested much in Moses; however, that preparation was not enough. Experience and preparation had to be mixed with obedience. God required his family to be circumcised. Moses failed to circumcise his son before returning to Egypt. This was so important to God that He was going to kill Moses if he did not uphold his commandment. "At a lodging place on the way, the Lord met Moses and was about to kill him" (Ex. 4:24).

Are there any areas in your life that have not come under the lordship of Christ? Is there any lack of obedience that will prevent you from being used fully by the Lord? Ask Him to show you this today so that you might be fully used of God.

July 8

Living as if You Were Dead

In the same way, count yourselves dead to sin but alive to God in Christ Jesus. Romans 6:11

What are the things that arouse the strongest emotions in you? Perhaps it is a rude motorist who cuts you off in traffic. Perhaps it is the anger you feel when you are wrongfully accused. Perhaps it is frustration that results from not having enough money to meet perceived needs. When do emotions turn into sin?

Whenever our peace is upset over events and circumstances in life, we have moved past emotions into sin. Sin says that circumstances of life now dictate anxiety, worry, fear, or anger. Consider the attributes of a dead man. He does not get angry when slandered. He does not worry about the future. He does not fear what can be done to him. Why? Because he is dead. Nothing can harm a dead man.

Christ said we are to live as if we are dead—dead to the temptation of responding to stimuli in our life that are designed to stir up the sinful nature that resides in each of us. We do not have to respond to that nature; we can consider it dead. Christ said He is enough. When He is our all in all, nothing can move us. If we are moved, then Christ is not our all in all.

July 9

Becoming a Valued Draft Pick

...Men will rejoice when they see the plumb line in the hand of Zerubbabel....   Zechariah 4:10

As children in grammar school we often played pick-up football. Two captains would alternate making the best choices among schoolmates to make up the two teams. I was often chosen first because I was a good athlete. It felt good to be valued by others for what they perceived I could contribute. Conversely, it must have felt crummy to be the last chosen or not chosen at all.

Such was the case for Zerubbabel. He was a man chosen by God to rebuild the temple. God saw something in Zerubbabel that He could use for His purposes. The people also recognized that Zerubbabel was a man in whom they could place their faith.

So the Lord stirred up the spirit of Zerubbabel son of Shealtiel, governor of Judah, and the spirit of Joshua son of Jehozadak, the high priest, and the spirit of the whole remnant of the people (Haggai 1:14a).

Are you part of the remnant of businesspeople whom God is calling out today? Do not let the busyness of today's marketplace sidetrack you from the importance of God's agenda for you. Can you recall the day God's Spirit rested on you? Have you walked in that anointing since that day? Satan's strategy is to keep us distracted with the urgency of the moment versus the importance of eternity. Ask God what your priorities should be today. Make His priorities your priorities.

***

July 10

Walking in the Anointing

So Samuel took the horn of oil and anointed him in the presence of his brothers, and from that day on the Spirit of the Lord came upon David in power....   1 Samuel 16:13

Has the Spirit of the Lord rested on your life? Can you cite the time when God's Spirit began demonstrating His power through you?

David knew the day the Spirit of the Lord began a special work in him. That Spirit was different from most leaders. Instead of seeking power and control, he led in response to a need. Instead of being a perfect person, he learned from mistakes and acknowledged them among those he led. Instead of placing confidence in his own abilities, he sought wisdom from the only real Commander in charge. David never lost a battle through his many years of leading Israel. He failed God by sinning with Bathsheba and by numbering the troops, but he learned from those failures, and he had to pay a price for them. However, God's Spirit never left David. He never left because of David's willingness to keep a soft heart toward God, even when he failed.

God wants to do the same in you and me, but He will not allow that Spirit to rest on us if we seek to control outcomes and manipulate out of our need for power. Servant leaders know that they are only a tool in the Master's hand. They do not value themselves more than they ought. David's heart was fully the Lord's. Is your heart fully the Lord's to do with what He wills?

July 11

Called to the Mission Field

To one there is given through the Spirit the message of wisdom, to another the message of knowledge by means of the same Spirit.
1 Corinthians 12:8

"I'm called to the mission field," said the beautiful young woman.

It was my first real encounter with the woman. As she spoke the words to me, I heard these words, "She's called to the mission field, but it's not what she thinks." I quietly kept this to myself until the following week when I felt compelled to share these words with her. She was taken back as I conveyed what I felt the Lord was saying to her. She questioned my motives, thinking I might simply be trying to gain her heart.

Sometimes God speaks through others to move His purposes forward in an individual's life. He will speak through those willing to listen and speak. It is exciting to know God speaks to us and through us at times. Henry Blackaby, author of *Experiencing God*, believes God speaks by the Holy Spirit through the Bible, prayer, circumstances, and the Church (His Body) to reveal Himself, His purposes, and His ways.

After three days passed, the woman called me on the telephone and said, "I have sold all that I have to go to the mission field but have not been accepted as yet. I believe what you said is true. I've had a history of thinking the Lord was doing one thing in my life only to end up as another."

As the days progressed, God made it known these words were, in fact, true. She was called to the mission field of marriage and the marketplace with her husband, this writer.

July 12

Independence That Leads to Sin

So he got up and went to his father. But while he was still a long way off, his father saw him and was filled with compassion for him; he ran to his son, threw his arms around him and kissed him. Luke 15:20

The two young men had worked for many years in their family business. One day one of the sons decided he wanted to venture out on his own. He had been under the employment of his dad's business long enough. He felt he had learned all he needed to know. He wanted his independence. He wanted to take his stock options early, which would allow enough capital to begin on his own. The other son remained behind, working day in and day out, faithfully doing his job.

The first son went out on his own only to find it was more difficult than he had ever imagined. The immediate cash gained from the advance from his dad's business was a temptation that was too great for him. He spent all of the money, fell into sin, and failed to invest it in another business. He failed miserably. Finally, he came crawling back to his dad, seeking to be taken back as a mere laborer. The father took him back with open arms, fully restoring him to his original place. He experienced grace and love in a way he had never known before.

When we desire independence so much that we launch out without God's full blessing, we can expect to fall on our face. When pride enters our lives, it discourages us from dependence on anyone but ourselves; yet God says that we are to depend on Him alone. If we think we can go it alone, we will fail. On the other hand, in spite of the prodigal son's failure, he learned a great lesson of grace that he had not known before. This resulted in a humility of heart that had a lasting impression for the rest of his life. Therefore, God even turns our failures into successes spiritually when we are willing to admit our failure.

Pride always goes before a fall. Check your heart today and ask God if there is any pride that is encouraging independence from total trust in God.

July 13

Overlooking Offenses

A man's wisdom gives him patience; it is to his glory to overlook an offense.
                                                                Proverbs 19:11

I have a friend who tells a story of a lesson the Lord taught him through his wife. It seems that every time he and his wife would get in the car to travel somewhere, his wife had a strong need to direct his driving. She would tell him where to turn and when to turn, even in their own subdivision. It was such a horrible habit that it drove my friend crazy and became the source of many an argument. Finally, one day my friend concluded that the Lord was trying to teach him some-thing through this experience. He decided he would let go of his need to be free from this correction. He began to affirm his wife and even thank her for her input. It was excruciatingly painful to do this from where he sat.

A few months passed. He let go of the entire situation and actually got to a place where it just didn't matter to him anymore. An interesting thing happened a few months later. One day his wife looked at him and said, "John, I just realized that I have been directing your driving all these years and now realize why I do that. It goes back to my childhood when I had to direct my younger brothers and sisters. I am so sorry I have been doing that." My friend nearly fell out of his seat!

Whenever we work close to another person, whether in an office or home, small offenses can become the source of great conflict. Resent-ment and irritability soon follow. God brings these "offenses" into our lives to develop character qualities in us. He uses individuals in our lives to accomplish his goal of making us more Christlike. So the next time you complain or resist a habit or action from someone close to you, ask God if it has been placed there to develop some quality in you.

Pride is the root source of the need to change another person. A man's wisdom gives him patience—to let go of little offenses. This is where spiritual maturity is seen in the day-to-day activity of life. Is there someone close to you who has some habit you really want to change? Give up that desire to the Lord. Who knows, He may even change it after you let go of the need to change it.

July 14

The Works of the Flesh

You may say to yourself, "My power and the strength of my hands have produced this wealth for me."　　　　Deuteronomy 8:17

We've all heard someone say, "He's a self-made man." What are they saying in this statement? Are they saying that this individual achieved success by his hard work and sweat? Many a person has achieved success through honest hard work. There is a danger for any of us who may have achieved significance through our work. That danger is the belief that we achieved it through our own efforts apart from God's grace and mercy. When we live in this belief, we assert that we are entitled to certain rights and privileges because of the position we have earned and feel we deserve.

The prodigal son's brother who refused to celebrate the wayward son's return was a man who felt he was entitled to certain rights. He saw himself as one who had been faithful to his responsibilities and deserving of more attention. He could not appreciate his brother's failure and the pain of falling into a sinful life because, in his mind, he had never failed. This pride kept him from experiencing God's real grace. This is how legalism develops in believers. It grows into a cold heart and an insensitive attitude toward others who may have stumbled in their lives. This same brother did not truly understand the love of his father apart from works; for he felt he gained acceptance only by doing his job.

Do you feel accepted by God, regardless of what you do? Have you wrongfully viewed your works as something you alone have achieved? These are the minefields of which each of us in business must be aware. God has gifted us to accomplish anything through His grace, not by our works.

July 15

Seeing Us for What We Will Become

..."The Lord is with you, mighty warrior."   Judges 6:12

God always looks at His children for what they will be, not what they are now. The Lord already had seen Gideon as a leader of others, not just a laborer who threshed wheat.

Gideon was an Israelite who lived during a time of oppression from the Midianites. God had allowed Israel to be oppressed because of its rebellion. However, the Israelites cried out to God, and He heard their cry for help. He decided to free them from the oppression of their enemies. God chose a man with little experience in such matters to lead an army against Midian.

When God came to Gideon through a visit by an angel, the angel's first words to him were, "The Lord is with you, mighty warrior." God always looks at His children for what they will be, not what they are now. The Lord had already seen this man as a leader of others, not just a laborer who threshed wheat.

The apostle Paul said, "I can do everything through Him who gives me strength" (Phil. 4:13). God has reserved an inheritance for you and me. He has foreordained that we should accomplish great things in His name—not so that we will be accepted or become more valued, but to experience the reality of a living relationship with a God who wants to demonstrate His power through each of us.

What does God want to accomplish through you today? He used Gideon, with only 300 men, to deliver Israel from an army of more than 100,000. He demonstrated His power through one man who was willing to let God use what little faith he had to free a nation from oppression and bring glory to the God of Israel. The Lord delights in showing Himself strong through those who will trust Him.

July 16

God's Selection Process

So Gideon took the men down to the water. There the Lord told him, "Separate those who lap the water with their tongues like a dog from those who kneel down to drink." Judges 7:5

Would you ever take on an army of 100,000 with only 300 men? Sound preposterous? I agree. However, this is exactly what happened with Gideon. It was bad enough that he began with 10,000 against 100,000, but this was too many men according to God. He would not allow Gideon to fight with this many soldiers, because the temptation would still remain to believe that it was the strength of his army that won the victory. God told Gideon to pare down his army to a mere 300. This would ensure that God would receive total credit for the victory. This is a law in the Kingdom of God. All glory must go to Him. "Announce now to the people, 'Anyone who trembles with fear may turn back and leave Mount Gilead.' So twenty-two thousand men left, while ten thousand remained" (Judg. 7:3).

Now there are 10,000 men left but that was still too many. God gave Gideon an interesting selection method for the 300 as he took the men down to the water. There the Lord told him, "Separate those who lap the water with their tongues like a dog from those who kneel down to drink" (Judg. 7:5b). What was the significance of this? Those soldiers who lapped water like a dog were soldiers who were more aware of the enemy around them compared to those who kneeled to drink. The lappers were men who were on constant guard to the danger around them, keeping their eyes up and looking about them. The others could be easily picked off.

If you and I are going to be one of God's elite, we must be battle ready. We must be sensitive to the spiritual dangers around us. We must be trained to go about our business while, at the same time, discern when the enemy of our souls is prowling about seeking to destroy us. "Be self-controlled and alert. Your enemy the devil prowls around like a roaring lion looking for someone to devour" (1 Pet. 5:8). Beware of the spiritual dangers around you.

July 17

Making the Lord our Banner

Moses built an altar and called it The Lord is my Banner.
Exodus 17:15

The Amalekites came and attacked the Israelites at Rephidim. God instructed Moses to stand on top of the hill with the staff of God in his hand. Moses' staff represented something that God said He would use to bring glory to Himself. The staff represented what Moses had done for most of his life—shepherding. It was his vocation. When God first called Moses at the burning bush, He told him to pick up the staff; He would perform miracles through it.

God wants to perform miracles through each of our vocations. At Rephidim, God defeated the Amalekites only when Moses held his staff to Heaven. It was a symbol of dependence and acknowledgment that Heaven was the source of the Israelites' power. When he dropped his hand, the power was removed and they began to lose the battle.

Each day we are challenged to reach toward Heaven and allow God to be the source of victory in the marketplace or be defeated. God calls us to let His banner reign over the marketplace so that others may know the source of our victory. "Then the Lord said to Moses, 'Write this on a scroll as something to be remembered and make sure that Joshua hears it, because I will completely blot out the memory of Amalek from under heaven' " (Ex. 17:14). The Lord wants those behind us and around us to know that He is the source of our power and success. With each victory is a testimony that is to be shared with our children and our associates.

Is the Lord your banner today? Reach toward Heaven today and let His banner wave over your work so that He might receive glory from your life.

July 18

Unlimited Potential

I can do everything through Him who gives me strength.

Philippians 4:13

What might God want to accomplish through you in your lifetime? As a businessperson, you may yet have your greatest contribution to society. Such was the case of Cyrus McCormick, born in 1809. Raised on a farm by an inventor father, Cyrus McCormick sought to invent a mechanical reaper to harvest wheat. His father's attempts at inventing a successful machine had failed until Cyrus, at 22, created one that worked. McCormick had to overcome many setbacks including the loss of his patent 14 years after his first invention. This opened up competition. Then, in 1837 he went bankrupt due to the bank panic of 1837. However, these setbacks did not prevent McCormick from achieving his goals.

He expanded his market by trying to sell his machine to European farmers in 1851. A long series of honors compensated for the lack of recognition and praise from his American compatriots. By 1856, he was not only a world figure but his factory produced more than 4,000 reapers a year.

McCormick was a committed believer. He lived during the time of D.L. Moody and gave $10,000 to Moody to start the Chicago YMCA in 1869. That building burned along with his Chicago factory in 1871. By this time, McCormick was over 60 and wealthy enough to retire. Before his death in 1884, he had given $100,000 to help open Moody Bible Institute. His son, Cyrus Jr., was to become the first chairman of the school's board. Cyrus McCormick was a devoted Christian who passed his faith on to his son who later met up with J. Pierpoint Morgan to become the first president of a combined reaper firm, the famed International Harvester Corporation. [John Woodbridge, ed., *More Than Conquerors* (Chicago, Illinois: Moody Press, 1992), 328-331.]

What might God want to accomplish through your life? Surely you can do *all things* through Christ who strengthens you.

July 19

Knowing Our Limits

He who works his land will have abundant food, but the one who chases fantasies will have his fill of poverty. Proverbs 28:19

Webster's defines *entrepreneur*: "one who organizes, operates, and assumes the risk in a business venture." [*Merriam-Webster's Collegiate Dictionary*, Tenth ed. (Springfield, Massachusetts, 1993), "entrepreneur."] Entrepreneurs can smell an opportunity a mile away. However, what is often their greatest asset can become their greatest downfall. The road is littered with entrepreneurs who have been successful in one venture only to fail in countless others. Is this the natural way for an entrepreneur, or is there a better way?

King David was an entrepreneur. He grew up as a shepherd boy and later became Israel's greatest warrior. He responded to opportunities, like the time when no one would fight Goliath. He saw this as an opportunity. He ultimately became king of Israel and faced many opportunities placed before him. David learned an important lesson somewhere along the way that each of us as businesspeople should learn.

As an entrepreneur the greatest danger is engaging ourselves in activities in which God never intended us to be involved. This is poor stewardship of what God has entrusted to us. When the Philistines attacked David, he always inquired of God as to if and when he was to counterattack. When he was attacked a second time on one occasion, David inquired of God as to whether he was to attack yet. This time God said yes, but with a condition, "Wait until you hear the sound of marching in the balsam trees" (see 2 Sam. 5:24). This story tells us that David had learned an important lesson about staying vertical in his relationship with God at all times. David had learned the important principle of staying focused on what God wanted for him, not what seemed logical. He was an opportunist, but only through the filter of the Holy Spirit in his life.

How do you approach opportunities? Do you consider the merits of the opportunity only? Or do you inquire of God as to whether He desires you to pursue? It may be a wonderful opportunity, but it may not be God's will for you to be involved. Ask the Holy Spirit to direct you as you seek to use the skills He has given you.

July 20

A Faithful Man

A faithful man will be richly blessed, but one eager to get rich will not go unpunished.   Proverbs 28:20

There is a distinct difference between the businessperson who operates based on living in the Promised Land versus the one who operates in Egypt. In Egypt, the businessperson sweats and toils to generate an outcome. The final objective is foremost in their mind. Outcome is everything.

In the Promised Land, we learn that obedience is the only thing that matters. We are called to execute, and leave outcome to God. Sometimes that outcome is very positive, yielding a return. In other cases, we may not yield a corresponding return. We may even get a negative outcome. The difference is that we know that we have been faithful to what God has called us to and we yield results to God. God often blesses obedience beyond what we deserve. If God brings wealth to your life, it should come as a by-product of obedience, not an end in itself.

God may call each of us to be obedient to situations that may not yield immediate, positive results. It is in these times that our faith must be obedience-based versus outcome-based. What if Jesus had considered the immediate ramifications of whether He would go to the cross? Based on the immediate outcome, the decision would have been an easy one. Who wants to die on a cross? However, for Him there was a higher purpose in that obedience. We are called to this same kind of obedience. This means putting our own flesh on the line daily, dying to our own self-will.

This is what it means to be a faithful man. Pray that God will make you a faithful man today.

July 21

Expectations

I eagerly expect and hope that I will in no way be ashamed, but will have sufficient courage so that now as always Christ will be exalted in my body, whether by life or by death.　Philippians 1:20

Have you ever had expectations that did not get fulfilled? Perhaps a coworker let you down. Perhaps you were trusting God for something in your life that never materialized. Perhaps you became devastated by an unmet expectation that you felt you were entitled to. Expectations can be a difficult trap for each of us if we are not fully committed to God's purposes in our lives.

Paul wrote this verse from prison to the people of Philippi. He had an expectation that his life would bring glory to God, whether through his continued ministry or his death. His joy in living was not based on his expectations getting fulfilled, but on remaining true to the purpose for which God made him.

When we react to circumstances with bitterness and resentment as a result of unmet expectations, we are saying that we know better than God, and that God has made a mistake in not meeting our expectations. The process of resolving unmet expectations may require full disclosure to the individual who was the source of the unmet expectation, and of how the unmet expectation made you feel. This is not to make the person feel obligated to meet the expectation, but simply to share your feelings about it. If God was the source, then it is important to share this with the Lord. However, once we have done this we must let go of the situation and allow God to work in our hearts the grace that is needed to walk in freedom from the pain of the unmet expectation. If we do not do this, we will allow the seed of bitterness and resentment to enter in. This seed of bitterness will create leanness in our soul and eventually will spread to others.

Ask yourself today if you have any unmet expectations. How have you responded to them? Have you processed this with the Lord and others who may be involved? These are the steps to freedom from unmet expectations.

July 22

Beware of the Thief

> *But understand this: If the owner of the house had known at what hour the thief was coming, he would not have let his house be broken into.* Luke 12:39

What are the times when you and I are most vulnerable to being caught off guard by the enemy of our souls? One of those times is just after you've had a great victory. Consider Jesus when He was baptized and was about to begin His public ministry. He was taken away into the desert to be tempted by satan.

Leisure time is another place in which satan seeks to take us off our normal routine of personal quiet times. In the normal routine of life, our senses are tuned to the need to draw upon God's Spirit to see us through the activities of each day. However, when we get away from our routine and go on vacation, we can often drop these routines. We wrongfully think that we do not need to spend time with the Lord during leisure times. This is a grave mistake. The vacation becomes a test of character. During vacations we turn freely to what we love most. It reveals to us what is at the core of our existence.

A teacher in a large school reportedly said, "The greatest difficulty we encounter is the summer vacation. Just when we have brought a student to a certain discipline and place in their study habits, we lose him; when he comes back we have to begin all over again." It is the same in our spiritual lives. It only takes a small crack in the door of our heart to lose our spiritual focus.

This summer, be on guard when times of retreat are made available to you. Use these times for spiritual refreshment, not just physical refreshment, and you will keep the thief from entering your house.

July 23

Second Chances

> ..."I knew that You are a gracious and compassionate God, slow to anger and abounding in love, a God who relents from sending calamity." Jonah 4:2

Have you ever gone through a time of disobedience with God? Jonah was a prophet of God who decided he didn't want to prophesy for the Lord. God wanted him to deliver a message to Nineveh to warn them against impending destruction if they didn't turn from their ways. Jonah had developed a hardened heart toward the people of Nineveh. He didn't really care if they repented or not; so rather than travel to Nineveh and deliver the message, he hopped a boat in the opposite direction. You probably know the rest of the story. He was eaten by a fish and spent a few days thinking about his decision.

There is a place where we all will obey. What circumstances must take place for us to become obedient? For some of us, it requires a good shakeup. For Jonah, it required a big shakeup because he was God's man to save 120,000 people. He was chosen by God to be used by God, and God didn't give up on him.

God understands our disobedient heart. He sees what we really are, yet He gives second chances. God gave Jonah a second chance. He gave the people of Nineveh a second chance. It is a lesson of love from a heavenly Father who specializes in second chances. Have you blown it? Have you disappointed someone close to you? God is the God of second chances. All we have to do is acknowledge our waywardness. He will restore. He will give grace. Ask Him.

July 24

Finding Meaning in Our Labor

But I said, "I have labored to no purpose; I have spent my strength in vain and for nothing. Yet what is due me is in the Lord's hand, and my reward is with my God."   Isaiah 49:4

Have you ever felt like you're spending your life using your talent for nothing? Life is often spent doing mundane activities that seem to have little eternal purpose.

The great prophet Isaiah was struggling with his own purpose. He knew he was chosen to be a voice for God, yet life became purposeless for Isaiah. We all go through periods when our purpose seems to be clouded with the mundane. We see little meaning in life. On the other hand, Isaiah didn't stay in this place. We read in this passage that he knew the truth of his existence. He could look past his present circumstance and know that his real reward and purpose would be revealed in eternity. He knew that God was just and fair, so he placed his faith on this truth.

When life appears to lack meaning and purpose, remember that if you devote your life to the purposes He has for you, the fruits of your labor will be manifested in due time. "The one who calls you is faithful and He will do it" (1 Thess. 5:24).

July 25

Experiencing God in Your Business

Now faith is being sure of what we hope for and certain of what we do not see.   Hebrews 11:1

The CEO walked into the president's office after reviewing his new marketing plan for the next year. It was a well-prepared, thoughtful plan.

"This will not do!" exclaimed the CEO. "This plan describes how you will achieve these objectives through your own planning. I am certain you can achieve these objectives through normal business operations; however, you have allowed no room for faith in your plan. Now you must determine what God wants us to trust Him to accomplish through this business. You must go beyond what you can naturally achieve."

What was this CEO saying? If you and I want to experience God in business at the practical level, we must be willing to trust Him for more than what our natural abilities can accomplish. God likes to show Himself in the midst of unlikely circumstances. This is the place that God receives the glory. God always forced Israel to trust Him for the supernatural. This is how glory was brought to the Father. It is no different in our lives.

The world is looking for real faith. Perhaps you are the instrument that He wants to use to demonstrate real faith to the unbelieving business world. It will require courage, faith, and action; also, it will require risk. You may risk finances, reputation, and being misunderstood. This was the risk of all leaders in the Bible. It was a risk worth taking. Are you willing to see God move in your business life? Ask Him what this might mean for you.

July 26

Being an Overcomer

> *I have told you these things, so that in Me you may have peace. In this world you will have trouble. But take heart! I have overcome the world.*   John 16:33

"Why does it seem that those involved in Christian enterprise find the way so hard? It seems as though it is harder for those who are committed Christians in business. Have you found this to be true?" This was the comment from a business associate recently. My answer was a definite yes. In fact, if you were not a Christian and sought to do a similar business without regard to maintaining a biblical philosophy, the way would be much smoother sailing. It makes us think of the prophet who asked, "Why do the wicked prosper?" (see Jer. 12:1)

It is a spiritual principle of which we speak. When the Israelites crossed the Jordan before they entered the Promised Land, they fought only two battles. Then after they entered the Promised Land, they fought 39 battles. The way of the cross is not paved with lilies; it is paved with grace. When we seek to honor God in our business life, we will be met with opposition from the spiritual forces of this world. This is why each of us must commit ourselves to walking in the power of the Holy Spirit and to be as gentle as doves but as wise as serpents.

Do not be surprised when you find the way harder as a believer than when you were a non-believer. You now have more at stake among the spiritual forces that desire you to be defeated and ineffective.

Stand firm against the evil forces that desire to keep you from walking in freedom in the Promised Land. Jesus is your victory for every battle you will encounter. Call on His name.

July 27

Small Things

Who despises the day of small things?....   Zechariah 4:10

Life is filled with a series of small things that can amount to something big. Have you ever considered why the God of the universe came to earth and spent 33 years identifying with mankind through work? Jesus grew up as a carpenter's son and, no doubt, learned the trade from His daily routine of helping His father. For 30 years He worked. When it was time for Him to begin to fulfill His purpose for mankind, He told countless stories of people and their work. He told stories of landowners, farmers, fishermen, tax collectors, and so on. He related to the everyday man because He Himself was one. This is why it was important for Him to have some personal work experience.

Life is filled with daily routines. Every now and then, God takes us to the mountaintop to experience His presence in a dramatic way. This is not the norm. It was not the norm for those in the Bible either. Moses spent 40 years in preparation. Paul spent a great deal of his life working toward the wrong purpose until a dramatic event changed his life. Jacob spent 20 years working for Laban.

God uses work to develop character qualities that He plans to use at the appropriate time. In the small things we develop trustworthiness with God. The day-in and day-out grind of working life molds us and makes us into what God desires. God may still be preparing you for something far greater. For now, however, you are learning the daily lessons of small things. Pray that you will be faithful.

July 28

When the Lord Tarries

For the revelation awaits an appointed time; it speaks of the end and will not prove false. Though it linger, wait for it; it will certainly come and will not delay. Habakkuk 2:3

God has a storehouse of blessings that He has reserved for you and me. However, our timing to receive those blessings may not be the same as our Lord's. God has a specific timetable that He requires to accomplish His purposes in the life of the believer. Sometimes that timetable seems excruciatingly cruel and painful, yet it is needful.

When we read that Joseph remained a slave in Egypt and was then placed in prison after being wrongfully accused, it would be easy to second-guess the God of the universe. *Oh, how cruel and uncaring*, we might think. Joseph thought he was going to be delivered from prison when he interpreted a dream for a court official, but then he was forgotten another two years. Why? An early release would have disrupted God's perfect plan.

God takes time to develop character before anything else. God could not afford to have a prideful 30-year-old managing the resources of an entire region of the world.

We can sometimes delay this timetable if we refuse His correction.

Although it is sometimes difficult to understand, the Lord is just and gracious in His dealings with His children. When He does decide to move on our behalf, we will appreciate the delay and will often understand the reason it was needed. Yet the Lord longs to be gracious to you; He rises to show you compassion. For the Lord is a God of justice. Blessed are all who wait for Him! (Is. 30:18)

If you are awaiting the fulfillment of a vision in your life, ask the Lord for His grace to sustain you. It will be worth the wait.

July 29

Presumption Versus Faith

> *The Lord's anger burned against Uzzah, and He struck him down because he had put his hand on the ark. So he died there before God.*
> 1 Chronicles 13:10

A life of faith often requires us to leave God's work alone. Responding to a need out of a desire to help move a vision along can be the greatest challenge for a Christian entrepreneur. There is a fine line between presumption and faith.

Uzzah learned that presumption can cost him his life. He was part of the crew that was to move the ark with the help of a team of oxen. When the way became rough, Uzzah responded in a natural way. He grabbed the ark to steady it. When he did, he was immediately struck down. God said it was forbidden to touch the ark. King David mourned the death of his servant and argued with God about this loss.

July 29—Day 210

Walking with God in the marketplace requires sensitivity to balancing our God-given talents and operating in the power of the Holy Spirit in and through our business life. A mentor once told me, "You almost have to hold back your natural gifting to ensure that God is the one who is guiding you. If not, you will not know if it is through your skill versus His hand that you are accomplishing the work." I find this the most challenging aspect of a walk with God in the marketplace.

You can only grow in your understanding of this balance by being accountable to others in the process. By having other committed Christians walking close to you, they become the safety net to keep you from presumption and the deceit of the heart. God also gives godly spouses to help many in this area.

July 30

Bad Alliances

> *"Woe to the obstinate children," declares the Lord, "to those who carry out plans that are not Mine, forming an alliance, but not by My Spirit, heaping sin upon sin; who go down to Egypt without consulting Me; who look for help to Pharaoh's protection, to Egypt's shade for refuge."* Isaiah 30:1-2

Have you ever entered a business relationship with someone you knew you were not supposed to? Throughout the history of Israel, the people were called to come out of an old way of life. Egypt represented that old way; when things got tough, the Israelites reverted to what was comfortable. They always knew they could take a trip to Egypt and find what they lacked. Perhaps this was their reasoning: "If we can't get it accomplished under the new way, why not go back to the way we used to do it? At least we know we can get it there."

When God calls us into a walk of faith, we can expect to be tested in this walk. If we enter into alliances that God has not ordained, it will only bring heartache. Such was the case for Israel. "But Pharaoh's protection will be to your shame, Egypt's shade will bring you disgrace" (Is. 30:3).

Beware what you perceive as an alliance that may advance your business. It may actually bring you great distress if God has not directed you to align it. Ask yourself what the motive is behind this possible alliance. Make sure that it is not based on fear or a quick fix. Get confirmation that God is leading you to make such an alliance. Then you will not end up in the way of Israel, experiencing shame and disgrace.

July 31

Waiting for the Lord

Wait for the Lord; be strong and take heart and wait for the Lord.
Psalm 27:14

Hearing and doing God's will are two important steps that often get confused as one step. However, these are two distinct processes. When we hear God's voice, this is only 50 percent of the process. The next important step is to know when to move. It is one thing to hear; it is another to know when to act.

There was a time when the Lord showed me I was to write. This was a major change in my life from what I was doing. As I began to write, I attempted to find a publisher for my work. This became a real frustration. I encountered many false starts, and many well-intentioned people wanted to assist but their efforts resulted in further delays.

Finally, my wife asked me, "Os, have you completed the book you are working on?"

"No," I replied.

"When you complete the book, God will provide a publisher if He has called you to write. You need to complete the book."

A few months later I was in discussions with a publisher about my work. They were going to be in my city and wanted to meet with me. The day we met they offered me a contract on my book. It also was the exact day that I had completed the book. I thought back to the words my wife had said.

Corrie ten Boom was a prisoner in the German Holocaust who lost her sister in the concentration camps. She tells a story about her father taking her on trains. She always wanted to get the ticket from her father ahead of time. He never gave her the ticket until she was about to get onto the train.

God is always on time. He is never late, and He is seldom early. Ask God for the wisdom to discern His will and His timing for the events in your life.

August 1

Being a Vessel to Bless Others

One man gives freely, yet gains even more; another withholds unduly, but comes to poverty. A generous man will prosper; he who refreshes others will himself be refreshed.   Proverbs 11:24-25

One of the reasons God entrusts money to us is to bless other Christians by meeting their needs. God uses the transfer of money within the Body of Christ to build unity among Christians. Sometimes we withhold money that God has designated for someone else. He wants to bless through us, but His will cannot be accomplished through us if we are disobedient.

This was the case for a business owner who tells of the time when God told him to forego a company bonus one year. God directed him to share his year-end bonus with an employee to show his appreciation for him. He wrestled with God for three full days before obeying the Lord on the matter. When he finally met with the employee to give him his check, the man said he had been praying about a financial need he had three days earlier. He had decided to borrow the money to meet his need. The amount of money he borrowed was the exact amount the business owner gave him.

God had already planned to provide for the employee through the business owner, but because he was hesitant, he almost missed the opportunity to be an instrument of God in this man's life. Even so, he could have prevented the man from having to borrow money. It was an important lesson for the business owner.

How many people do we let down because we feel the "harvest" God provides is all ours? In America the pressure is always on to move up the ladder of material accumulation. Jesus warned us about this. If our focus is on accumulation, we will not look for opportunities to be God's vessels of financial blessing to others. Ask the Lord if you have an open hand when it comes to finances.

August 2

The Door of Full Surrender

But He knows the way that I take; when He has tested me, I will come forth as gold. Job 23:10

I was recently sitting with the leader of a marketplace organization as he described a question he poses to businesspeople. "What if there were two doors to choose from; behind one door was the complete will of God for your life and behind the other door was how life could be according to your own preference. Which door would you choose?" The struggle for most lies in the desire to follow God completely and the fear of what might be behind the door of full surrender. Most of us desire to follow God, but few of us will do it at any cost. We do not really believe that God loves us to the degree that we are willing to give Him complete permission to do as He wills in us.

If we desire to fully walk with Christ, there is a cost. We may give intellectual assent and go along with His principles and do fine; however, if we are fully given over to Him and His will for our life, it will be a life that will have adversity. The Bible is clear that humans do not achieve greatness without having their sinful will broken. This process is designed to create a nature change in each of us, not just a habit change. The Bible calls it circumcision. Circumcision is painful, bloody, and personal.

If God has plans to greatly use you in the lives of others, you can expect your trials to be even greater than those of others. Why? Because, like Joseph who went through greater trials than most patriarchs, your calling may have such responsibility that God cannot afford to entrust it to you without ensuring your complete faithfulness to the call. He has much invested in you on behalf of others. He may want to speak through your life to a greater degree than through another. The events of your life would become the frame for the message He wants to speak through you.

Do not fear the path that God may lead you on. Embrace it. For God may bring you down a path in your life to ensure the reward of your inheritance. "For our light and momentary troubles are achieving for us an eternal glory that far outweighs them all" (2 Cor. 4:17).

August 3

Angels in the Marketplace

> *For He will command His angels concerning you to guard you in all your ways; they will lift you up in their hands, so that you will not strike your foot against a stone.* Psalm 91:11-12

For years Sergis ran his small retail business from his store in a local shopping center. Every week a visitor would drop by to collect a percentage of his sales. The visitor wasn't his landlord; the mafia had taken control of business in his small country.

Through the ministry of a marketplace Christian, Sergis came to faith in Christ, and God began a deep work in his life. One day Sergis decided he could no longer give God's money to the mafia.

A few days later his "friends" paid him a visit. They kidnapped him, blindfolded him, and placed him in a jail cell located in the middle of a mafia-controlled house. During the night Sergis sat in the jail cell discouraged. Two locked doors with guards separated Sergis from his freedom. Suddenly, in the middle of the night Sergis awoke to a voice: "Sergis, get up. Follow me." Sergis awakened to a real, in-the-flesh, angel of God sent to deliver him. The angel opened the doors while the guards remained asleep. Sergis and the angel walked quietly past the guards to freedom. Sergis immediately went to his Christian brothers to share the miracle that had just taken place.

This true story is living proof that we serve a God who still does miracles on behalf of His servants. Ask God for the miracle you need today.

August 4

Blessing God's Chosen

The Lord bless you and keep you; the Lord make His face shine upon you and be gracious to you; the Lord turn His face toward you and give you peace.   Numbers 6:24-26

Recently, a friend from London sent this personal account of an experience he had:

"I was walking passed the Stock Exchange in the City of London when I overtook an Orthodox Jew with his black hat and long grey beard. As one does, I put my arm on his shoulder and gave him the blessing which God gave to Moses to give to Aaron with which he was to bless the Jews.

" 'The Lord bless you and keep you; the Lord make His face shine upon you and be gracious to you; the Lord turn His face toward you and give you peace.'

"The Jewish gentleman turned round with a smile. 'God said to Abraham, "Those who bless the Jews will be themselves blessed." You will be blessed!'

" 'I know,' I said. 'Ten years ago I blessed a Jew at Kennedy Airport and I was upgraded to Club class and this happened again on my next two transatlantic flights. Every time I blessed a Jew I was upgraded!'

" 'You're the man, you're the man!' cried my friend. 'I read
that article in the *Jewish Chronicle* and was just going to tell you
the story.'

"We ended up embracing each other on the pavement, no
doubt to the astonishment of passing stockbrokers and
bankers!"

Is there an opportunity to bless a Jew today? You might find
yourself blessed if you do.

August 5

Two by Two

*Two are better than one, because they have a good return for their
work.*   Ecclesiastes 4:9

Have you discovered yet that you are incomplete by yourself? During my "warrior" stage of life you would have been hard-pressed to convince me that I needed you or anyone else. I know few people willing to admit their need for others, but many who live according to this principle. However, sooner or later we discover God's truth regarding our need for others.

God made us to need others. We may not discover this until we fail—fail in a business, a marriage, a close friendship, a client relationship. We are incomplete without the ongoing input from others into our lives. An independent spirit is one of the most detestable sins from God's viewpoint. It is the highest form of pride. "Pride only breeds quarrels, but wisdom is found in those who take advice" (Prov. 13:10).

God has made each of us so that we have only so many gifts. He did not give any of us all the available gifts. Hence, we learn to depend on others and to humbly trust others to complete us where we are deficient.

David had Jonathan. Paul had Silas. John Wesley had George Whitefield. Martin Luther had Philip Melanchthon, who was 14 years younger. Martin Luther learned that he needed someone in his life to complete the work God called him to do. Luther had the greatest respect for this friend who helped him reform the Church of their day, and the Church as we know it at present. Luther learned a great deal from Melanchthon, who was a great scholar at a young age. He could speak several languages, and he became Professor of Greek at the new University of Wittenberg at 21 years of age. This was ten months after Luther posted his famous theses on the church door in Wittenberg. Melanchthon helped shape the Protestant movement of the sixteenth century through his research, writings, moral purpose, and religious conscience. Luther and Melanchthon became inseparable, and when they died, they were buried next to each other.

Who has God placed in your life to complete you? Perhaps it is a mate. Perhaps it is a close friend. Perhaps it is a business partner. If you lack this in your life, I encourage you to seek someone out who can speak into your life. If you have someone like this, tell him or her how much you appreciate the role he or she plays in your life.

August 6

"May I Pray for You?"

Do not be anxious about anything, but in everything, by prayer and petition, with thanksgiving, present your requests to God.
Philippians 4:6

I walked into the office. The secretary seemed physically struggling with her breathing and her countenance was different than normal.

"Are you okay?" I asked.

"Allergies," she replied. "Sometimes it gets so bad I can hardly breathe."

"May I pray for you?" I asked.

"Oh, I don't want to take up His time with something as menial as me. I'd rather not waste it on me. You should pray for someone much less fortunate than me. My mother always taught us to pray at the dinner table for those less fortunate than us," she replied. The woman was touched that I would offer to pray for her.

The next day I told her my prayer group was praying for her. She could not believe that I would do such a thing for her.

It is interesting what happens when you offer to pray for someone. Offering to pray for someone can be the most genuine and loving thing you can do for another person. It can be the one means of getting a conversation on a spiritual plane that cuts across religious stigmas and gets to the root of the problem—the person's real need. It immediately reveals your own values and sets the stage for future encounters. All it takes is a little holy boldness to step through the door when the opportunity seems to present itself.

Is there anything too small to pray about? Do we, in fact, bother God when we make any request that is not dealing with only the poor in Calcutta? Paul clearly tells us in this passage that prayer is talking with God. It is having such a relationship with Him that we can bring anything to His attention.

We've all heard the housewife's prayer for a parking spot or other such seemingly trivial prayer requests, but is this trivial to God? If God is our closest and most intimate friend, then it becomes very natural to talk to Him as you would a friend who might be sitting next to you in the car. Yes, God desires to have such close communion with you and me that we can pray about *anything*—even a parking spot.

As you enter the marketplace today, ask a coworker if you can pray for him about something. You may be surprised at what doors will open as a result.

August 7

Being a Shelter for Those in Need

> *Each man will be like a shelter from the wind and a refuge from the storm, like streams of water in the desert and the shadow of a great rock in a thirsty land.* Isaiah 32:2

Have you ever walked in a dry, hot climate for an extended time? The sun beats down, sweat begins to pour off your brow, and your throat and mouth are parched with thirst. A little shade, a slight breeze, or a cool drink becomes the greatest thing one could value at the moment.

When you and I walk with Christ in the marketplace, we become that kind of oasis for non-Christians. However, they may not recognize it at the time. Let's face it, the marketplace is pretty tough, especially when Christ is not in the center of it.

When a person becomes aware of their need of Christ through you or me, we have become a shelter from the wind. We become their refuge from the storms of life.

Someone once said that you and I may be the only Bible someone ever reads, so we need to be something worth reading. Are you available to be that shelter for a non-believing friend? If so, then you may open the eyes of someone who has been blind his whole life. What an incredible blessing to know you were the instrument God used to bring a person into the Kingdom of God.

Then the eyes of those who see will no longer be closed, and the ears of those who hear will listen (Isaiah 32:3).

August 8

The Causes of Failure

You cannot stand against your enemies until you remove it.
Joshua 7:13b

The first battle for the people of Israel traveling from Egypt was at Jericho, once they crossed the Jordan River. God had given them a great victory at Jericho, and Joshua was now ready to move to their next battle at Ai. After they spied out the enemy camp, they determined they needed only a few thousand men to gain victory. They went up against Ai only to fail miserably. They lost 32 men in a battle that should have been an easy victory, but instead they were forced to retreat. Joshua was devastated. "Ah, Sovereign Lord, why did You ever bring this people across the Jordan to deliver us into the hands of the Amorites to destroy us?" (Josh. 7:7a)

August 8—Day 220

In this case, the people fell short because they failed to uphold the standard God had set for them. God had told them not to take any plunder from their first battle. However, Achan hid some forbidden treasures, and God was now judging the entire nation for one man's sin.

Whenever we act without God's complete blessing on our activity, we can expect God to thwart our plans. God's word to Joshua was that he could not stand against his enemies as long as there was disobedience among his troops.

Whenever we launch a business endeavor, we should make sure there are no unclean things in our business dealings that would allow us to be vulnerable to a failed effort: unpaid vendors, disgruntled employees who were not treated fairly, lawsuits, dishonest dealings. Many of these things can hinder God from blessing our enterprises. These things can remove the shield of protection from our businesses, which God wants to bless, but cannot because He is committed to upholding righteousness. His name is blemished when unrighteousness is allowed to permeate our lives.

Is the Lord able to bless your enterprises today? If not, you may need to go back and clean up a few things before He can do so. Take whatever steps are needed to ensure the blessing of God today.

August 9

Embracing the Mess

Where there are no oxen, the manger is empty, but from the strength of an ox comes an abundant harvest.   Proverbs 14:4

My wife and I run together through a new home subdivision. Often we see the street filled with red clay from the land as bulldozers clear it to lay a foundation. The job site is littered with lumber, all sorts of trash from workers, and is generally a mess. The house looks ugly; it has all its insides exposed as it is being pieced together, yet this process is necessary to get to the finished product. When completed, the home is beautiful. The landscaping looks like it came out of a home-design magazine. Everything is clean and perfect in order for the new homeowner to move in.

Our walk with God is much the same process. Often we must go through a messy period of our lives in which all aspects of it are in disarray. It is in these times that God builds a new structure. He might remove some structural timbers in our lives and replace them with new ones. He might even add on another room. And unless this process takes place, we will never see the end product. The goal is more Christlikeness. In order to achieve this in us, He requires a period of removing all that is not of Him. It can be a painful process.

It would be impossible to keep oxen in a barn without having to clean up the mess from time to time. It just comes with the territory, but the result of the oxen is an abundant harvest. God may be allowing a mess in order to ensure a fruitful harvest in your life. Learn from Him so that you might experience the fulfillment of His purposes for you in these times.

August 10

Waiting on God

Yet the Lord longs to be gracious to you; He rises to show you compassion. For the Lord is a God of justice. Blessed are all who wait for Him!   Isaiah 30:18

Have you ever noticed that God is not in a hurry? It took 40 years for Moses to receive his commission to lead the people out of Egypt. It took 17 years of preparation before Joseph was delivered from slavery and imprisonment. It took 20 years before Jacob was released from Laban's control. Abraham and Sarah were in their old age when they finally received the son of promise, Isaac. So why isn't God in a hurry?

God called each of these servants to accomplish a certain task in His Kingdom, yet He was in no hurry to bring their mission into fulfillment.

First, He accomplished what He wanted in them. We are often more focused on outcome than the process that He is accomplishing in our lives each day. When we experience His presence daily, one day we wake up and realize that God has done something special in and through our lives. However, the accomplishment is no longer what excites us. Instead, what excites us is knowing Him. Through those times, we become more acquainted with His love, grace, and power in our lives. When this happens, we are no longer focused on the outcome because the outcome is a result of our walk with Him. It is not the goal of our walk, but the by-product. Hence, when Joseph came to power in Egypt, he probably couldn't have cared less. He had come to a place of complete surrender so that he was not anxious about tomorrow or his circumstances.

This is the lesson for us. We must wait for God's timing and embrace wherever we are in the process. When we find contentment in that place, we begin to experience God in ways we never thought possible.

August 11

Reflecting His Glory

> *They will tell of the glory of Your kingdom and speak of Your might, so that all men may know of Your mighty acts and the glorious splendor of Your kingdom.* Psalm 145:11-12

How do you measure your effectiveness in God, or should you even be thinking like this? The early Church turned the world upside down in that first century. What made them so effective? Was it their theology? Was it great preaching? Was it due to one man's influence apart from Jesus?

The Scriptures are clear as to what made the early Church effective. It is at the core of God's heart, and it is quite simple. God desires to reflect His nature and power through every individual. When this happens, the world is automatically changed because the world is affected by those who reflect His glory.

We serve a jealous God. He is a God who will not share His glory with anyone. God sets up situations in order to demonstrate His power through them. He has done this since the day He created man. His desire is to reflect His glory through you and me, so that all men may know of His mighty acts and the glorious splendor of His Kingdom.

The apostle Paul understood this principle: "My message and my preaching were not with wise and persuasive words, but with a demonstration of the Spirit's power, so that your faith might not rest on men's wisdom, but on God's power" (1 Cor. 2:4-5).

If you do not see His glory being reflected through your life, then you need to ask why. He has promised to do so if we will walk in obedience to His commands.

August 12

Business as Ministry

> *Whatever you do, work at it with all your heart, as working for the Lord, not for men, since you know that you will receive an inheritance from the Lord as a reward. It is the Lord Christ you are serving.*
> Colossians 3:23-24

The Bible is very clear that the purpose for our work life is to reflect Christ in and through our lives. It is an attitude that says our work is to have an overriding "ministry" objective to it. Our *work* is our *worship* to God. These two words even originate from the same Hebrew word, *avodah*.

Robert Laidlaw was born in Scotland in 1885 but grew up in New Zealand. Born to Christian parents, he committed his life fully to the Lord when he was 17. Laidlaw began working in a hardware merchant company as a traveling sales representative when he was 19. Later he had the idea for a mail-order catalogue business that sold everything imaginable including underwear, groceries, cosmetics, and farm equipment, all at bargain-basement prices. His concept proved successful and his business later merged with the Farmer's Union Trading Company. He became general manager and held that position for 50 years.

But this is not the most significant thing that can be said about Robert Laidlaw. He understood that his work life was a tool to affect others for Jesus Christ. He began giving ten percent of his income early in his business life. Later, however, he entered this into his journal: "September 1919, age twenty-five. I have decided to change my earlier graduated scale, and start now giving half (fifty percent) of all my earnings." This he continued for the next 60 years. [John Woodbridge, ed., *More Than Conquerors* (Chicago, Illinois: Moody Press, 1992), 351.]

The result of that commitment was countless numbers affected for Jesus Christ through the resources he gave to mission groups and other worthy Christian causes. He was personally involved in ministry. He wrote a small book that gave a thoughtful answer to basic questions about life and faith. It was titled *The Reason*. Many hundreds of thousands came to faith in Christ because of this 46-page booklet. He publicly spoke to many of his faith in Christ and became very involved in the Soldier's and Airmen's Association when World War II broke out. Robert Laidlaw understood what it meant to view business with an overriding ministry objective.

Does the Lord have complete control of your life? If so, you will be able to see your business life as an extension of His life in you. Let the Lord live in and through your business life today.

August 13

The Faithfulness of God

The Lord is faithful to all His promises and loving toward all He has made. The Lord upholds all those who fall and lifts up all who are bowed down.　　　　　　　　　　　　Psalm 145:13b-14

Have you ever had a relationship with someone who was faithful? You knew you could depend on that person to do what he said. You learned that his word was completely trustworthy. If he said he would call you, he would. If he said he'd be somewhere at a certain time, he'd be there. In fact, if he was late, you began to wonder if he had an accident because it was so contrary to his nature. It's great to have friends who are faithful.

God is faithful. He is faithful to fulfill every promise in His Word. Sometimes we think God isn't faithful because it appears He has not fulfilled a desire that we have. Sometimes we think He is not faithful because of a crisis event that seems to say God isn't faithful. We must remember that God is more concerned about accomplishing His ultimate purpose in the life of every believer than giving us the desires of our heart. Sometimes this results in hardship.

The Bible is full of accounts of God's faithfulness that was often accompanied by hardship. He brought Joseph out of slavery to be greatly used in a nation. He delivered the people from Egypt and brought them into the Promised Land. He gave Abraham the son of promise late in his life. He delivered David from his enemies and made him a king. In story upon story, we learn of God's faithfulness.

Are you a faithful man or woman? The marketplace needs faithful men and women. Take an inventory of your life today and ask God if you have been faithful with what He has entrusted to you.

August 14

Things I Cannot Understand

Surely I spoke of things I did not understand, things too wonderful for me to know. Job 42:3b

If there was any one man on earth who had reason to question God's love, it was Job. He lost his family, his health, and his wealth—all at the same time. His friends came to his side only to question his spirituality.

God had already answered the question of his integrity. Job was described in the opening verses of the book as "blameless and upright" (see Job 1:1). His calamities were not born from sin. Job acknowledged God's right to do anything in his life until one day he could take it no longer. He questioned God's motives.

God answered Job, but not in the way he wanted to hear. God answered him with a series of questions that represents the most incredible discourse of correction by God to any human being. Three chapters later, Job realized that he had questioned the motives of the Author of the universe, the Author of love. He fell flat before his Creator and realized his total depravity. "Surely I spoke of things I did not understand, things too wonderful for me to know."

Have you ever questioned God's activity in your life? Have you questioned His love for you based on circumstances that came your way? The cross at Calvary answers the love question. He sent His own Son in replacement for your sin. If you were the only person on earth, He would have done the same. His ways cannot always be understood or reconciled in our finite minds. That must be left for a future time when all will be understood. For now, entrust your life to Him completely. Embrace Him in the hard times and the good.

August 15

Blameless

> *For the Lord God is a sun and shield; the Lord bestows favor and honor; no good thing does He withhold from those whose walk is blameless.* Psalm 84:11

If you were running for political office, what approach would your opponent take against you? If he wanted to launch a smear campaign, would there be any ammunition for him to use? Think how you would feel if the director of the opposing campaign came to you afterwards and said, "Sir, we tried to find something negative to play up in our campaign against you, but we couldn't."

What does it really mean to be a person who is blameless before God? Being blameless before God does not mean we are perfect. No human being is perfect. It means that we so fully trust in God that we are willing to make things right when we fail. We are willing to humble ourselves continually before the throne of God. "...blessed is the man who trusts in You" (Psalm 84:12). God has a specific plan for the people who fully trust in Him. He promises to be their shield, to bestow honor on them. He will not withhold any good thing from them. What a promise! What motivation to be all that we can be in God.

Imagine living a life that God views as blameless which allows Him to withhold no good thing. Pray that God would make you and me that kind of person.

August 16

Rejected for Christ

And they took offense at Him....   Matthew 13:57

Jesus taught in the synagogue in the community He grew up in. He was raised as a local carpenter's son. No one saw any miraculous powers in this young boy's life. But something changed as He became older. "Where did this man get this wisdom and these miraculous powers?" Those in the community could not reconcile God's work in someone they thought they knew simply as the carpenter's son. God brings every person who is committed to Him out of their normal routine into a new revelation of Himself that impacts others.

Is the move of God so evident in your life that it invites scrutiny from friends or coworkers? Jesus confronted the issues of His day without fear of being rejected. A life of obedience will be an affront to the systems of this world. When God begins His deeper work in you, it will be a stumbling block to those around you. When you are rejected for Christ, consider that Christ is affirming His call on your life and you are becoming a threat to the kingdom of darkness. How many of satan's workers do you suppose have been assigned to thwart God's activity in your life? Those who sit in a pew from week to week and never speak the name of Christ in the marketplace require few opponents because they represent no threat to the kingdom of darkness.

How are you impacting the kingdom of darkness? God has called you and me to impact the lives around us for His Kingdom. Your words may be an affront to those around you; do not fear this. God will use your words and life to draw others to Himself. You are His ambassador in the marketplace. He has placed you there for this time to extend life to those who live in darkness.

August 17

Mixing Faith With Commerce

"Your servant has nothing there at all," she said, "except a little oil."
2 Kings 4:2b

Her husband had died. There was no way to fulfill her debts. Her creditors decided to take her two sons as slaves for payment of the obligations that still remained. She pleaded for assistance with the only man of God she knew.

"Is there anything in your house?" Elisha asked.

"Nothing at all," she said, "except a little oil."

Elisha then instructed her to go and collect all the empty jars that her neighbors might possess. "Ask for as many as you can," he instructed.

When the jars were collected, he instructed her to pour what little oil she had into the jars. The oil was more than enough to fill the jars. In fact, there was more oil than jars to fill. "Go, sell the oil and pay your debts. You and your sons can live on what is left" (2 Kings 4:7b).

God often mixes faith with the tangible. The widow believed she had no resources to meet her need. God said she had more than enough resources. She did not see the one jar of oil as a resource. It did not become a resource until it was mixed with faith. Her need was met when her faith was mixed with the practical step of going into the marketplace to sell what she had in order to receive her needed income. In fact, there was so much income she was able to pay her debts and live on the money derived from the sale.

Quite often we forget that God works through commerce to provide for our needs. It is wrong to place total trust in commerce without *faith* in God. God often requires simple obedience to an act that seems ridiculous to the logical mind. It is this faith mixed with the practical that God honors.

Do you have a problem that is perplexing to you? Do you see no way of meeting your need? God may have already given you the skills and talents to meet your need. However, He may be waiting for you to mix them with faith. Ask God to show you the steps necessary to solve your problem. Be willing to take the next step.

August 18

The Response of Faith

…"Everything is all right"….   2 Kings 4:26

The prophet Elisha often would travel through the town of Shunem, and in that town was a well-to-do couple who extended hospitality to him. At first, they simply offered Elisha a meal when he came through town. Then, seeing that Elisha needed a place to stay and study, they built a room for him above their house so that each time he came through town, he had a place to stay. He was so appreciative of their kindness that one day he asked the wife what he could do for her. His servant Gehazi later informed Elisha that the woman was barren and her husband was old. " 'About this time next year,' Elisha said, 'you will hold a son in your arms' " (2 Kings 4:16). A year later the son arrived.

One day the father was working in the field, and the son became ill and died.The woman ran to meet Elisha to inform him. When Elisha asked what was wrong, she did not panic and react in fear. Her response to Elisha seemed almost unnatural. "Everything is all right," she said.

Elisha went to the boy and raised him from the dead. It was a glorious miracle. (See Second Kings 4.)

Faith looks at situations through God's eyes, not the eyes of our limited understanding. This woman did not panic, for she knew something more than the current circumstance. Faith does not panic, but realizes that what looks like devastating circumstances may be God's plan to bring glory to Himself by demonstrating His power. When Jesus appeared on the water to the disciples in the middle of the night, they exclaimed, "It's a ghost!" (see Mt. 14:26) First appearances can bring great fear upon us even to the point of paralyzing us. Find the Lord in your circumstance today. Exercise your faith today and trust Him for His outcome in the situation.

August 19

Overcoming All Odds

> …*"Because you have prayed to Me…."*   Isaiah 37:21

Have you ever had your back against the wall so badly that if something didn't happen to change your situation, you were sunk? King Hezekiah was one of Israel's greatest godly kings. One of the greatest challenges to his reign came when the king of Assyria threatened to attack Israel and wipe them out. The Assyrians were the local bullies of the region and had wiped out all other enemies in their region.

They mocked the idea of having a God who could save them.

> *Do not let Hezekiah deceive you. He cannot deliver you! Do not let Hezekiah persuade you to trust in the Lord when he says, "The Lord will surely deliver us; this city will not be given into the hand of the king of Assyria"* (Isaiah 36:14b-15).

The marketplace is full of "Assyrian kings" who mock the idea of a living God who delivers. Without God's help, Israel would not overcome. Their backs were against the wall. They would be destroyed.

King Hezekiah saved Israel because of one act. He prayed; and because he prayed, God moved on his behalf. In fact, God moved so powerfully that Hezekiah did not even have to fight the battle.

Then the angel of the Lord went out and put to death a hundred and eighty-five thousand men in the Assyrian camp. When the people got up the next morning—there were all the dead bodies! (Isaiah 37:36)

The king of Assyria was even murdered by his own sons. Imagine seeing your enemy totally destroyed without one hand raised in battle!

God wants to act on behalf of His children if they will call on Him. One of the motives Hezekiah had in seeking God's help was "so that all kingdoms on earth may know that You alone, O Lord, are God" (Is. 37:20). This is what happened. God was glorified.

God wants to let your marketplace know that God is a living God. He can deliver. Seek Him today for the crisis in your life. Keep your motive pure and God will surely answer.

August 20

New Things

> *Forgetting what is behind and straining toward what is ahead, I press on toward the goal to win the prize for which God has called me heavenward in Christ Jesus.*   Philippians 3:13b-14

Our past can be a hindrance or a help in moving toward God's purposes for each of us. For some, the past has meant pain and heartache, and grace is required so that we do not let our past dictate our responses to the future. If we allow our past to make us a victim, then we have not entered into the grace that God has for us. If we live on memories of past successes and fail to raise our vision for new things, we again are victims of our past.

"See, I am doing a new thing! Now it springs up; do you not perceive it? I am making a way in the desert and streams in the wasteland" (Is. 43:19). Our past should only be viewed for what we can learn from it. We must move forward and avoid viewing the negative or the positive for more than what we can learn. Many have allowed their past to dictate their future. God is always about doing new things in our lives. He gives fresh revelation of His purposes in our lives. Do not live in the past. Do not hold onto bitterness that may hinder God from doing new and exciting things in your life. He turns our wastelands into streams of water to give life, not death.

How have you viewed your past? Has it hindered you in some areas of your life? Have you relied on past successes to dictate what you will do in the future? Put aside such thoughts and allow God to do a new thing in your life. Ask Him to help you see the new things He wants to do in and through you today.

"When your memories are bigger than your dreams, you're headed for the grave" [Author unknown].

August 21

Free to Stand

> *That is why the Israelites cannot stand against their enemies....*
> Joshua 7:12

It matters not how strong you are. It matters not whether you have the greatest resources and talent. It matters not if you have the best plans and procedures. It will all fail if you have a break in your armor.

This is the message God told Joshua when he attempted to go against a small army at Ai, which was the Israelites' second battle in the Promised Land. Sometimes we try to figure out why we are not successful in an endeavor. We look at all aspects of our performance to see what went wrong. For the people of Israel, it was not easily seen on the surface. Everything seemed just as it should be from Joshua's vantage point, so when his army was soundly defeated, he cried out to God, "Ah, Sovereign Lord, why did You ever bring this people across the Jordan to deliver us into the hands of the Amorites to destroy us?" (Josh. 7:7a)

The people had been defeated because God could not bless them. One person had violated the covenant with God. They were not to take any possessions from the first battle, but one person failed to live up to this, and the whole army suffered.

Sin makes our armor vulnerable to attack from satan, who then gains permission from God to attack us in the area where we have failed to uphold righteousness. If we break down in moral purity, satan comes in and establishes a stronghold. If we give place to bitterness and unforgiveness, we will break fellowship with God and others. If we become money-focused, we will fall into greed and deception. It is a vicious cycle.

Examine your armor today. Make sure you are not susceptible to attack. Begin from a solid spiritual foundation and your chances of success will be great.

August 22

Drawing Near to Darkness

The people remained at a distance, while Moses approached the thick darkness where God was. Exodus 20:21

Like the nation of Israel, we are each called to the mountain of God, but few are willing to pass through the darkness to get there. God wanted to reveal His glory to the children of Israel, but they were afraid to enter into His presence. They only wanted to know *about* God, rather than know him personally like Moses did. This grieved the heart of God.

Why wouldn't the people of Israel risk entering the darkness if it meant being in the presence of God? What did the people fear?

Perhaps they had fears like each of us. The fear of the unknown. The fear of what might happen. The fear that God might not like what He sees. Or, perhaps even the greatest fear: the fear of darkness itself and what lies behind that darkness.

Many of us have been satisfied to hear about God from God's messengers. But there is a greater calling for each of us--a calling to enter into His presence. Sometimes entering into His presence means we enter through an unexpected door—a door that appears to have nothing good behind it.

We do not need to fear entering the presence of God even if it means entering through a period of darkness. Above all else we must believe that God is a God of love. If He calls us into darkness in order to enter His presence, then that darkness will become an entry to new levels of relationship with a God who longs for fellowship with you and me.

August 23

The Art of Waiting

By day the Lord went ahead of them in a pillar of cloud to guide them....   Exodus 13:21

How are you at waiting on God? How do you determine if God is giving you the green light to move forward? Many businesspeople make the mistake of adding up all the pluses and then concluding that God has given them the green light. Several factors go into making a decision from the Lord.

It is important to do three things before you make a decision on a matter. First, you should gather facts. Fact gathering allows you to determine all the realities of a given situation. However, this does not ultimately drive your decision, but it can put a stop to it. For instance, if you were planning to build a shopping center and you knew the only way to lease the space was to rent to a porn shop, your decision would be made. God would not lead you to enter into unrighteous ventures.

Second, is the Holy Spirit guiding you in your decision? "If the Lord delights in a man's way, He makes his steps firm" (Ps. 37:23).

George Mueller cites that the steps are also "by the Lord." God puts hedges around us, but many times we bull our way through the hedges under the guise of tenacity and perseverance. This too is unrighteousness. One wise businessperson stated that the greatest success one can have in business is to know when it is time to pull the plug rather than keep forcing a situation. Not all businesses last forever.

Third, has your decision been confirmed? God has placed others around us to be used as instruments in our lives to confirm decisions and keep us from the deceit of our own heart. "Every matter must be established by the testimony of two or three witnesses" (2 Cor. 13:1b). This is God's way of keeping us within the hedge of His protection.

"Write your plans in pencil and give God the eraser."

August 24

God's Recruitment Strategy for Leaders

Saul got up from the ground, but when he opened his eyes he could see nothing. Acts 9:8a

When God calls one of His servants into service, there is often much travail. There are many examples where God makes His presence known through circumstances that tax the individual to his very soul.

Consider Paul, who was stricken blind on the Damascus road.

Consider Peter; when he denied Jesus after the Crucifixion, he was in total despair.

Consider Shadrach, Meshach, and Abednego, who were thrown into the fiery furnace.

Consider Daniel, who was thrown into the lion's den.

Consider David, who was forced to flee his former employer for many years and lived as a fugitive.

It may seem strange to us that God uses such incredible adversity to prepare His servants for greater service, but this is God's way. God knows that the human heart is incapable of voluntarily stepping into situations that take us beyond our comfort zone. He intentionally brings us into hard places to prove us and to drive us deeper into the soil of His grace.

In arid regions of the world, trees cannot survive unless their roots grow deeper to where the water table can be found. Once they reach the water, these trees become stronger than any tree that can be found in tropical climates. Their root systems ensure that they can withstand any storm. In the same way, God brings us into extremely difficult situations in order to prove His power and drive our spiritual roots deeper.

Friend, God may take you through times when you will question His love for you. In such times, you must cling to His coattail so that you see His purposes in it. Do not throw away your confidence; it will be richly rewarded.

> *You need to persevere so that when you have done the will of God, you will receive what He has promised. For in just a very little while, "He who is coming will come and will not delay. But My righteous one will live by faith. And if he shrinks back, I will not be pleased with him"* (Hebrews 10:36-38).

August 25

True Repentance in a Nation

> *When the king heard the words of the Law, he tore his robes.*
>
> 2 Chronicles 34:19

Josiah was a godly king in Israel. However, before he came to power, the nation had fallen into all kinds of evil. One man, Manasseh, had brought the nation to a condition of inexorable evil. God finally had enough.

Therefore this is what the Lord, the God of Israel, says: I am going to bring such disaster on Jerusalem and Judah that the ears of everyone who hears of it will tingle. I will stretch out over Jerusalem the measuring line used against Samaria and the plumb line used against the house of Ahab. I will wipe out Jerusalem as one wipes a dish, wiping it and turning it upside down (2 Kings 21:12-13).

Josiah came into power just before this judgment. He began to clean up the evil by burning all the idolatrous temples, ridding prostitution and homosexuality from the streets, and destroying occult shrines. He did this without the benefit of even reading God's Word, but through the Holy Spirit working in his heart. Then one day the ancient Scriptures were discovered in the temple that had lain dormant for years. They had a profound impact on King Josiah.

When the king heard the words of the Law, he tore his robes. He gave these orders to Hilkiah, Ahikam son of Shaphan, Abdon son of Micah, Shaphan the secretary and Asaiah the king's attendant: "Go and inquire of the Lord for me and for the remnant in Israel and Judah about what is written in this book that has been found. Great is the Lord's anger that is poured out on us because our fathers have not kept the word of the Lord; they have not acted in accordance with all that is written in this book" (2 Chronicles 34:19-21).

Josiah was broken. He tore his robes in repentance. He fell to his knees and repented for the wickedness of his nation. He stood in the gap and God honored Josiah; however, it wasn't enough. God still had to judge the nation for its previous wickedness under the reign of Manasseh.

"Because your heart was responsive and you humbled yourself before God when you heard what He spoke against this place and its people, and because you humbled yourself before Me and tore your robes and wept in My presence, I have heard you, declares the Lord. Now I will gather you to your fathers, and you will be buried in peace. Your eyes will not see all the disaster I am going to bring on this place and on those who live here." ... (2 Chronicles 34:27-28).

God spared Josiah during his reign, but after he died judgment came upon the nation.

No nation is immune from God's judgment. Pray for your nation today. Pray that your nation will have a repentant heart among the leaders and the people.

August 26

Our Plans and God's Plans

Many are the plans in a man's heart, but it is the Lord's purpose that prevails.   Proverbs 19:21

Have you ever heard of someone who spent years of preparation for one vocation only to end up doing something completely different? Perhaps this could be said of you. Quite often we have in our minds what we believe we want to do only to have a course correction. Often the course correction comes through a major crisis that forces us into an area that we would never have considered.

Such was the case for Samuel Morse. Born in 1791, Morse grew up desiring to be an artist, and he eventually became very talented and internationally known. However, it was difficult to make a living as an artist in America during that time. A series of crises further complicated his vocational desire when his wife died; then his mother and father also died soon after. He went to Europe to paint and reflect on his life. On his return trip aboard a ship, he was captivated by discussions at dinner about new experiments in electromagnetism. During that important occasion, Morse made the following comment, "If the presence of electricity can be made visible in any part of the circuit, I see no reason why intelligence may not be transmitted by electricity." In the face of many difficulties and disappointments, he determinedly perfected a new invention, and, in 1837, applied for a patent that became what we know today as the telegraph. He also created Morse code. It was only later, after many more setbacks and disappointments, that his projects received funding.

Samuel Morse later commented, "The only gleam of hope, and I cannot underrate it, is from confidence in God. When I look upward it calms any apprehension for the future, and I seem to hear a voice saying: 'If I clothe the lilies of the field, shall I not also clothe you?' Here is my strong confidence, and I will wait patiently for the direction of Providence." Morse went on to create several other inventions and can be recognized today as the father of faxes, modems, e-mail, the Internet and other electronic communication. ["Glimpses," Issue #99 (Worcester, Pennsylvania: Christian History Institute, 1998).]

God's plans may not always seem to follow our natural inclination. Perhaps God has you taking a path that may not lead to His ultimate destination for you. Trust in the Lord, lean not on your own understanding, acknowledge Him in all you do, and He shall direct your path (see Prov. 3:5-6).

August 27

Grace

…"Peace be with you!" John 20:19

How would you respond to a group of fellow workers if you were their leader and you poured your life into them, teaching them all you know for three years, only to have them disband and go their own way when troubles came? What would you say to them after you were reunited for the first time? Perhaps you might scold them. Perhaps you might cite each one's offense. At the least, you might shame them for their lack of faithfulness and courage.

After Jesus was crucified and raised from the dead, He appeared to the disciples. His first words to them were, "Peace be with you!" The word *grace* means "unmerited favor." When someone loves you unconditionally, without regard to your behavior in return, it becomes a powerful force in your life. Such was the case for the disciples when Jesus appeared to them. They could have expected reprimand. Instead, they received unconditional love and acceptance. He was overjoyed to see them. They were equally overjoyed to see Him.

Jesus understood that the disciples needed to fail Him as part of their training. It would be this failure that became their greatest motivation for service. Failure allowed them to experience incredible grace for the very first time. Grace would transform them as human beings.

Have you experienced this grace in your life? Have you extended grace to those who have hurt you? Can you let go of any wrongs that have come through friends or associates? The grace you extend may change their lives—and yours.

August 28

Motivations to Call

> …*"Cheer up! On your feet! He's calling you."*   Mark 10:49

Do you recall the circumstances when God first called you into relationship with Him? Were you in need of something? Were you in a crisis situation? Every day God calls someone into relationship with Him through different circumstances. More often than not, the circumstances relate to a need in their life that only God can meet.

Bartimaeus had the need to see again. He was a poor blind beggar, who had heard about Jesus and the miracles He had done. The crowds rebuked him for seeking Jesus. Yet he continued to cry out. "Many rebuked him and told him to be quiet, but he shouted all the more, 'Son of David, have mercy on me!'…Throwing his cloak aside, he jumped to his feet and came to Jesus" (Mk. 10:48,50). That day, Bartimaeus saw for the first time. But more than that, he saw with spiritual eyes for the first time.

Each business day, we rub shoulders with someone who has not met this Jesus we know personally. God uses needs to draw us to Himself. What need has He placed in a coworker that only Christ can meet? Perhaps you are the instrument He wants to use to introduce that person to Himself. It requires availability and a willingness to look for people with needs; then point them to Christ to meet their needs. Pray for divine appointments today.

August 29

Going Against the Flow

But the whole assembly talked about stoning them.

Numbers 14:10a

Have you ever had to stand up against the majority for a cause that wasn't popular? God brought the Israelites out of Egypt and promised He would lead them into a land of milk and honey. The process of moving out of Egypt was difficult. They could no longer do things the old way, for the old ways didn't work in the desert. God provided for them during this journey. But there came a point in which the people forgot what God had said. Their discomfort changed their belief about God.

Whenever God is slow to answer our prayers, what we believe about God is revealed. Do we change our plans and move in a different direction when pressure mounts? Or do we continue on the path God has directed for us? Four men believed what God said and were willing to stand; however, the crowd wanted to stone them.

Then Moses and Aaron fell facedown in front of the whole Israelite assembly gathered there. Joshua son of Nun and Caleb son of Jephunneh, who were among those who had explored the land, tore their clothes and said to the entire Israelite assembly, "The land we passed through and explored is exceedingly good. If the Lord is pleased with us, He will lead us into that land, a land flowing with milk and honey, and will give it to us. Only do not rebel against the Lord. And do not be afraid of the people of the land, because we will swallow them up. Their protection is gone, but the Lord is with us. Do not be afraid of them." But the whole assembly talked about stoning them. Then the glory of the Lord appeared at the Tent of Meeting to all the Israelites (Numbers 14:5-10).

Notice Joshua and Caleb's response to the situation. They had spied the land. They believed God. They challenged the crowd. They seemed to know that if the Lord was not pleased with them they would not enter into the Promised Land. Those who grumbled did not enter the Promised Land. Only Joshua and Caleb and a new generation saw the fulfillment of God's promise.

Has God called you to stand for a cause bigger than yourself? You will have opposition to His call; sometimes it even comes from those in your own camp. But if God has called you, then you can be sure He will make a way. He has already opened the way before you. But you must walk in faith, joined with Him to take the land.

...Be strong and courageous. Do not be terrified; do not be discouraged, for the Lord your God will be with you wherever you go (Joshua 1:9).

August 30

Defining Moments

As he neared Damascus on his journey, suddenly a light from Heaven flashed around him.   Acts 9:3

- For Moses, it was the burning bush.
- For Peter, it was walking on water.
- For Shadrach, Meshach, and Abednego, it was walking through the burning furnace untouched.
- For Paul, it was being blinded and spoken to by Jesus on the Damascus road.
- For Daniel, it was deliverance from the lions' den.
- For Joshua, it was parting the Jordan River and crossing into the Promised Land.

There have been many defining moments in the lives of human beings that changed their lives forever. These defining moments often set the course for the balance of their lives.

We could go on and on. Each of these servants had years of preparation leading up to their defining moment. These moments forced the servants to be involved in something beyond their human experiences. It took them outside their own paradigms of life. God had to move them outside their own boxes. And when He did, their lives were never the same.

You may be in one of three stages of life: You may not have had your "defining moment" yet—God may be preparing you with many important life experiences. You may have had your defining moment and you are living out your call. Or, you may be toward the end of your journey and you have already experienced what I speak of.

We are all called to a relationship with God; and we are all called vocationally, which is often ushered in by a defining moment. And there can be more than one defining moment, each pointing you down a path that God foreordained from the foundation of the world. The secret of a great life is often a man's ability to discern the defining moments given to him, understanding them, and learning to walk in the path that leads him to his ultimate destination.

Once you have had a defining moment, you are never the same. Pray that you have eyes to see and ears to hear when your Master brings a defining moment into your life.

August 31

True Repentance

Godly sorrow brings repentance that leads to salvation and leaves no regret, but worldly sorrow brings death. 2 Corinthians 7:10

What does it mean to repent? When you or I wrong another person, or we sin against God, do we simply say we are sorry and move on?

A few years ago I was involved in a business situation that taught me a great lesson. A client severely wronged me and ultimately took our company for $160,000. In a court of law, I probably would have won the dispute. However, after I had already filed suit against the man, I realized that there was one aspect of the matter that I was wrong about, involving a third party that could no longer be held accountable. I could not effectively resolve the matter without taking the first step in owning the responsibility for my part in the matter.

I made a decision to drop the lawsuit. However, after calling my attorney, I discovered the client had already filed a countersuit. This made the situation even scarier. I was completely exposed if I dropped my suit.

I was unable to reach the business owner because he would not return my calls. I got his secretary on the line. "I want you to take this message down and give it to your boss, word for word. Please do not change the words at all. 'I have sinned against you. I know I do not deserve your forgiveness, but I ask your forgiveness for filing the lawsuit against you. You are no longer obligated to pay the balance you owe me if you feel you do not owe it.' " The secretary knew me and the gravity of what I was saying. She began to weep. She could not believe what she was hearing.

A few hours later I received a call from this client. He said, "I received your message. I accept your request and I forgive you." He dropped his countersuit. A few days later, I went to see the man and had dinner with him. He did not offer to pay any of the balance. It took three years to pay the vendors related to this situation. It was difficult because I knew he was not taking any responsibility for his contribution to the problem. However, I knew I was to let go of it. The Lord was glorified in this situation and He provided for my needs.

Is there anyone you need to seek forgiveness from? Acknowledging our sin is the first step. Humbling ourselves and taking actions to restore is the next step.

September 1

Faithfulness to Convict

> *When He comes, He will convict the world of guilt in regard to sin and righteousness and judgment.* John 16:8

I had recently come back from a mountaintop experience. As I attempted to get back into my routine, I found a great cloud of oppression come over me. Each day I attempted to press through it, but with no success. Fear, anxiety, doubt, and unbelief were setting in. I knew I was fretting over my future. I had been in a long period of transition in my business life and was tired of the place of waiting. Yet I didn't understand the oppression. It was definitely spiritual warfare.

That night I was reading a book regarding our calling from God. The author made mention that we can become envious of others when we get into a place where we are dissatisfied. Suddenly, I realized I was guilty of envying where other businesspeople were in their lives. I was "subconsciously" angry that the calling God had placed on my life had such adversity. I had to repent.

As if this were not enough, the next day the Holy Spirit confirmed my assessment in the most unusual way. That morning I turned on my computer to read my own Marketplace Meditation that is sent to my computer. The message was on "Envying Others" and included the same Scripture reference as the author's in the book. Imagine God using my own words to convict me of sin! The nerve of Him! To make matters worse, at lunchtime I tuned into the local Christian radio station to hear an interview with the same author as he cited the very passage I had read the day before. I was shocked to realize how the Holy Spirit could be so precise in His ability to convict and give proof of His activity in my life.

Do you question if the Holy Spirit is active in your life? The Lord has promised that the Holy Spirit will convict us of sin when we move away from Him. It is His responsibility as our guide.

September 2

Triumphant Defeats

This was now the third time Jesus appeared to His disciples after He was raised from the dead.   John 21:14

William Wallace was a Scotsman who sought freedom from a tyrannical king of England in the 1200s. He initially took up this cause in retaliation for his own personal family losses. His cause grew among the people, and it became an insurrection against England. Wallace entreated Robert the Bruce, the future king of Scotland. However, Bruce betrayed Wallace in return for lands from the king of England. Wallace was turned over to the king of England to be tortured to death for crimes against England. Bruce realized his betrayal against Wallace and his own country. This remorse led to real repentance and a return to his commitment to the people of Scotland. He finally took ownership of the mission to free Scotland from England. He led the people of Scotland into subsequent battles against England and freed them. Wallace's defeat ultimately led to victory through Bruce. It took the lives of many, including Wallace, for victory to be accomplished. [James Mackay, *William Wallace, Brave Heart* (Edinburgh, Scotland: Mainstream Publishing, 1995).]

So often defeat is what is required before victory can be won. Jesus said that unless the seed dies and goes into the ground it cannot bring forth fruit (see Jn. 12:24). The death of a vision is often required before the fulfillment can really take place. Have you failed at something in your life? Have you not seen the vision fulfilled you thought you were given? The vision may yet happen.

The disciples thought they suffered their greatest defeat when Jesus died on the cross. However, this defeat became the greatest victory on earth. Christ's death gave liberty. Forgiveness came to all men. New life came forth—new strength for the disciples. Resurrection and new life came as a result of a "defeat."

"There are triumphant defeats that rival victories" (Montaigne, French philosopher).

September 3

Moving With the Cloud

Whether by day or by night, whenever the cloud lifted, they set out.
Numbers 9:21b

God brought the Israelites out of Egypt, and they had to pass through the desert on their way to the Promised Land. God was their guide by means of a cloud that appeared overhead. When it moved, they moved. When it stopped, they stopped—sometimes a day, a week, even a year.

Imagine living with the uncertainty of this situation. One day you work at getting your "house" in order, only to have to pick up the stakes and move. Your ability to plan is totally gone. But even greater is the temptation to move when the cloud did not move because you felt it was time to move. For the Israelites, perhaps the grass was no longer green. Perhaps the water was not easily accessible. Perhaps the bugs were a problem. Whatever the case, they were strictly prohibited from moving if the cloud did not move.

It is still the same today. We are not to move unless the Holy Spirit instructs us to do so. We are not to make that business deal on the basis of whether or not it makes sense, but on the leading of the Holy Spirit's "cloud" in our life. It is a difficult process to move only when we are directed, and to remain if we are not. The pressure is always upon us to move, to plan, to act. But if we act, we may move into a place where the presence of God may not be. Hence, the rub. The Christian businessperson must learn to move when God says move; it is a sign of complete surrender and dependence on God's Spirit to direct our steps.

Ask God today if you are sitting under His cloud. Or, have you moved when He said stand still? He will show you.

September 4

Changing Our Paradigm

> *While Peter was still thinking about the vision, the Spirit said to him, "Simon, three men are looking for you. So get up and go down-stairs. Do not hesitate to go with them, for I have sent them."*
>
> Acts 10:19-20

Peter had never preached to the Gentiles. In fact, he believed it was against Jewish law to associate with the Gentiles. God needed to change Peter's attitude about this, so during the night God gave Peter a vision that showed him it was permissible to preach to the Gentiles. The Spirit came to Peter and informed him that some men were about to come visit him, and he was to go with them. He went with them, and the Lord did great miracles in the lives of Gentiles through Peter.

Sometimes we are so bent on our particular belief that the Holy Spirit must do something miraculous to change our paradigm.

I was once asked to attend a conference overseas. At the time, finances were such that the very idea was ridiculous to me. The very next day a man I had met only once before informed me of this event and asked if I would come if my expenses were covered. I was dumbfounded! The Lord had sent a messenger to change my paradigm because He knew I didn't have the faith to think of the possibility. He knew I needed help.

Do you need a paradigm shift in some area of belief? The Lord still intervenes in the lives of His people every day. Don't be surprised when God begins to change your paradigm by giving you a vision or sending you a messenger of His choosing.

September 5

Significance

May the favor of the Lord our God rest upon us; establish the work of our hands for us— yes, establish the work of our hands.

Psalm 90:17

Many of us begin our careers with the goal of achieving success. If we haven't entered our work as a result of God's calling, we will eventually face a chasm of deep frustration and emptiness. Success flatters but does not provide a lasting sense of purpose and fulfillment. So often we enter careers with wrong motives—money, prestige, and even pressure from parents or peers. Failing to match our work with our giftedness and calling is like trying to fit a square peg into a round hole. If that happens over an extended period, a person crashes.

At this time, many make another mistake. Businesspeople think that beginning a new career in "full-time Christian work" will fill the emptiness they feel. However, this only exacerbates the problem because they are again trying to put another square peg into a round hole. The problem is not whether we should be in "Christian work" or "secular work," but rather what work is inspired by gifts and calling. If there is one phrase I wish I could remove from the English language it is "full-time Christian work." If you are a Christian, you are in full-time Christian work, whether you are driving nails or preaching the gospel. The question must be, are you achieving the God-given calling for your life? God has called people into business to fulfill His purposes just as much as He has called people to be pastors or missionaries.

It is time for businesspeople to stop feeling like second-class citizens for being in business. It is time businesspeople stop working toward financial independence so that they can concentrate on their "true spiritual calling." This is the great deception for those called to business.

Significance comes from fulfilling the God-given purpose for which you were made. Ask Him to confirm this in your own life.

September 6

The Necessity of the Desert

..."I have become an alien in a foreign land."   Exodus 2:22

God's preparation of a leader involves training, extended times of waiting, pain, rejection, and isolation. Are you ready to sign up?

Moses was brought up in Pharaoh's court. He had the very best of everything—education, clothing, food, and personal care. But there came a time when the man God would use to free an entire people from slavery was going to have to learn to be the leader God wanted. At age 40, when most of us want to be thinking about winding down instead of beginning a new career, Moses was forced to flee to the desert.

Like Joseph and Abraham, Moses had to endure some difficult years of preparation that first involved removal from his current situation. He went from notoriety to obscurity, from limitless resources to no resources, from activity and action to inactivity and solitude. And, most importantly, waiting. And waiting. And waiting. He probably thought he would die in the land of Midian.

Then one day, a full 40 years from the day he arrived, God appeared to Moses in a burning bush. Everything changed. God said, "It is time." The years had seasoned the vessel to prepare him to accomplish the work.

God is preparing many businesspeople today. The circumstances may be different. The time frames may not be quite as long. But the characteristics of the training are still the same. Do not try to shortcut the desert time of God. It only leads to cul-de-sacs, which force you to revisit the lessons you are meant to learn. Embrace them, so that He can use your life for something extraordinary.

September 7

Dying for Lack of Knowledge

The Lord's anger burned against Uzzah, and He struck him down because he had put his hand on the ark. So he died there before God.
1 Chronicles 13:10

A business friend of mine confessed that he did not like to read. He found it a difficult discipline. I replied, "If you do not commit yourself to knowing what is in God's Word and following it, you will fail to know and experience God. God's Word is life to our souls. It provides knowledge that leads to life." The prophet Hosea tells us, "My people are destroyed from lack of knowledge. Because you have rejected knowledge, I also reject you as My priests; because you have ignored the law of your God, I also will ignore your children" (Hos. 4:6).

God has given us His Word that has specific laws and principles that must be followed if we expect His blessing. King David forgot to follow one of those laws related to the ark. "...But they must not touch the holy things or they will die..." (Num. 4:15). When they were transporting the ark, Uzzah innocently reached to steady the ark but was immediately stricken dead when his hands touched the ark of God. Did David know this law or did he simply forget? Did Uzzah know this law? If so, did he really believe it? David thought it was okay to carry the ark the way Uzzah did. A man lost his life for his presumption.

Many businesspeople I know take God's Word lightly. They believe they can violate His Word without consequence. This is not true; the Lord stands by to uphold His Word. It can be life, or it can bring death. When God provides instructions, we need to follow them.

Knowing this about God brings a healthy fear of the Lord. "David was afraid of God that day and asked, 'How can I ever bring the ark of God to me?' " (1 Chron. 13:12) We must all have a fearful respect of God's Word. For truly, it is life or death.

Do you take God's Word seriously? Is it life or death for you? Do you feed upon His Word daily so that you might know Him and know His precepts? Feed upon this knowledge and be blessed of God.

September 8

Spiritual Warfare

> *For our struggle is not against flesh and blood, but against the rulers, against the authorities, against the powers of this dark world and against the spiritual forces of evil in the heavenly realms.*
>
> Ephesians 6:12

My wife walked out of the airport restroom. She looked as if she was going to throw up. We were about to go through the airport checkpoint when we paused.

"I feel awful. It came on suddenly. I don't know if I should go," she said.

We were going on an overnight trip to meet with a marketplace ministry about a possible joint venture project. It was important for me to have her there. But she was feeling so badly and would probably be miserable traveling in her condition.

"You may be right. Perhaps you should not go."

We were both disappointed. We began to transfer my clothing into my bag. We prayed together and I proceeded to the gate. I was disappointed, perplexed, and a bit angry.

"Lord, I don't know about this. If this is not of Your hand, I pray against it in Jesus' name. I pray for Angie's healing right now and I bind this spirit of infirmity."

I got to the gate about ten minutes later. As I was waiting to check in, I looked up and there was Angie.

"I'm going. I kept asking if I should go and a voice said, 'No.' I changed my mind three times. But I finally decided that I am not dead and I should be going on this trip."

We got on the plane and within a few minutes, the symptoms of illness were completely gone. The symptoms were a counterfeit. She was fine the rest of the trip. It was critical for her to participate with me because it became a major turning point in my own spiritual pilgrimage. She needed to experience what I was going to experience.

There is the spiritual and there is the physical. The spiritual involves two forces. One is good. One is evil. We must realize that the spiritual is more real than the physical. Satan has his agents in the world to thwart God's purposes. We need to recognize when these are at work. Pray that you might have spiritual eyes and ears to discern these forces today in your work.

September 9

The Way of God

If My people would but listen to Me....   Psalm 81:13

God has a specific training ground for leaders. There are three patterns of preparation that have been common among most of God's leaders. First, there is a time when the leader is separated from his old life. Consider Moses, Joseph, Abraham, and Paul. In order for God to mold and shape them into His nature, it appears that He had to remove them from the life of comfort. A teacher once said, "You cannot go with God and remain where you are."

Next, there is usually a time of solitude. God often brings leaders into a time of solitude in order to speak to them without other distractions. Hosea 2:14b says, "I will lead her into the desert and speak tenderly to her." Paul was sent to Arabia for two years for a time of solitude. Joseph spent years in the solitude of prison. Moses spent 40 years in the desert herding sheep.

The third characteristic of God's preparation for leaders is discomfort. The setting in which the preparation takes place usually is not a place of comfort. Abraham traveled through the difficult deserts. David lived in caves fleeing Saul. Paul was frequently persecuted.

Are you ready for the classroom of leadership preparation? If God chooses to bring you into this class, you may have one of three reactions to the events. First, you may say, "I don't need it." Perhaps you know intellectually that you do need this, but God wants you to know it in your heart. Pride prevents us from entering this classroom. The second reaction may be, "I'm tired of it." You decide you've had enough. If so, this will disqualify you from leadership. Finally, God's desired response from us in this preparation is, "I accept it." To accept it with joy is the place of maturity in Christ. God often keeps us in these places until we come to accept and agree that Jesus is enough. Is He all you need?

Like the people of Israel, I think we have something to do with the timetable of our education. "If My people would but listen to Me, if Israel would follow My ways, how quickly would I subdue their enemies and turn My hand against their foes!" (Ps. 81:13-14)

Are you ready for the process required for being a godly leader? Ask for His grace to willingly embrace these times of preparation.

September 10

The Spiritual Realm

So what shall I do? I will pray with my spirit, but I will also pray with my mind; I will sing with my spirit, but I will also sing with my mind.   1 Corinthians 14:15

September 10—Day 253

How real is the spiritual realm? My lawyer friend from Nigeria tells a personal story of how he was preparing for an important case. He knew that he must be prepared to argue five separate points. He was to appear before his country's supreme court, so it was a very important case.

As he neared the time in which he was to go to court, he began to pray about how he was to argue the case. He spent much time in legal preparation and intercessory prayer. As he went to court, the Spirit spoke to him and said, "Do not argue point one, point two, point three, or point four. Only argue point five." Imagine my friend's struggle of faith. If he were reading this wrong, the shame and professional fallout would be devastating.

The time had come to present the case before the judge when my friend said, "Judge, I wish to withdraw points one through four. I wish to argue only point five."

The opposing counsel stood up and objected. "Your honor, he cannot do that!"

"Objection overruled, counsel," said the judge.

My friend went on to present his case around point five only, and then sat down. When the opposing counsel stood to present his case, he stood speechless for 12 minutes. He could not get a word out of his mouth. He finally mumbled a few words and complained to the judge that he was going to have to yield. It seems that the opposing counsel had prepared to argue only points one through four, but failed to prepare for point five. The judge ruled in favor of my friend.

The unseen Lord wants to help us in the physical realm of our work life. We must acknowledge His presence and tap into this incredible resource He has given to each of us. Seek Him today and ask Him to reveal His perfect plan for you this day.

September 11

Unless the Lord Goes With Us

> *Then Moses said to him, "If Your Presence does not go with us, do not send us up from here."*   Exodus 33:15

Moses was in the middle of his journey through the wilderness, leading the people of Israel out of Egypt. The people had just sinned by worshiping the golden calf. Moses interceded for them and God spared them their lives. Moses then talked one on one with the Lord. He knew he could not lead this stubborn people without God's presence. He had come to realize that without God's presence, he could not do anything.

How will anyone know that You are pleased with me and with Your people unless You go with us? What else will distinguish me and Your people from all the other people on the face of the earth? (Exodus 33:16)

Moses did not want to move farther without the assurance that God was moving with him. He knew it was a life-and-death situation. He sought the Lord with his whole heart on this one matter.

The question is a good one. If we are to be effective in anything we do for the Lord, the Lord must be in the midst of it. Unless the Lord's power is seen among us, we will be just another person who has religion. Unless we manifest His life to others, they will see only good behavior that is easily counterfeited by moral people.

Moving out in presumption will end in failure and frustration. Ask the Lord today to assure you of His presence and power in your activities. Then you will be assured that you will be distinguished among all the other people on the face of the earth.

September 12

Will You Enter?

Then Moses raised his arm and struck the rock twice with his staff.
Numbers 20:11a

Will you fulfill the destiny God has for your life? Perhaps you have never thought about it. God had a perfect plan for Moses to lead the people out of Egypt and into the Promised Land. It's been said the hardest place to score a touchdown is from the goal line. You're almost there. But there is something about crossing over that makes those last few yards the most difficult. Moses failed at the goal line, and it prevented him from finishing well a glorious life of service for God.

The people of Israel were complaining that they did not have water to drink. It was another of many tests for Israel. Moses inquired of God and God said, "...Speak to that rock before their eyes and it will pour out its water" (Num. 20:8a). Moses, in his frustration and anger with the people, began to act on his own and made a strategic mistake. Instead of speaking to the rock, he struck the rock twice with his staff. In spite of his disobedience, the rock poured forth water.

God was calling Moses to a different dimension. Moses was to use his words to speak the miracle. However, he not only lost his temper, but he also took credit and dishonored God. He used his staff, the symbol of his work life as a shepherd, to force the provision.

When we become callous, we can use our skills and abilities to force what we believe should happen. We take control. When we do this, we are in danger of failing to enter the Promised Land of blessing from God. Living in life's spiritual dimension requires patience and obedience. Beware of solving problems in your own strength. God wants to bring you into the Promised Land of His blessing. But it will require walking in the spiritual dimension.

September 13

The Butterfly Principle

The Lord hardened the heart of Pharaoh king of Egypt, so that he pursued the Israelites, who were marching out boldly. Exodus 14:8

Overprotective parents do their children a great injustice. The caterpillar that lies inside the cocoon will never become the beautiful butterfly if someone cuts open the cocoon prematurely. It is the struggle itself that allows the butterfly to emerge as a strong, new creature of nature.

God understands how necessary this process is. That is why we are allowed to experience difficult, often life-changing events. He even orchestrates them—all for our benefit. What the Israelites thought was a cruel joke when Pharaoh sent troops to pursue them after they had been freed and penned against the shore of the Red Sea became the stage for the most publicized miracle of all time—the parting of the Red Sea. Generation after generation has heard this incredible story of deliverance. God puts us against the "Red Seas" in order to show His power in and through us. If we do not know God can deliver, then we can never learn to trust Him. Circumstances that go beyond our capabilities of solving them place us at God's complete mercy. This is how He likes it.

Do not fear the calamity that comes your way. If you are faithful to Him in the test, you will see God's power manifested like never before. Just as the Israelites were able to sing a song of deliverance, you too will have your own testimony of the Lord's faithfulness; and you will be able to recall it for others to build your faith and theirs.

September 14

Calling by Name

These were the chiefs among Esau's descendants: The sons of Eliphaz the firstborn of Esau: Chiefs Teman, Omar, Zepho, Kenaz.

Genesis 36:15

God is big on giving meaning to names. Names often are specific indicators of God's plans and purposes for that individual. A young boy grew up as Moses' servant. His Hebrew name, Hoshea, means "salvation." As the lad grew, Moses could see that he had a "different spirit" from the rest of the Hebrew men. He was selected to be one of the 12 men whom Moses chose to spy out the land of Canaan. Before the expedition, Hoshea was given a new name by Moses—Joshua, which means "the Lord saves." Joshua became the new leader of Israel who would lead them into the Promised Land. He would, in fact, save an entire nation.

In my own journey I had learned that God gave me a name that had something to do with my future call from Him. I was 44 years old and had just gone through two of the most difficult years of my life. During that time, God brought a man into my life who discipled me in areas where I had never been trained. I was discovering many new spiritual truths about myself and Christians in the workplace. I came to identify with the struggles of Esau and Joseph in their desire to understand their own birthrights. I began to write about these discoveries to help other businesspeople understand their own callings through business. One morning on a weekend getaway in the mountains, my friend looked at me and said, "Do you know the meaning of 'Omar'?"

Omar is my first name. My real name is Omar Smallwood Hillman III. Dr. Smallwood had delivered my grandfather. No one, not even my mother, knew the origin of "Omar." They put the "O" and the "S" together to call me "Os."

"You need to know the meaning of 'Omar.' It has something to do with your future," said my friend.

Startled by his assertion, that night I looked up the name of "Omar" on a computer program. Here is what I found:

> Arabic for "first son" and "disciple," Hebrew for "gifted speaker," and German for "famous." Rooted in the Middle East, this name is rarely used in the West. Omar was the grandson of Esau. [http://www2.parentsoup.com/babynames/baby/o.html]

I was shocked. I had just completed 300 pages of material on the relationship of Christian businessmen to the life of Esau. My friend quickly concluded that God had called me to free Christian businessmen and women from the "Esau life." And He had allowed me to receive a name that related to the person of Esau. It was the closest thing to a burning bush experience I'd ever had. Could the Lord be this personal with us? Yes, Matthew 10:30 tells us He knows the very hairs of our head.

September 15

A Tool for Miracles

> *With the tip of the staff that was in his hand, the angel of the Lord touched the meat and the unleavened bread. Fire flared from the rock, consuming the meat and the bread. And the angel of the Lord disappeared.* Judges 6:21

How does God call people into His service? There is a clear pattern in the way God calls men and women into service for Him. Almost every major leader has been called while he or she was in the midst of performing his or her everyday vocation. Peter was a fisherman; Matthew, a tax collector; Luke, a physician; Paul, a tentmaker; Moses, a shepherd; Jesus, a carpenter; and so on.

When God called Gideon to free the people of Israel from the oppression of the Amalekites, he did so while Gideon was threshing wheat in a winepress. Like Moses, Gideon argued with God, saying his family was nothing special, so how could he be used of God to save Israel? Gideon acknowledged God by preparing an offering to Him. The angel did an interesting thing with Gideon's offering; he took the tip of his staff and touched the meat and the unleavened bread. Fire flared from the rock, consuming the meat and the bread. As with Moses, God chose to do a miracle with a staff, the instrument that symbolized Gideon's work life. Why would God do this? It is because God wants us to know that the tools He has given each of us are the tools He wants to use to demonstrate His power. However, in order for that to happen, we must yield our tools to Him for miracles to be manifested through them.

Have you yielded your tools to the Lord? God wants you to have an overriding ministry objective to your work life. He doesn't want you to leave your work; He wants to work through your work. Allow Him to do that today.

September 16

Why God Blesses

> *And David knew that the Lord had established him as king over Israel and that his kingdom had been highly exalted for the sake of His people Israel.* 1 Chronicles 14:2

King David learned an important lesson every business leader must learn if he is to ensure God's continual blessing. He knew why God blessed him. It wasn't because he deserved it, though he was a man who sought God with his whole heart. It wasn't because of his great skill, though he was a great military strategist. It wasn't because he was perfect, for he committed some horrible sins during his reign as king. No, it was for none of these reasons. God blessed David for the "sake of His people Israel."

God never blesses an individual just for that person's exclusive benefit. God calls each of us to be a blessing to others. So often we forget this last part. R.G. LeTourneau, a businessman who built heavy construction equipment, came to realize this only after God took him through many trials. Once the Lord had all of LeTourneau, he came to realize that the question wasn't whether he give 10 percent of what the Lord gave him. Rather, the question was, "What amount does He want me to keep?" LeTourneau was known for giving 90 percent of his income toward the end of his career and was a great supporter of world missions. But the Lord doesn't bless businesspeople just for the ability to give financially. God has given businesspeople many more gifts beyond the financial.

What is happening with the spiritual fruit of God's blessing on your life? Is it clogged, or is it freely flowing to others? Ask the Lord to free you to be a blessing to those in your circle of influence.

September 17

The Error of Positive Thinking

> ..."Not by might nor by power, but by My Spirit," *says the Lord Almighty.* Zechariah 4:6

God's people should be the most positive, joyful people on earth. This joy should be a by-product of a healthy, intimate relationship with Jesus. In today's business climate, we are barraged with every possible means of becoming more productive businesspeople. Positive thinking and self-help philosophy are promoted as tools for businesspeople to fulfill their potential and overcome the mountains in their lives. God calls each of us to be visionary leaders, but we must be careful that vision is born out of His Spirit, not the latest self-help program. These ideas lead us away from dependence on God to a self-based psychology designed to give us more power, prosperity, and significance.

The result is heresy. Our faith in God becomes faith in faith. It is born out of hard work and diligence rather than obedience to God's Spirit. The problem lies in that these philosophies sound good, and can even be supported by Bible verses. Beware of anything that puts the burden of performance on you rather than God. There are times in our lives when God doesn't want us to climb every mountain. Sometimes He wants us to go around. Knowing the difference is the key to being a man or woman led by the Spirit.

God has called us to affect the marketplace through His Spirit, not by our might. Have you tapped into the real power source of the soul? Ask the Lord to reveal and empower you through His Spirit today. Then you will know what real positive thinking is.

September 18

Called to Craftsmanship

> *Then the Lord said to Moses, "See, I have chosen Bezalel son of Uri, the son of Hur, of the tribe of Judah, and I have filled him with the Spirit of God, with skill, ability and knowledge in all kinds of crafts—to make artistic designs for work in gold, silver and bronze, to cut and set stones, to work in wood, and to engage in all kinds of craftsmanship.* Exodus 31:1-5

Bezalel was called by God to perform a most important work for Him. I am sure that Bezalel believed that he was naturally gifted with his hands to make fine crafts with gold, silver, and bronze. He probably did not associate it with God's work. But the Scripture tells us that God chose him and filled him with God's Spirit to enable him.

Does God call men and women into their vocations to fulfill His purposes—to fulfill that which needs to be accomplished throughout the world? Have you ever thought about how many occupations there are in the world? How did that balance of interest among each human throughout the world happen? Did it just happen? Was it by chance that we have only so many doctors, only so many accountants, only so many geologists?

Your interest in your vocation is not born of your own making. So many businesspeople and even pastors have made the mistake of encouraging us who have a deep desire to walk with Christ in the workplace to pursue vocational ministry. To remove us from the marketplace where the greatest harvest is yet to occur would be to remove us from where God called us. Do not take this bait. Serve the Lord in the marketplace where He has gifted you and called you.

I almost made this same mistake when God drew me to Himself when I was 28 years old. I concluded that I must be called to be a pastor. I took steps to fulfill this by leaving my job and entering a Bible school for training. Upon completion, I took a job as an assistant pastor in a church. But God's mercy allowed me to be removed from that position only three months into it. I was "forced back into business," where God wanted me in the first place. It was a great lesson. I was never cut out to be a pastor in a church, but a "pastor" in the marketplace.

September 19

Discovering the Source of Problems

After that, God answered prayer in behalf of the land.
2 Samuel 21:14b

During the reign of David, there was a famine in the land for three successive years. So David sought the Lord regarding this famine, "Why is there famine on this land?" The Lord answered David, "It is on account of Saul and his blood-stained house; it is because he put the Gibeonites to death" (2 Sam. 21:1b).

Years earlier, Joshua made a peace treaty with the Gibeonites. This, too, was an act of disobedience. When God called Israel to come into the

Promised Land, they were to destroy all the enemies of God. Joshua failed to see through the ruse of deception when the Gibeonites portrayed themselves as travelers. The Israelites signed a peace treaty only to discover who the Gibeonites were after the fact. Now, they had to honor the treaty. However, this led to intermarriages and much sorrow for Israel. Years later, Saul made a decision to kill the Gibeonites.

The nation was now receiving the punishment for their sin of disobedience through a famine. David knew that famines could have a spiritual source, so he inquired of God and God answered. The source was Saul's murder of the Gibeonites. Once David knew the source of the problem, he took action. He repented on behalf of the nation and made restitution. The famine was then lifted.

Do you have a problem that seems to be a continually unresolved issue? Have you asked God to tell you the reason for the problem? It may have a spiritual root that is still unresolved with God. He may be allowing this pressure to bring attention to an issue He wants you to take care of. Ask the Lord today to give you revelation on your problem. As a loving Father, He desires to make known anything that stands in the way of fellowship between you and Him. However, His righteousness must always be upheld.

September 20

The Pitfall of Being Entrepreneurial

> *When they came to the threshing floor of Kidon, Uzzah reached out his hand to steady the ark, because the oxen stumbled. The Lord's anger burned against Uzzah, and He struck him down because he had put his hand on the ark....* 1 Chronicles 13:9-10

There are good things we can do, but only God-things we should do. Those activities not born out of the Spirit will result in wood, hay, and stubble. What seems good in our eyes may be an abomination in God's eyes. For instance, if you decide to build an orphanage but God has never directed you to do so, then that work will not be seen as good by God; it was born out of your own strength, even though it was a "good work."

The most difficult challenge a Christian businessperson will ever have is to know what things to be involved in and what things not to be involved in. Many businesspeople have a great ability to see opportunity. What appears to be a "slam dunk" may come back to haunt us if God never ordains us to enter that arena.

There are many good things we can be involved with. However, there are God-things we are supposed to be involved with. Uzzah was a good man in David's sight. It was a time of celebration, and David and the people were transporting the ark of God. However, the ark hit a bump, and Uzzah reached for the ark to hold it steady. He touched the ark, and he immediately died. David became very upset with God about this situation; he questioned whether he could serve God.

God's ways are not our ways. The most important quality God desires to develop in us is our dependence on Him and Him alone. When we begin to make decisions based on reason and analysis instead of the leading and prompting of the Holy Spirit, we get into trouble with God. David later learned the importance of this principle in his own life. This encounter was one of the stepping-stones in his pilgrimage. David was an extraordinary entrepreneur. He ran the nation very successfully, but he, like each of us, had to learn the difference between "good things" and "God-things."

Are you involved in anything in which God has not directed you to be involved? Do you seek God about every decision, every action before you take it? This is where God wants you and me to be. Ask Him to show you how to walk with Him in this way.

September 21

When a Problem Turns Into a Calling

As for the donkeys you lost three days ago, do not worry about them;
they have been found. And to whom is all the desire of Israel turned,
if not to you and all your father's family? 1 Samuel 9:20

Saul and his servant were out seeking his father's lost donkeys. This was symbolic of the waywardness of the nation of Israel. The people of Israel had just asked the prophet Samuel to have a king rule over them. This saddened God greatly, yet God granted their request.

Saul and his servant heard of a man of God named Samuel. "Perhaps this man of God can tell us where to find our donkeys," said the servant. Isn't that just like us? We seek God to solve the issues related to material life. Saul was about to receive the greatest opportunity of his lifetime. He was about to be crowned as king of Israel. His life would never be the same. What was he concerned about? His donkeys. We don't have to be worried about the material things of life if we are about the things He's called us to do.

God called Saul to be the next king in order to free the people from the Philistines. God sent a messenger, the prophet Samuel, to inform him of his new career. The messenger also had to ease his mind about his donkeys. Donkeys often represent commerce in the Bible. They were the primary means of transporting goods; therefore, in essence, what was Samuel saying to Saul? He was saying, "You don't need to worry about your business if you respond to the call of God on your life. All the material things will take care of themselves."

Jesus said the same thing to the disciples years later. "But seek first His kingdom and His righteousness, and all these things will be given to you as well" (Mt. 6:33).

When God calls us, it often involves making major adjustments in our lives. Saul went from one kind of business to another. He went from working for his father to being a king. What changes is God calling you to make today in order to join Him in His work?

September 22

Gently Leading

So let my lord go on ahead of his servant, while I move along slowly at the pace of the droves before me and that of the children, until I come to my lord in Seir.   Genesis 33:14

Business often determines that we move at a pace that can put incredible stresses upon people and relationships. Jacob was a man who learned to manipulate and control outcomes. He even stole the birthright of his brother, Esau, through trickery. The Bible speaks of Jacob as a man who strived with God. He knew how to force situations to his advantage. It took years for God to break down all the rough edges of Jacob so that he could be worthy of becoming the patriarch of the 12 tribes of Israel. God saw something in Jacob that He could use.

Robert Hicks, in his book *Masculine Journey*, describes five biblical stages of manhood that must be passed through before a man becomes a mature man of God. One of those early stages is known as the "warrior stage." In this stage of manhood, the man is known by what he does, what he accomplishes, and he is totally defined by his performance. It can be a tumultuous time for the man and those close to him. It is often signified by broken relationships because the goal is often more important than the way the goal is accomplished. When I meet with a man, I can easily determine what stage of life he is in by hearing him talk.

Jacob had successfully passed through these five stages based on the verse above. It takes someone mature to be able to "move along slowly at the pace of the droves before me and that of the children." Leaders who never come to understand this may be successful materially but fail at the most important aspect of leadership—leading at a pace that his followers can maintain. The roads are full of wives, children, and workers who cannot keep up with the pace of leaders and are left behind with broken dreams, broken hearts, and unfulfilled promises.

Are you a person who is more concerned with outcome than how you achieve the outcome? Can the people around you describe you as someone who leads at a pace that ensures respect and admiration? Ask the Lord for the ability to be a godly leader who understands the condition of his flock and the pace in which you can lead without alienating.

September 23

Your Irrevocable Calling

For God's gifts and His call are irrevocable. Romans 11:29

It is dangerous to align your calling and your vocation as dependent on each other. God calls us into relationship with Him. That is our foremost calling. It is from this relationship that our "physical" calling results. Whether that is to be a teacher, a stockbroker, a nurse, a pastor, or any number of vocations, we must realize that when He calls us, the change in vocation never changes His call on our lives. It is a mere change in the landscape of our calling. This is why it is dangerous to associate our purpose and calling too closely with our work. When we define our work life exclusively as our calling, we fall into the trap of locking up our identity into our vocation. This promotes aspiration because of a need to gain greater self-worth through what we do.

Os Guinness, author of *The Call*, describes the great artist Picasso, who fell into this trap.

"When a man knows how to do something," Pablo Picasso told a friend, "he ceases being a man when he stops doing it." The result was a driven man. Picasso's gift, once idolized, held him in thrall. Every empty canvass was an affront to his creativity. Like an addict, he made work his source of satisfaction only to find himself dissatisfied. "I have only one thought: work," Picasso said toward the end of his life, when neither his family nor his friends could help him relax. [Os Guiness, *The Call* (Nashville, Tennessee: Word Publishing, 1998), 242.]

What happens when you lose your job? Do you lose your calling? Do you lose your identity? Do you lose your sense of well-being? No. Calling involves different stages and experiences in life. Disruptions in your work are an important training ground for God to fulfill all aspects of His calling on your life. Trust in your God who says your calling is irrevocable and that all things come from Him.

September 24

God's Messengers

*Surely the Sovereign Lord does nothing without revealing His plan
to His servants the prophets.*   Amos 3:7

"You are called to free businesspeople from the Esau life." Those
were the words spoken to me years ago by someone God sent into my
life. I had been in the midst of trying to understand some catastrophic
events that shook my world. Years later, I was able to see that God gave
this person supernatural insight that revealed God's calling on my life.

God still uses His prophets today to reveal His plans in the lives of
His people. I have seen this Scripture proved over and over in the lives
of people. It is as though God sends out His "scouts" to inform His servants what is ahead for them. Sometimes He does this because He
knows the event will require such changes in that person's life and so
He wants to assure them of His love. I have experienced the Lord using
me in this way in the life of other individuals. God did this in the life of
Moses. He came to Moses at the burning bush to reveal His purposes for
the people of Israel and His call on Moses to free them. The apostle Paul
had Cornelius come to him to let him know God had called him to
preach to the Gentiles.

Has God placed individuals in your life to speak His plans for you?
Are your eyes and ears spiritually sensitive so that you will know who
are messengers of God? Elisha had a servant who could not see or hear
with spiritual eyes and ears until Elisha prayed they would be opened.
Then the servant could see the great army of God protecting them (see
2 Kings 6:17). Pray that you might see and hear with the Spirit. He may
desire to reveal His purposes and plans through another individual.

September 25

A Shoe Salesman

Jesus looked at them and said, "With man this is impossible, but with God all things are possible." Matthew 19:26

Dwight L. Moody was a poorly educated, unordained, shoe salesman who felt God's call to preach the gospel. Early one morning he and some friends gathered in a hay field for a season of prayer, confession, and consecration. His friend Henry Varley said, "The world has yet to see what God can do with and for and through and in a man who is fully and wholly consecrated to Him." Moody was deeply moved by these words. He later went to a meeting where Charles Spurgeon was speaking. In that meeting Moody recalled the words spoken by his friend, "The world had yet to see!…with and for and through and in!…A man!" Varley meant any man! Varley didn't say he had to be educated, or brilliant, or anything else. Just a man! Well, by the Holy Spirit in him, he'd be one of those men. Then suddenly, in that high gallery, he saw something he'd never realized before. It was not Mr. Spurgeon, after all, who was doing that work; it was God. And if God could use Mr. Spurgeon, why should He not use the rest of us, and why should we not all just lay ourselves at the Master's feet and say to Him, "Send me! Use me!"

D.L. Moody was an ordinary man who sought to be fully and wholly committed to Christ. God did extraordinary things through this ordinary man. Moody became one of the great evangelists of modern times. He founded a Bible college, Moody Bible Institute in Chicago, that sends out men and women trained in service for God.

Are you an ordinary man or woman in whom God wants to do extraordinary things? God desires that for every child of His. Ask God to do extraordinary things in your life. Begin today to trust Him to accomplish great things for His Kingdom through you.

September 26

Situational Ethics

Lord, who may dwell in Your sanctuary? Who may live on Your holy hill? He whose walk is blameless and who does what is righteous, who speaks the truth from his heart. Psalm 15:1-2

"I cannot believe they are not going to honor my bonus agreement," said the executive who was about to take another position in a new city. Her understanding of her present work agreement called for a bonus at the end of the year. Management saw the situation differently. "It's not right. I am entitled to that bonus," she complained.

It was time to leave. The company had given her a laptop to use. However, when she left, she decided that because the company was not going to pay her the bonus she was entitled to, she would simply keep the laptop as compensation due her. "And they would never miss it," she reasoned. She was now in the employment of the new company. As each day passed, she grew more uneasy about her decision. She could not get it off her mind. Finally, she concluded that the Holy Spirit was telling her this decision was wrong and that she needed to call her former boss to confess her action. She called him and confessed what she had done and why she had done it. Her boss accepted her confession and forgave her. Strangely enough, he allowed her to keep the laptop computer.

Truth never changes. It is absolute. When we make decisions based on other actions that are taken, we move into making decisions based on the situation, not truth and righteousness. The executive may indeed have been wronged, but she had to address the wrong in the appropriate way. Trying to compensate for the wrong by doing something that violates another scriptural principle is called situational ethics. If the executive had never been wronged by the employer, do you think she would have felt justified in taking the computer? Probably not. When you isolate the two situations, you see that one action was taken in response to the other action.

Have you had any experiences in which you have used situational ethics? The Lord desires His people to have a higher standard, even at the cost of being wronged. Ask the Lord to reveal any business practices that may indicate situational ethics. You might be surprised what will happen when you do the right thing.

September 27

A Joseph Story

For God so loved the world that He gave His one and only Son, that whoever believes in Him shall not perish but have eternal life.
John 3:16

"I'd like you to help us develop our marketing program beginning in January," said the CEO of a sports product company. The consultant was delighted to have the opportunity. It was the first new business opportunity he'd had in some time. He had just come out of some very difficult business and personal circumstances in the last few years. A few months into the relationship, the CEO asked the consultant to manage the entire marketing department, placing him over the current marketing staff. It appeared that God was blessing his efforts with several successful initiatives. The consultant began to build a relationship with a few of the executives. One day, the sales manager came into his office and asked for help on a personal crisis. One thing led to another, and two months later, the consultant found himself leading the sales manager in the sinner's prayer in the sales manager's office.

God prepares His servants in many ways to accomplish His purpose. The story of Joseph is repeated every business day in the lives of His people. The circumstances may be different, but the results are the same. God trains His servant through sometimes difficult "boot camps." When that training is complete, He places them in strategic places to be a provider—both physically and spiritually.

Is God preparing you to be a provider in the marketplace? Do not fret at the difficult training ground you may be required to endure. He has a plan. If you'll allow Him to carry out His plan, you'll be privileged to be used by the Master's hand. I know because I am that consultant.

T G I F   281

September 28

Be as Little Children

> *How great is the love the Father has lavished on us, that we should be called children of God! And that is what we are!*   1 John 3:1a

"I have an important business meeting in the morning. Would you please set the alarm for 5:30 a.m.?" I said to my wife.

"Oh, that won't be necessary. Just tell the Lord what time you want to wake up. He does it for me all the time," my wife said.

I rolled my eyes in disbelief. "Well, I'd feel more comfortable if we set the alarm."

"Okay, ye of little faith. But just to prove my point I am going to ask the Lord to wake us up just before 5:30."

The next morning I awoke before the alarm went off. I looked at the clock. It read 5:15. I looked at my wife, who had just awakened at the same time with an I-told-you-so smile.

Sometimes we wrongfully view God as someone we go to for only the "big things." The idea of "bothering God" for such a trivial matter seems foolish and presumptuous. However, when you were a child and had to get up in the morning for school, didn't your mom or dad come wake you up? They were your parents, and you could come to them with the most trivial concerns or requests. Why would our heavenly Father be any less approachable? Perhaps our problem is that we simply have not developed a level of intimacy with God so that we feel the freedom to approach Him at these daily, routine levels. We often operate with an unwritten code that says our needs must have a certain degree of importance or crisis before we come to God with them. This is not God's character towards us.

Does the Lord desire this level of intimacy with you and me? The apostle Paul exhorted us to "pray without ceasing" (1 Thess. 5:17 KJV). There is never a caution to pray only about matters of greater importance.

Today, go to God with matters that you might view as trivial and would normally avoid bringing to God. Ask God to increase your level of intimacy with Him. You may even be able to get rid of your alarm clock.

September 29

Visions and Dreams

In the last days, God says, I will pour out My Spirit on all people.
Your sons and daughters will prophesy, your young men will see
visions, your old men will dream dreams. Acts 2:17

"I need to meet with you," said the man from England during a break at a conference overseas. We walked outside to have a coffee break and sat down. "God wants you to know that He removed your finances in order to reserve His reward for you in Heaven. He has done you a great service."

I was shocked. I'd never met this gentleman before. How would he have known I had lost a half million dollars in the previous few years, virtually all of my financial net worth, to some unusual calamities? We shared for the next several minutes.

That week, during our lunch and dinner times, I had been enjoying wonderful, juicy oranges from this island in the Mediterranean Sea. It came time for the gentleman and I to conclude our coffee break. We bowed in prayer. As we prayed, the man began to describe a picture he was seeing in his mind.

"I see a picture of a large orange tree. The tree is full of large, ripened oranges. They are beginning to fall to the ground. You are the tree!"

Again, I looked at the man with shock and amazement, and now tears in my eyes.

"You are the third person in three years that has had a similar vision during a prayer time like this. The first two people were also strangers to me."

I went back into the meeting rejoicing that God could be so personal in my life. He used a servant who had gone through similar trials to supernaturally speak a word of encouragement in a way that I would know it was God who was speaking.

There are times when God supernaturally speaks into our lives. He does this to demonstrate His power, His love, and His intimacy with us. Do not be surprised if God sends one of His messengers to speak into your life when you need it most. Be open to how God might want to speak into your life today.

He is like a tree planted by streams of water, which yields its fruit in
season and whose leaf does not wither. Whatever he does prospers
(Psalm 1:3).

September 30

The Booster Rocket

After the death of Moses the servant of the Lord, the Lord said to Joshua son of Nun, Moses' aide: "Moses My servant is dead. Now then, you and all these people, get ready to cross the Jordan River into the land I am about to give to them—to the Israelites.

Joshua 1:1-2

A rocket launch is truly an amazing phenomenon to me. Tons of weight is stacked vertically to the sky with thousands of gallons of fuel exploding in a matter of moments. Soon the rocket drops its take-off boosters and uses additional boosters to move the rocket to the next stage of the mission. The first engines have a unique purpose...to get the rocket to the next stage.

Joshua was known for almost 40 years as "Joshua, servant of Moses." God's preparation for him required years of selfless service, training in the desert, and tests of faith. Those preparation years were booster rockets designed to move Joshua into each new stage of his development and his ultimate calling.

God allows each of us preparation times to lay a foundation that He plans to build on. Some of those foundation times appear to be laborious and meaningless, yet these varied experiences are what God is using to frame your life for the message He plans to speak through you. Without these foundational experiences, the Jordan River can never be crossed and we cannot enter the Promised Land.

Embrace these times of seeming inactivity from God. They, too, are a rocket booster to your next stage of your walk with God.

Being confident of this, that He who began a good work in you will carry it on to completion until the day of Christ Jesus (Philippians 1:6).

October 1

Changing Our Paradigm of Experience

So Moses thought, "I will go over and see this strange sight—why the bush does not burn up." Exodus 3:3

Have you ever heard someone say, "God doesn't work that way? He would never do that." Well, there are times when God chooses to confound the foolish in order to change our paradigm of experience. Moses had never seen a bush that burned but did not burn up. It got his attention and it drew him to God.

When Jesus appeared on the water in the middle of the night during a storm, the disciples exclaimed, "It's a ghost!" They had never seen a man walk on water. This led to a great miracle—Peter walked on the water, too. When Jesus asked Peter to catch a fish and get the coin from its mouth to pay their taxes, you can imagine what Peter must have thought about those instructions. When Moses got to the Red Sea, he ran out of options. God had an unexpected solution to the Israelites' problem—He parted the Red Sea to demonstrate His power and allow the people of Israel to cross over to flee the Egyptian army.

Each of these new paradigms was a stepping-stone of an encounter with God so that the individual would experience God in a new way. God used these times to enforce the principle that His ways are not our ways. Whenever we try to predict that God will act in a certain way, He changes the paradigm to keep us from becoming our own little gods.

Have you ever been guilty of judging someone for an experience they've had that you've never had? Did you dismiss it as extreme or something not of God? God is in the business of changing our paradigm from no personal experiences to God-experiences. However, if you operate on a level of rigid logic, you may never have the privilege of having the God-experiences. Keep your heart free to experience new paradigms with God today.

October 2

The Goal of Life

"For I know the plans I have for you," declares the Lord, "plans to prosper you and not to harm you, plans to give you hope and a future."
Jeremiah 29:11

For many people in the world, real meaning in life is the next vacation, career success, or stepping up the income ladder. It is a life based on pleasurable experiences. Many a human being has toiled their whole life to gain a pleasurable lifestyle only to find a life that is empty and meaningless. You only have to watch television for one evening to discover that advertisers want us to believe this is the goal of life. The work-to-play theme is consistent with most advertising messages.

Solomon was a man who had nothing withheld from his appetite. He was a great builder, a great businessman, and a great lover of women. Every imaginable pleasure was his. Nevertheless, he was to discover that these things alone could not satisfy the human soul.

A recent trip to a beautiful island left me grateful that God had allowed me to understand the futile trap of the work-to-play lifestyle. It is great to experience times of refreshing and visit beautiful places as long as we don't fall into the trap of thinking that these experiences equal a meaningful life. God's beautiful creation can so easily become a prison of emptiness if Jesus is not in the center of it. The apostle Paul said there is only one way to find meaning and purpose in life:

I keep asking that the God of our Lord Jesus Christ, the glorious Father, may give you the Spirit of wisdom and revelation, so that you may know Him better. I pray also that the eyes of your heart may be enlightened in order that you may know the hope to which He has called you, the riches of His glorious inheritance in the saints, and His incomparably great power for us who believe... (Ephesians 1:17-19).

Knowing Christ brings the only real meaning and purpose to the human soul. Spend time today getting to know the Lord in a more intimate way. Then you will discover real meaning and purpose in life.

October 3

The Need to Control

"You acted foolishly," Samuel said.... 1 Samuel 13:13

The prophet Samuel had anointed Saul the first king of Israel. Saul was now 30 years old and was leading the nation in battle against the Philistines. The Philistines had gathered at Micmash to come against Saul and his army. The Lord was directing Saul through the prophet Samuel. Samuel instructed Saul to go ahead of him to Micmash, and he would follow in seven days. He would then offer a burnt offering on behalf of the people of Israel.

The pressure began to build as the Philistines gathered around Micmash preparing for battle. The people of Israel grew fearful and began to scatter throughout the countryside. Saul was also afraid. Samuel did not show up on the morning of the seventh day. Finally, Saul, fearing the impending attack, took it upon himself to offer the burnt offering. After he had done this, Samuel showed up.

> ..."You have not kept the command the Lord your God gave you; if you had, He would have established your kingdom over Israel for all time. But now your kingdom will not endure; the Lord has sought out a man after His own heart and appointed him leader of His people, because you have not kept the Lord's command" (1 Samuel 13:13-14).

Saul believed he needed to take control of the situation. Whenever we try to take control of a situation out of God's will, we demonstrate that we are led by fear. Many a boss is so driven by fear that he attempts to manage by overcontrolling his people. This results in codependent relationships in which the employees are fearful of making the wrong decisions, and are driven to please the manager at all costs. This results in loss of respect for the manager. Many times the employees make poor choices just to please their manager; as a result, resentment begins to build among the employees due to the manager's overcontrol.

Do you see any signs of overcontrol in how you relate to others? Can you allow others the freedom to fail? Do you find yourself changing directions in midstream when you see something you don't like? Are you fearful of failure? These are all symptoms of a Saul-control spirit. Pray that God will allow you to walk in the freedom of trusting in Him and those around you.

October 4

A Fine-Tuned Instrument

...I will refine them like silver and test them like gold. They will call on My name and I will answer them; I will say, "They are My people," and they will say, "The Lord is our God."   Zechariah 13:9

My business career has been as an owner of an advertising agency. Over the years, I have had the privilege to work on many different and prestigious accounts. One of those accounts was Steinway Pianos, the maker of the world's finest pianos. Each piano has always been made from scratch; it takes over a year to make one Steinway. The most impressive scene as I toured the manufacturing plant was the place where the soundboard is stretched to its maximum tolerance and allowed to sit for an extended period until it remains in the curved design. This was done in an off-to-the-corner part of the plant. If the wood were alive, it would be crying out for mercy.

After an extended time of stretching, the wood will never spring back to its original state. It is permanently changed. The piano is becoming a fine-tuned instrument. After this process takes place, the next step requires another point of stress. It takes 11 tons of pressure on a piano to tune it. Each step in the process moves the piano closer to a finished product that will ultimately be played by the world's finest musicians. These musicians desire a particular sound that only a piano like this can make.

God looks at each of us as a fine-tuned instrument. However, we begin as rough wood that He desires to transform into gold. Tuning us requires certain experiences that will stretch our faith, our frame, and our very life. Sainthood springs out of suffering. If we can stand the strain of this intense process, we will come forth as gold—as a sweet-smelling offering to our Maker. When we are in the midst of these times, it feels like fire. It is painful to be stretched beyond our perceived limits, but the Lord knows this is necessary for us to become an instrument that can play a beautiful song that others will seek after.

Let the master Craftsman have His way in your life today. You will be pleased with the instrument He fashions.

October 5

Confrontation With God

They will be called oaks of righteousness, a planting of the Lord for the display of His splendor.   Isaiah 61:3b

"God, is this the way You treat someone who is faithful to You?" I yelled out loud on the top of the wooded hill where no one but God could hear me. "I have waited and waited and now this! I hate You, God! I have had enough!" Those were my words that day as I wrestled with news of an event that devastated me to the point where I broke down weeping.

As I sat there among the trees deciding what else I could say to God, I was speechless. I was angry. I was confused. I wondered if He even existed. If He did, I felt like He really didn't honor my faith and obedience. I sat for hours wrestling internally with my feelings.

Finally, without answers and sensing that God wasn't answering me, I turned to leave. I had been sitting on an old oak tree that was broken at the base. The tree pointed toward the base of another huge oak tree. Finally, a still quiet voice inside said, "Today, like this broken oak tree you are sitting on, you are a broken man. But this brokenness was needed in order for you to become this large oak tree you see."

Months and even years had passed with many struggles. But God was true to His word from that day. He began to replace the pain and disappointment with an inner joy that only His grace could provide.

Have you ever wrestled with the events of life, feeling that God has deserted you? Have you been honest with God? He is the kind of Father who is willing to have those difficult conversations. He won't always change things, but His purposes will be accomplished and peace will come if you trust. Trust Him this day with those things that are most difficult.

October 6

Understanding What God Has Given

We have not received the spirit of the world but the Spirit who is from God, that we may understand what God has freely given us.
1 Corinthians 2:12

God desires for us to know what He has freely given to us. One of the responsibilities of the Holy Spirit is to reveal His plans and purposes to us. They may be hidden for a time, but if we seek Him with our whole heart, we can know what He has given to us.

John the Baptist understood this principle. When asked if he was the Messiah, he replied, "A man can receive only what is given him from heaven" (Jn. 3:27). John understood his role in the Kingdom of God. He came to pave the way for the Messiah; he was not the Messiah himself. His ministry on earth was very brief, yet Jesus described his life in this way: " 'I tell you the truth: Among those born of women there has not risen anyone greater than John the Baptist; yet he who is least in the kingdom of heaven is greater than he' " (Mt. 11:11).

Once we understand what God has given to us, we can walk freely in our calling. However, if we strive to walk in a role that He never gave us, it will result in frustration and failure. God wants to reveal His plan to us by His Spirit. This requires a willingness to seek and accept what He gives us. It may be different from what we thought. It may require adjustments to follow His path for our lives. As we learn from the life of John the Baptist, obedience requires death to our own wills.

Ask God to reveal what He has freely given to you. Pray that you receive and embrace only those things He has reserved for you to receive and to accomplish in your life. Then you can be assured of a life full of meaning and purpose, and you can look forward to hearing those all-important words someday, "Well done, My good and faithful servant."

October 7

Redeeming the Time

Philip, however, appeared at Azotus and traveled about, preaching the gospel in all the towns until he reached Caesarea.   Acts 8:40

Many times I've heard a businessman or woman say they cannot participate in an event, a service, or activity for God because of the time it will take away from their business. God has called each of us to be good stewards of our time and our resources. It is just as important to learn how to say yes as it is to say no, and we must be faithful to our employers if we do not have freedom to take time away. However, many times I sense that businesspeople justify a lack of obedience under the guise of stewardship.

Philip was one of the first businessmen who was given a commission to preach the gospel. He was in the city of Samaria preaching when many miracles began to take place and the crowds came to see what was happening. Then in the midst of this great move of God, the angel of God spoke to Philip and told him to leave Samaria and go to a desert road that led from Jerusalem to Gaza. Imagine how Philip must have questioned the logic of this decision when he was seeing such results in Samaria. But Philip was obedient to the angel. Along the road, he met an Ethiopian eunuch who wanted to have the Scriptures explained to him. Philip explained the Scriptures to the Ethiopian, who was the treasurer of Ethiopia under Queen Candace, and led him to the Lord, then baptized him in a nearby lake. A few moments later, Philip was supernaturally transported many miles northwest of his location to Azotus, where he preached Christ along the way toward his final destination of Caesarea.

So often we think that if we give our time outside our business life, our business will suffer. God redeemed the time for Philip by supernaturally transporting him to the next place he was to be. God always blesses those who serve Him. He can redeem lost time for those who willingly give of themselves for His purposes. Do not fall into the trap of believing that God cannot redeem the time you give for Him. If He calls you to give outside your normal business life, be assured He can make up that time. I have heard countless examples of businesspeople who experienced God's supernatural financial provision for time given for the sake of the gospel through unexpected business or unusual income that resulted after they made the commitment to take time away from their business for service to God.

God desires that we respond as Philip did in order to be used by Him in the life of another person. Listen to the voice of the Holy Spirit so that you can go and speak when He says go and speak. Do not fear the consequences of what that might mean if it requires leaving your business interests for a time. God will make it up. He always takes care of those who are obedient. He is more concerned about obedience than the bottom line.

October 8

A Faithful Woman

> *Her children arise and call her blessed; her husband also, and he*
> *praises her.*   Proverbs 31:28

She was the Vice President of Household Affairs for her entire adult life. She had a husband, four daughters, and one son whom she managed. Her calling was not to the marketplace; it was to the home. It was a calling that she fulfilled well. She often went beyond her job description to fulfill menial tasks like sewing clothes for her twin girls, playing dolls, and even playing catch with the only boy in the clan.

Things were going along well until midway in life a telephone call came that changed everything. The caller informed her that the love of her life had been killed in an airplane crash. She was in her early 40's, still beautiful, with five kids to raise on her own in spite of the fact that she hadn't worked in the business place for nearly 20 years. The death of her husband removed their steady upper middle-class income, and she was now faced with the greatest test of her life. At her lowest moment, wondering how she was going to make it, she cried out to God. God answered, "Trust Me, Lillian." Those audible words became the strength that she needed to care for her family for the next 40 years. From that moment on, she came to know her Savior personally and shared Him with her family. Her children came to know Him as well. Grandchildren became the recipient of her prayers, and they came to know Him too. She was building an inheritance in Heaven, one prayer at a time, one soul at a time. She never remarried; Christ became her Husband.

Whatever wisdom and encouragement has come to you through these devotionals, it is only as a result of one who answered the call to the greatest and most important workplace there is: the home. You can thank my mom, Lillian Hillman, for whatever grace you have gained from these messages throughout the year because she remained faithful to the call to invest in those she was called to love and serve. *"Her children arise and call her blessed; her husband also, and he praises her."*

October 9

Mount Horeb

So he got up and ate and drank. Strengthened by that food, he traveled forty days and forty nights until he reached Horeb, the mountain of God.   1 Kings 19:8

Elijah and Moses were men of great zeal. They were passionate about their causes. Moses sought to free the Hebrews from the tyranny of slavery by killing an Egyptian with his own hand. Elijah, after calling down fire on the evil prophets of Baal, found himself spent physically and emotionally to the point he asked God to take his life.

Immediately after these two events, 500 years apart from one another, both men were led to the same Mount Horeb, the mountain of God. In Hebrew, *Horeb* means "desolation." This barren environment mirrored the condition of Moses and Elijah. For Moses, it was 40 years of barrenness. For Elijah, it was 40 days without food. Elijah became tired of standing alone for God.

As businesspeople we often become so focused on the goal we forget to meet God at our own Mount Horeb. This was the place God met both Moses and Elijah. It was a place of renewal, a place of new beginnings, a place of personal encounter with the living God.

Perhaps Elijah's greatest virtue was his zeal. Indeed, we shall see that twice in his communication with God, Elijah speaks of having been "very zealous" for the Lord. But zeal, unattended eventually becomes its own God; it compels us toward expectations, which are unrealistic, and outside the timing and anointing of God.

To remain balanced, zeal must be reined in and harnessed by strategic encounters with the living God. We otherwise become frustrated with people and discouraged with delays. We step outside our place of strength and spiritual protection. Many of us become so consumed with our battles that we are no longer aware of the presence of Jesus. We have been traveling in our own strength. [Francis Frangipane, *Place of Immunity* (Cedar Rapids, Iowa: Arrow Publications, 1994), 5.]

Pray that Jesus will teach us that intimacy with Him is the greatest measure of success. Lord, guide us to the mountain of Your presence.

October 10

Covenant Relationships

> *But I will establish My covenant with you, and you will enter the ark—you and your sons and your wife and your sons' wives with you.*
> Genesis 6:18

The Bible is filled with covenants made between God and people. Six of those covenants were made with Old Testament figures: Noah, Abraham, Isaac, Jacob, Moses, and David. The seventh was made with His own Son, Jesus Christ. God is always the strongest partner in a covenant relationship.

God made a covenant with Noah in order to preserve the human race. This covenant involved Noah's participation by building an ark. He'd never built an ark before. He'd never had a boat. It was a totally new concept to Noah and the rest of the world. Why would he need a boat in a dry land?

Noah did not have to invent the ark; God gave him the plans—in specific dimensional detail. He did not have to gather the animals—God led them into the ark. God even closed the door when they all came on board. God made it rain to prove why the ark was needed.

The covenant provided all Noah needed to complete his mission in life. When God spoke to Noah to do this thing, he needed only to respond to God's call to do it. Noah could rest in knowing the covenant made with God was going to be fulfilled if he fulfilled his part.

If you have entered into a covenant relationship with God, you too can be assured that God will uphold His part of the covenant relationship. He is committed to fulfilling His covenant with you and to fulfill His purposes in and through your life. It only requires one thing on your part—obedience. He will even provide grace and faith to you to help you fulfill your part of the covenant.

Each of us has a covenant with God. But we also enter covenants with others in our personal and business lives. How are you doing in fulfilling covenants to others? God has given us the example to follow. Ask God if you have any unfulfilled covenants you need to honor. He has called you and me to be covenant keepers.

The one who calls you is faithful and He will do it (1 Thessalonians 5:24).

October 11

The Place of Obedience

Saul got up from the ground, but when he opened his eyes he could see nothing. Acts 9:8a

There is a place of obedience for all of us. For Paul, it was being struck blind on the Damascus road. God literally knocked him off his horse with a blinding light. A voice from Heaven asked Paul why he was persecuting Him (Jesus). When Paul arose, he could not see. Jesus told him to go to Damascus and meet a man named Ananias. There, Jesus restored Paul's sight through Ananias.

Each of us has a place of obedience. For some, it requires only a nudge of pressure to gently lead us toward God. For others of us, a lightning bolt is necessary to get our undivided attention. Many who are hardhearted rebel against the living God. Yet God's love for these individuals is so great that He takes extreme measures to gain their attention—and their hearts. When you come in contact with people like this, do not fear their arrogance. Instead, see them as God sees them—as people who need the Savior and who could be a powerful force in the Kingdom if God saved them. It is a sign to begin praying for them.

We've all heard the saying, "The bigger they are, the harder they fall." In many cases this is true. God has called many hard cases into His

Kingdom through miraculous circumstances in order to save their lives from the pit of hell and transform them into a sweet-smelling fragrance. Do not let the hard exterior fool you. These are needy people who are crying out for help in their own prideful way.

Whenever God begins this process in the life of a sinner, He has others standing by to assist. Ananias was the person in Paul's life. He found it unbelievable that Paul really could have been saved. An angel had to convince him. Has God placed such an individual in your path? Perhaps God desires to use you to be an "Ananias" in the life of one of His wayward children. To do so requires a willingness to come alongside that one who needs your help. Who knows, that person could be the next apostle Paul.

October 12

An Audience of One

> *Do not conform any longer to the pattern of this world, but be transformed by the renewing of your mind. Then you will be able to test and approve what God's will is—His good, pleasing and perfect will.*
> Romans 12:2

What audience do you play to? Each day you are seen by many who will make a judgment about the way you handle yourself among different audiences. Politicians have learned to play to their audiences, customizing messages for the needs of their particular groups. Musicians have learned to play to their audiences. Pastors play to their congregations each Sunday morning. Businesspeople play to the audiences who will buy their product.

Christ has called us to play to one audience—the audience of Himself. When you seek to please any other audience in your life, you become susceptible to situational ethics and motivations based on the need for the moment. Your audience becomes a pawn in your hands because you know what they want. Is that wrong? Sometimes it is, sometimes it isn't.

Pure obedience to pleasing God in our lives will often meet the needs of those around us. It is God's will that you and I love our spouses, provide good services to our customers, and look to the interests of others before ourselves. This will result in meeting many needs of the audiences in our lives.

However, there are other times when our audiences are asking for something contrary to God's will. Politicians are often forced to appease their audiences, even though it may go against God's laws. When we are asked to go with the flow, we discover which audience is most important in our lives. Is it the audience of One, or the audience of many?

Today, be aware of which audience you are playing to. Ask yourself why you are taking a particular action. Is it to please the audience of One? Or is it to please the audience of others who might negatively impact you should you not play to their tune?

October 13

When Plans Are Thwarted

But the prince of the Persian kingdom resisted me twenty-one days. Then Michael, one of the chief princes, came to help me, because I was detained there with the king of Persia.   Daniel 10:13

I left at 5:00 a.m. to fly to another city to present some possible joint initiatives in ministry with another organization. I would have only an hour or so to meet with the board. I got into the city and taxied to the hotel. *This is great*, I thought. *No glitches. I am even here an hour early.* I asked where the meeting was. There was no record of such a meeting, even though my contact was staying at the hotel. I made several calls, to no avail. What had I missed? I continued trying to reach someone. An hour and a half later I reached my wife. She located a letter that seemed to indicate the meeting might be downtown. I took a cab and arrived at the location. "I am sorry, sir, there are no seventh-floor offices in use yet in this building."

"That cannot be. My letter says different." After I insisted, she let me go up. I arrived on the seventh floor. Nothing but concrete. Perplexed, I called my wife again. We made contact with yet another person who gave us another number to call. Finally, we located where the meeting was taking place. I got into the cab for another $30 cab ride. Forty-five minutes later the cab driver was lost. We stopped at a dry cleaners and he asked the people there, where the street was located. I was past the point of anger. I was laughing at this situation. A few minutes later, we arrived at our destination, three and a half hours after our scheduled time.

Plans do not always go as we hope. Sometimes they are hindered for our purposes. Sometimes we are dealing in a spiritual realm in which we realize we are truly in a spiritual battle. And sometimes we are even hindered to protect us. After looking at this situation, I believe I was being hindered from getting to this meeting. However, perseverance and God's grace allowed me to make the meeting. Important initiatives resulted from the brief time I was there.

The next time your plans are thwarted, begin asking what is at the root of the calamities. Ask God for discernment on what is taking place. Just as He revealed to Daniel, God will show you what is behind such events.

October 14

Tested for Abundance

> *We went through fire and water, but you brought us to a place of abundance.* Psalm 66:12b

It is nice to hear that God desires to bring us into abundance. In fact, many a preacher has promoted the goodness of the Lord and His ability to prosper His children. Alas, my experience is that this gospel of material abundance has little to do with the gospel of the Kingdom as our Lord works in the realm of the sanctified soul. The passage above tells us that God does in fact bring us into places of abundance. However, upon further study of the entire passage, we learn the route to this abundance.

> *For you, O God, tested us; You refined us like silver. You brought us into prison and laid burdens on our backs. You let men ride over our heads; we went through fire and water, but You brought us to a place of abundance* (Psalm 66:10-12).

God's economy of abundance often has little to do with material blessing. In God's economy, abundance is often measured in wisdom and knowledge of Himself. It is then that we are truly blessed. Wisdom cannot be gained through intellectual pursuits. Wisdom comes only through experience. Real wisdom comes from the kinds of experiences that come only through the deepest tests. Lessons of refinement, including prison accompanied by burdens, lead us through the fire and water. This is the territory that must be traveled to reach that place of abundance. It would seem strange that a loving God would use such means with His children. What we often fail to realize is that God's measuring stick is the character and likeness of Jesus Christ Himself in each of us. This cannot be gained through a life of ease and pleasure. Ease and pleasure fail to refine.

Is God using your marketplace to refine you today? Has He placed you in a prison or laid burdens on your back? Take heart if this is the place you find yourself, and realize that if you are faithful through the tests, you will enter a place of abundance that few will ever attain. The darkest hour is just before daybreak.

October 15

The God of the Valley

The man of God came up and told the king of Israel, "This is what the Lord says: 'Because the Arameans think the Lord is a god of the hills and not a god of the valleys, I will deliver this vast army into your hands, and you will know that I am the Lord'."   1 Kings 20:28

Whenever we stand on the mountain, we are able to see clearly. It is the best vantage point to see what lies ahead. Wouldn't it be great to live on the mountain all the time in order to anticipate what is ahead? God allows us to experience the mountaintop at times. Joseph's first mountaintop experience was as a young man. He had the favor of his father, Jacob. He was given a fine coat and even had a dream about his future. As a young man, Joseph had a sense of destiny about his life. God often gives us a picture of our future so that we will remember this picture when we are being tested to trust Him in the valley. This picture usually does not reveal how God intends to bring about the visions for our life.

However, none of us really derive the character qualities God desires for our lives while we are on the mountain. It is in the valley where the fruit is planted and harvested. It cannot grow on the mountain; it must grow in the valley. God is a God of the mountain, but he is even more a God of the valley. In the valley, it is more difficult to see ahead; the clouds often cover the valley and limit our sight. Joseph was thrust into a deep valley that left him wondering if the God of his father had forsaken him. Jesus hoped that He might be able to avoid the valley that caused Him to sweat blood. There is a valley that each of us must enter, usually unwillingly, in order to experience the God of the valley— and to experience His faithfulness in the valley. Once we have spent time in this valley, we come out with something we would have never gained if we had not entered it. The valley brings much fruit into our lives so that we might plant seeds into the lives of others. God does not waste valley experiences. If we are faithful in the valley, we will enter a new dimension with God that we never thought possible. There is a harvest of wisdom and virtue that can only be grown in the valley.

Has God brought you into the valley? Know that the valley is a place of fruitfulness; it is a place of testing. It is where God brings what you know in your head into your heart. The only value of knowledge is when it becomes part of your heart. Look for God in the valley today.

October 16

When Insecurity Turns Evil

Rejoice with those who rejoice; mourn with those who mourn.
Romans 12:15

Saul was the King of Israel. David was in Saul's army and beginning to build a reputation as a great warrior. One day when David came back from a battle, the women danced and sang: " 'Saul has slain his thousands, and David his tens of thousands' " (1 Sam. 18:7).

Saul was very angry; this refrain galled him. "They have credited David with tens of thousands," he thought, "but me with only thousands. What more can he get but the kingdom?" (1 Samuel 18:8)

This statement caused something to snap in King Saul. From this point on, Saul was never the leader God intended him to be. He allowed insecurity to drive his every decision. Insecurity leads to the need to control people and circumstances. The need to control leads to anger once we realize we are unable to control the circumstance. King Saul could not accept, much less rejoice, over David's success. David's life would never be the same, because Saul sought to kill David every chance he had. Saul had a choice; he could have seen David as an up-and-coming general in his army who could have become an important part of his team and made the kingdom of Israel even stronger. Instead, he looked at him as a threat.

When you hear good news about fellow workers or associates, do you rejoice with them? If you find yourself comparing your life's circumstances to others and don't feel you measure up, recognize that this is one of satan's greatest ploys to destroy you.

Christ has given you all things in Him. He has a unique plan for you that cannot be compared to another. He alone is your security. Trust in the purposes He has for your life. And remember, "My God shall supply all your need according to His riches in glory by Christ Jesus" (Phil. 4:19 KJV).

October 17

The Benefits of Obedience

This is what the Lord says—your Redeemer, the Holy One of Israel: "I am the Lord your God, who teaches you what is best for you, who directs you in the way you should go."   Isaiah 48:17

My career has been in marketing and advertising. Early on, I learned to distinguish the difference between features and benefits. Features represent characteristics of a product or service. Benefits are those things that directly profit or benefit me by using the product or service. For instance, my new computer has incredible speed and lots of memory (feature). This allows me to do things more quickly and easily (benefit). People are more concerned about the benefits than the features.

God tells us in the above verse that there are some direct benefits to the features of His nature. He is a God who is committed to teaching His children in the way they should go. What is the real benefit of His teaching? He answers this in the next verse. "If only you had paid attention to My commands, your peace would have been like a river, your righteousness like the waves of the sea" (Is. 48:18).

The Lord tells us that the benefit of allowing God to teach us and lead us in the way is peace and righteousness. Here is a guaranteed promise from God. I often use guarantees in my advertising claims. Here is God's immutable guarantee: You will have peace like a river and righteousness like the waves of the sea! What a great promise!

Are you trusting God with the very details of your life so that He can lead you in the way you should go? Are you allowing Him to teach you? Seek the Lord today for what He wants to teach you and allow Him to lead you, and you will ensure peace and righteousness in your life.

October 18

The Power of Unity

That all of them may be one, Father, just as you are in Me and I am in You. May they also be in Us so that the world may believe that You have sent Me.   John 17:21

What is the greatest power that allows the unsaved to make a decision for Jesus Christ? It isn't prayer, though this is important. It isn't good deeds, though deeds indicate a fruitful relationship with God. It isn't good behavior, though Christ commands us to be obedient as sons. The greatest power God's children have over darkness is unity. Jesus talked a great deal about His oneness with the Father and the importance of unity in the Body of Christ. It is the most difficult command Jesus gave to the Church, because it wars against the most evil aspect of our sin nature—independence.

In the last days we are seeing God's Spirit convict His children of the lack of unity among His Church. We are seeing God move between blacks and whites, ethnic groups, denominations, and parachurch groups. There is much work to be done. The walls of division and competition among His Body are a stench in God's nostrils. He sees the competition and the pride of ownership and weeps for the lost who cannot come to Him because they cannot see Him in His Body. When His Body is one, the unbelieving see that Jesus was sent by God. It is like a supernatural key that unlocks Heaven for the heathen soul. The key is in the hand of Christ's Church.

When there is unity, there is power. Scripture tells us five will chase 100, but 100 will chase 10,000 (see Lev. 26:8). There is a dynamic multiplication factor in unity of numbers. We are a hundred times more effective when we are a unified group. Imagine what God could do with a unified Church.

Jesus prayed that we all might be one, as the Father and He are one. He wanted the same love God has for Jesus to be in each of us. When this love is in us, we are drawn to each other with a common mission. The walls fall down. The independent spirit is broken. Competition is destroyed. Satan's accusations are thwarted. Our love for each other is manifest to the world around us. Lost souls begin to seek this love that is so foreign to them.

Have you contributed to an independent spirit within His Body? Are you seeking to break down walls of competition among Christians, churches, denominations, and ethnic groups? Until we walk in the spirit of unity, we will hinder those in whom God has reserved a place in Heaven. Pray for His Church to be unified.

October 19

Are You Salty?

Everyone will be salted with fire. Mark 9:49

Jesus used parables to communicate principles of the Kingdom of God. He said each believer's life should have the same impact on his or her world as salt has on food. Salt gives food flavor and brings out the best, while at the same time it serves as a preservative.

What allows a Christian to become salty? Fire. God knows that each believer needs a degree of testing by fire in order for Christ's fragrance to be manifested. We cannot become salty without this deeper work of the Holy Spirit's fire in our lives. Fire purifies all that is not of Christ. It takes away all the impurities that prevent His nature from being revealed in us.

In this you greatly rejoice, though now for a little while you may have had to suffer grief in all kinds of trials. These have come so that your faith—of greater worth than gold, which perishes even though refined by fire—may be proved genuine and may result in praise, glory and honor when Jesus Christ is revealed (1 Peter 1:6-7).

Are you a salty Christian? If not, pray a prayer that the immature are unwilling to pray. Pray that God makes you a salty Christian. It will result in praise and glory at the throne of God.

October 20

Avoiding Detours

Trust in the Lord with all your heart and lean not on your own understanding; in all your ways acknowledge Him, and He will make your paths straight.　　　　　　　　　　Proverbs 3:5-6

I turned off the interstate to get gas for my car. I was returning from a speaking engagement and it was very late. As I turned onto the road, I looked for the entrance ramp to get back on the interstate. It was dark and I could not see any signs. I made a turn to the right that appeared to be the turn I needed to make. I could see the interstate was next to the road. As I continued down this road, the interstate was on my left. It soon became obvious it was not the entrance road but rather a frontage road. I assumed it would take me to the next interchange. However, the road soon turned away from the interstate. It grew darker and darker. The road became a dirt road. I realized I was not going to get to the interstate on this road. Being a bit frustrated that I had made the wrong turn, I turned around and went back, losing valuable time.

It is easy to make assumptions about the path we are on. If God's Spirit has not enlightened our reasoning, we are inclined to make the wrong choices. Our choices seem right at the time, but later we discover these choices have led us away from God because they were based on our own reasoning.

Acknowledge God in all your ways today. Lean completely on Him to reveal His direction for your life. If you do so, He will direct you to the desired destination He has for you.

October 21

David's Armor

David fastened on his sword over the tunic and tried walking around, because he was not used to them. "I cannot go in these," he said to Saul, "because I am not used to them." So he took them off.
1 Samuel 17:39

David, the young shepherd boy, heard the challenge from the Philistines to send someone to fight Goliath. No one volunteered to fight except David. King Saul reluctantly agreed and offered David his armor. David put on the weighty equipment, but quickly concluded he could not fight in this heavy armor.

God equips each of us in such a way that is unique to our strengths and abilities. David was trained as a shepherd to use another weapon. For David, it was a slingshot. David showed great maturity in realizing he could not be effective with Saul's armor.

What are the gifts and talents God has given to you? Have you ever tried to accomplish a task with tools you were not trained to use? God allows each of us to develop skills that are unique to our life. He will not call you to use someone else's tools.

However, this is only half of the equation. These talents must be mixed with faith. Talent alone is not enough. Faith alone is not enough. It is only when the two are combined that God's power is released and manifested in the physical realm.

Mix your unique gifts with faith today; you will be surprised at the power of God that will be manifested.

October 22

God's Double-talk

The Lord said to Moses, "When you return to Egypt, see that you perform before Pharaoh all the wonders I have given you the power to do. But I will harden his heart so that he will not let the people go." Exodus 4:21

Have you ever had a boss tell you to do something only to have him sabotage your ability to complete the task? Nothing is more frustrating than to begin to carry out a task and have your superior thwart your effort to do what he asked you to do.

Moses must have felt this way after God told him to go to Pharaoh and tell him to release the people of Israel. He said, "I am going to give you the power to release the children of Israel by the miracles I will do through you." Yet at the same time, He told Moses they would not be released because He was going to put a hard heart in Pharaoh. How do we reconcile this?

In my own life, I knew God called me to certain endeavors. Yet every time I turned around, a roadblock stood in my way. It took years of plodding along before the light came on as to why there was such a distance between what God called me to do and the manifestation of that calling. When David was anointed king of Israel, it was years before he realized the manifestation of that calling. There were a number of reasons for these delays.

In the case of Moses and Israel, God wanted to demonstrate His power in such a way that generations would be able to hear the story of their deliverance from their ancestors. God wanted greater glory from the situation. God also wanted to deal with Egypt by sending specific plagues. Finally, the very process built character in Moses and tested Moses to see if he would stay the course.

There is a time for everything. If God has called you to some endeavor and you are frustrated that it has not manifested, know that times of preparation and simmering are required before the vision can be achieved. Seldom does God call and manifest something at the same time. There is preparation. There is testing. There is relationship building between you and God that must take place. Once this is complete, you will see the vision materialize.

October 23

A Remnant That Prays

One day Jesus was praying in a certain place. When He finished, one of His disciples said to Him, "Lord, teach us to pray, just as John taught his disciples."   Luke 11:1

God is calling out a remnant of businesspeople throughout the world who understand the role of prayer in their business lives. These people have learned that prayer is not a five-minute exercise in the morning devotion time, but it is a vital strategic tool to discern and know God's will and purposes in their work lives. You see, they have learned that their business lives are their ministries to God and others.

These men and women have entered into covenant relationships with intercessory prayer partners who help discern the activities they should be involved in. Some even have paid staff who intercede for the decisions and activities in which they will be involved. They are a small remnant of businesspeople who know that skill and technique are not enough to fulfill God's purposes.

A servant of the Lord has well said: Prayer is the rail for God's work. Indeed, prayer is to God's will as rails are to a train. The locomotive is full of power: it is capable of running a thousand miles a day. But if there are no rails, it cannot move forward a single inch. If it dares to move without them, it will soon sink into the earth. It may be able to travel over great distances, yet it cannot go to any place where no rails have been laid. And such is the relation between prayer and God's work. Without any doubt God is almighty and He works mightily, but He will not and cannot work if you and I do not labor together with Him in prayer, prepare the way for His will, and pray "with all prayer and supplication" (Eph. 6:18) to grant Him the maneuverability to so work. Many are the things, which God wills to do, and would like to do, but His hands are bound because His children do not sympathize with Him and have not prayed so as to prepare ways for Him. Let me say to all who have wholly given themselves to God: Do examine yourselves and see if in this respect you have limited Him day after day. [Watchman Nee, *Let Us Pray* (New York, New York: Christian Fellowship Publishers, 1977), 11.]

Is prayer a vital part of your strategic business practices? Put prayer on the front lines, instead of making it an afterthought. You will begin to see renewed power in your work life.

October 24

Are You God's Next Deliverer?

But when they cried out to the Lord, He raised up for them a deliverer, Othniel son of Kenaz, Caleb's younger brother, who saved them.
Judges 3:9

Have you ever heard of a man named Othniel? Probably not. He was Caleb's nephew. When the people of Israel went into the Promised Land, they were victorious through the courageous efforts of Joshua and Caleb. As this generation grew older, a new generation began to emerge. Israel again fell into sin by worshiping idols. The anger of the Lord burned against Israel, and He allowed them once more to be enslaved by their enemies. However, the people again cried out to the Lord and God heard them.

Whenever God's people cry out to the Lord, He hears them. When they are truly repentant, He responds. He responds by raising up those whom He has prepared for such a time. Every soldier looks forward to the day he can use the training he has received. God had been preparing a nephew for such a time as this. He had the same Spirit as his uncle, Caleb.

> *The Spirit of the Lord came upon him, so that he became Israel's judge and went to war. The Lord gave Cushan-Rishathaim king of Aram into the hands of Othniel, who overpowered him. So the land had peace for forty years, until Othniel son of Kenaz died* (Judges 3:10-11).

Has God been preparing you for a time when you will be called upon to deliver God's people? Millions of men and women are enslaved to the god of mammon and idolatry in the workplace. Has He placed you there to be a deliverer? Pray that you will have the same Spirit as Joshua, Caleb, and Othniel.

October 25

How and Where God Speaks

> *The hand of the Lord was upon me there, and He said to me, "Get up and go out to the plain, and there I will speak to you."*   Ezekiel 3:22

God speaks in many different ways to His children. He spoke through a bush to Moses. He spoke through a donkey to Balaam. He spoke through prophets to His kings. He speaks through other believers. He speaks directly to us through the invisible Holy Spirit. And He speaks even through circumstances.

When God wants to speak a very important word directly to us without interruption from the noise of our busy lives, he will take us "into the plain." The plain is a place of no distractions and no other persons. It is a place of silence. It can be a place of great need as it often fails to have the normal provisions we are accustomed to. It can be a place we go to voluntarily to seek His face, or we can be moved there without choice by His supernatural ability. More often, it is the latter method that brings us into the plain. In modern times, it often means a separation from our normal activities such as jobs or families.

The plain can also be a place where we discover afresh that God's hand has been on us all the time. When we are so busy with life, we sometimes forget that God's hand is still there, gently leading our path. When our lives get so busy that we are not listening or responding to His gentle touch, He must take more aggressive measures to get our attention. Thus, the plain is one of those appointed times of one-on-one communication with our heavenly Father. No distractions, no people, no beautiful surroundings to capture our thoughts. It is a barren place designed to allow us to seek and hear clearly. When He speaks, we need to be able to listen. We hear much better in the plain.

Do you need to hear God's voice today? Is your life such that you cannot even hear His voice? Each day God calls us to our own mini-plain in order to speak to us and for us to hear. If we neglect this time of open communication, we may be invited to His plain in order to hear without distraction. Pray that you might make time to hear.

October 26

The Isolation Chamber

Be still and know that I am God....   Psalm 46:10

There is a time and place in our walk with God in which He sets us in a place of waiting. It is a place in which all past experiences are of no value. It is a time of such stillness that it can disturb the most faithful if we do not understand that He is the one who has brought us to this place for only a season. It is as if God has placed a wall around us. No new opportunities--simply inactivity.

During these times, God is calling us aside to fashion something new in us. It is an isolation chamber designed to call us to deeper roots of prayer and faith. It is not a comfortable place, especially for a task-driven businessperson. Our nature cries out, "You must do something," while God is saying, "Be still and know that I am God." You know the signs that you have been brought into this chamber when He has removed many things from your life and you can't seem to change anything. Perhaps you are unemployed. Perhaps you are laid up with an illness.

Most religious people live a very planned and orchestrated life where they know almost everything that will happen. But for people in whom God is performing a deeper work, He brings them into a time of quietness that seems almost eerie. They cannot say what God is doing. They just know that He is doing a work that cannot be explained to themselves or to others.

Has God brought you to a place of being still? Be still and know that He really is God. When this happens, the chamber will open soon after.

October 27

Going Without Jesus

> *...they were unaware of it.*   Luke 2:43

Mary and Joseph traveled to Jerusalem for the Feast of the Passover. Jesus was 12 years old. They were evidently very distracted by the excitement and business of the Feast. In fact, Mary and Joseph began their return trip to Nazareth only to realize well into the trip that Jesus was not with them. It would be three days before they would be reunited with their 12-year-old son. It caused quite a scare in Mary and Joseph, and they reprimanded Jesus for "wandering" off.

As a parent, I find this story truly amazing. How can parents of the Son of God not know their son is not in their presence? Yet this story illustrates how each of us can become so busy that we continue to operate not realizing that Jesus is no longer with us. Obviously, there was very little fellowship taking place between Jesus and His parents during the trip.

Are you experiencing daily, even moment-by-moment, fellowship with Jesus? If not, you will wake up one day and realize Jesus is not with you in your endeavors. It may, like Mary and Joseph, create a certain fear in you that you may have lost a very important relationship. Doing business without Jesus' presence leaves us powerless and prone to live in fear. Jesus said He would never leave or forsake His children. However, we can walk away from His fellowship by refusing to be with Him. Do not let this happen to you. He longs to have daily fellowship with you because He loves you.

October 28

Seeing What Others Cannot See

And Elisha prayed, "O Lord, open his eyes so he may see." Then the Lord opened the servant's eyes, and he looked and saw the hills full of horses and chariots of fire all around Elisha.　　　2 Kings 6:17

Several years ago, a movie was made called *Field of Dreams*. The story is about a man who had a vision to build a baseball field in the middle of a cornfield on his rural farm. He did not know why; he just knew he was to do it. To the chagrin of his neighbors, he built the baseball diamond in the farm community. One night some players showed up. The man realized these were no ordinary players, but were actually the great players from the past. When the skeptical neighbors came to view this phenomenon, they were unable to see what the farm owner could see. This made it even worse for him. Now he was really a lunatic in their eyes.

This fictitious story has a spiritual application for us. First, if God tells us to "build a ball field," we should do it. It is not for us to determine the reason we are instructed to do it. Once we are obedient, God will allow us to see what others cannot see. It is the rite of passage for those who are willing to risk all for God's purposes. God increases the spiritual senses to levels we never knew before. Those around us will observe this.

Do you want to see what others cannot see? If so, it will require a level of obedience that will go beyond human reason. It may require risk and ridicule from others. But you will see what others cannot see.

October 29

Moving in Presumption

Nevertheless, in their presumption they went up toward the high hill country, though neither Moses nor the ark of the Lord's covenant moved from the camp. Numbers 14:44

The people of Israel were brought out of Egypt to enter a new land—the Promised Land. This land was not handed over to them freely; it required the removing of God's enemies through battle. It required a partnership between God and the people. As long as the people remained true to God, they were victorious.

The people were camped at Kadesh Barnea, near the border entrance to the long-awaited Promised Land. All the hardships of their journey from Egypt were now culminating at this important crossing. However, Joshua and Caleb were the only scouts who proclaimed faith in God to take them into the land and conquer their enemies. The other spies saw all the dangers and refused to take the risk. The people of the camp shrank in fear because of their report. They decided not to enter in.

God was angered at the people for their lack of faith. Moses had to intercede on their behalf. Once they realized what they had done, it was too late. But they thought their repentance was enough to right their wrong. They presumed this was all that was necessary.

Moses informed them they were deceived in their presumption of God's favor. They went to battle against the Amalekites only to be soundly defeated. Those who returned did not understand why they lost the battle.

October 29—Day 302

It is important for us to know whether we have God's hand upon our endeavors. Presumption leads to failure. God's favor leads to success. Ask God to confirm His hand on your endeavors.

…"If Your presence does not go with us, do not send us up from here" (Exodus 33:15).

October 30

Fear Not!

For God did not give us a spirit of timidity, but a spirit of power, of love and of self-discipline. 2 Timothy 1:7

God calls each of us to engage in spiritual warfare at times. Whenever satan wants to come against one of God's children, he does so by trying to intimidate through fear.

Goliath's formidable size and arrogant boasting intimidated Saul and Israel's army. And because God's anointing had fallen from Saul, he was unable to respond with courage to Goliath's charge. Fear paralyzes and torments. That is why Saul could not respond.

The anointing had fallen on David, who was just a young boy, but mighty in spirit. David did not cower at the size or shouts of the giant Goliath. He saw Goliath through the eyes of God, who saw him as a mere speck. David had righteous indignation for an affront to the armies of the living God.

David did not weigh the risk of failure because his faith was resting totally in God. That is another important factor in overcoming fear—complete trust in God.

When the Lord began training me to confront fear, the training grounds were a groundless lawsuit, intimidations, and calamity that confronted my very existence. Learning that these were merely tactics of the enemy, designed to instill fear, allowed me to stand firm in God's power to overcome.

Do not fear sudden calamity if you are walking uprightly before God. It may be setting the stage for a great victory that will bring praise and honor to your heavenly Father. These battles are training grounds for greater victories to come.

October 31

Keeping Oaths

This is what we will do to them: We will let them live, so that wrath will not fall on us for breaking the oath we swore to them.

Joshua 9:20

Joshua and the people of Israel were in the Promised Land. They were winning battles and were feeling good about their progress. One day a band of Gibeonites came by dressed as travelers in order to fool Joshua. They wanted to make Joshua believe they were merely travelers instead of enemies. The Gibeonites asked Joshua to make a peace treaty with them. Since Joshua chose to believe their story, he did just that. That was a mistake on Joshua's part. The Bible says Joshua did not inquire of the Lord about the Gibeonites. This forced Joshua to uphold the peace treaty with the Gibeonites, even though it was made under false pretenses.

Keeping our oaths before the Lord is a serious matter. One might think that Joshua had every right to consider the agreement with the Gibeonites null and void since it was done on false pretense. However, Joshua knew how God viewed oaths. He knew that a man's word, once it was given, should be good as done. There was no reversing it. He also knew that if he did not keep his oath, he was subject to God's disfavor, which meant his ways would not be blessed.

Whenever we become a child of God, we represent Him. When His children follow unrighteousness, He takes this personally. Unrighteousness opens us up to satan's attack. God's protection shield is removed.

October 31—Day 304

So Joshua knew that if he did not honor his oath, he would be subject to God's judgment.

Is there any unfulfilled oath you have made to anyone? Ask God this morning if you have not fulfilled a commitment to anyone. Then, if there is, go and fulfill. Otherwise, you will be subject to God's judgment for your unrighteousness.

November 1

Worldly Planning

> *Or do I make my plans in a worldly manner so that in the same breath I say, "Yes, yes" and "No, no"?*   2 Corinthians 1:17

The apostle Paul was discussing his plans to come to the church at Corinth. He was acknowledging the serious nature of his trip and informing the Corinthians that he did not flippantly come to this decision to visit them. It was a matter that had been given serious prayer, not one made in the spur of the moment.

Planning from God's view is a process. It isn't merely an exercise in reason and analysis. It requires entering into the mind of Christ together with our minds to determine which course to take. In the Old Testament, the priests wore breastplates with the Urim and Thummim in a pouch on their breasts. It was like a roll of dice that the priests were required to perform to know which direction they were to take on a matter. It was the ultimate release of all decisions into God's hand. God did not want the priests to rely on their own intellects for final decisions.

We have an uncanny ability to make decisions based on our own needs and wants. However, God desires that we seek Him to know His plans for us. David was a skilled warrior who never lost a battle. He consulted God on every decision. He knew the results of the battle rested in God's hand. So, if he was to gain victory, he had to know God's mind on the matter. Sometimes this requires more time given to the process in order to hear His voice. Sometimes it may even require fasting and prayer. Sometimes it may require input from other godly friends.

Are you a man or woman who makes decisions based on God's purposes for your life? Do you take every major decision and put it before the throne to determine God's mind on the matter? If so, you will avoid making decisions in a worldly manner.

November 2

An Audience of One

Jesus answered, "If I want him to remain alive until I return, what is that to you? You must follow Me." John 21:22

For several weeks I awoke with heaviness over me. It seemed it did not matter how much I prayed or how much I read the Scriptures. Finally, one night I was reading a book by Os Guinness that described the conversation between Jesus and Peter. God had just commissioned Peter in the famous "Peter, do you love Me" passage of Scripture. This was after Jesus' resurrection. Jesus was calling Peter to feed His sheep, and He informed Peter of the death he would encounter for following Him. But Peter had a question. He wondered what was going to happen to John. Would John have the same trials, the same responsibility, as Peter? Jesus quickly retorted to Peter, "What is that to you?"

That night I realized I was guilty of envy. I had several friends who were now "making it" in business. I began to compare where I was in life. It brought me into a state of depression. Once I realized this, I asked the Lord to forgive me. I knew in my head I was to have only one audience— the audience of One. That knowledge needed to get to my heart. I also knew I was experiencing spiritual warfare in the area of unbelief.

The next morning I awoke, and as I normally do, I checked my e-mail to see what the devotional was for that day that is sent to other businesspeople. Although I write the devotional myself, I read it because I get letters from readers regarding the devotionals. To my shock, the devotional was on this same passage of Scripture. It talked about the sin of envy. I was amused by God's sense of humor, as He convicted me with my own devotional message. But that was not the end of it.

That day I went to lunch with a friend. After lunch I got into my car. I turned on the radio and Os Guinness, the author of the same book I was reading the night before, was being interviewed. They were talking about the discourse between Jesus and Peter and the sin of envy! I was floored! "Okay, God, I get the message!"

The Holy Spirit has an uncanny ability to communicate to us. The Lord wanted me to know that I am not to worry about someone else. God has called us to a unique life that may look totally different from anyone else's life. Once we begin to compare ourselves to others, we begin to live for others and ourselves.

There is only one audience we should be living for—the audience of One. Ask the Lord today if you are living solely for His pleasure.

November 3

The Root of Bitterness

See to it that no one misses the grace of God and that no bitter root grows up to cause trouble and defile many.   Hebrews 12:15

The enemy of our souls has a very specific strategy to destroy relationships. Whether these relationships are in business, marriage, or friendships, the strategy is the same. A conflict arises, judgments are made, and feelings are hurt. What happens next is the defining point of whether the enemy gains a foothold, or the grace of God covers the wrong.

When a root of bitterness is allowed to be planted and grown, it not only affects that person, but it also affects all others who are involved. It is like a cancer.

Breaking satan's foothold requires at least one person to press into God's grace. It cannot happen when either party "feels" like it, for none of us will ever feel like forgiving. None of us feel like talking when we have been hurt. Our natural response is to withdraw or lash out at the offending party. It is only obedience that allows God's grace to cover the wrongs incurred. This grace prevents the parties from becoming victims who will seek compensation for their pain.

The next time you are hurt by someone, realize the gravity of the crossroads where you find yourself. Choose grace instead of bitterness. Then you will be free to move past the hurt, and a root of bitterness will not be given opportunity to grow.

November 4

Face to Face

I have much to write to you, but I do not want to use paper and ink. Instead, I hope to visit you and talk with you face to face, so that our joy may be complete. 2 John 12

It is easy to fire off a letter to someone in this age of electronic communication because of its expediency. In business we call this being efficient. However, there are times when nothing but a face-to-face meeting is the appropriate means of communication. We know that verbal skills are a very small portion of communication. Body language, voice tone, and our expressions make up the majority of our overall communication. This cannot be seen through a letter or electronic medium.

Paul knew that being face to face with those he ministered to was important. And for Paul, it meant some major trouble to get from one place to another. It wasn't as simple as getting into a car or hopping onto an airplane. Paul's desire and determination to visit and talk face to face reinforces the importance of one-on-one personal communication.

I once had to confront a businessman about some problems we were having in a business deal. He lived in another town. The negotiations had stalled to some degree. I could have attempted to solve the problem over the phone. But I realized the serious nature of the issues required a face-to-face meeting. I drove two hours to his office and met with him face to face. It meant all the difference. It demonstrated to my friend I was serious enough about solving the problem to take a day to come see him. It also showed I valued him and he was worth the effort. This resulted in him giving greater emphasis to the issue.

Next time a situation arises that requires more focused communication, consider whether the situation requires a personal visit. You may find this will be the key to resolving issues that otherwise might end in a stalemate.

November 5

Leadership That Frees

Wives, in the same way be submissive to your husbands so that, if any of them do not believe the word, they may be won over without words by the behavior of their wives, when they see the purity and reverence of your lives. 1 Peter 3:1-2

"I am having a real problem with something that I need input from you guys," said the lady in our fellowship group. "My husband wants to make a major purchase that I am opposed to. We cannot afford it right now. I understand what the Bible says about headship in the home, but what do I do when I totally disagree with his decision?" The men in the group looked at each other, realizing the sensitive nature of such a question, especially in today's society.

Then someone said, "You really only have a few options if you adhere to the principle that God has entrusted the man as the leader in the home. God has placed you under the umbrella of His protection as well as your husband. There are times when he will not make the right decision. Does that mean God is not protecting you? No. There may be several things working here. God may be testing your own obedience to this principle. He may use you to open up your husband's spiritual life due to your obedience and submissive spirit. Your obedience may cost your family something, but it will be beneficial in the long term. Your alternative is to rebel and pay him back for his decision by withholding your love from him, which is often what a wife does in this situation. It becomes a vicious circle of paybacks. My suggestion is to tell your husband how you feel about his decision and the impact you feel it will have on you and your family. If he still wants to make the purchase, you must let him do it and support him. What happens next will rest in God's hand as your ultimate protector."

A few weeks later our sister in Christ came to our meeting. "I have some wonderful news. We did make the purchase. However, we were able to make it in such a way that we did not go into debt and I was able to support my husband. I have already seen a change in his attitude toward me by the way I responded to him in this. It has been a real lesson for me. I see him much more open to spiritual things since I made this decision and supported him, even though I disagreed with it."

God has made man and woman equal in His sight. Yet He has given each a different role to play in marriage. Husbands must answer to God for their leadership in the home. They will be judged for that leadership. When a wife submits to that leadership, God protects her from wrong decisions of that husband, although sometimes it may not appear that way at first.

You can trust God to protect you in your decisions that are made in obedience to His Word.

The one who calls you is faithful and He will do it (1 Thessalonians 5:24).

November 6

Divine Setups

Simon, Simon, satan has asked to sift you as wheat. But I have prayed for you, Simon, that your faith may not fail. And when you have turned back, strengthen your brothers.   Luke 22:31-32

November 6—Day 310

Have you ever perceived yourself to be at one place spiritually only to discover that you were actually far from this place? Peter perceived himself to be so spiritually strong that he was prepared to suffer greatly for his Master. Yet Jesus knew where Peter really was in his own pilgrimage. He knew that Peter's enthusiasm did not match his reality. He was suffering from an attitude of self-righteousness. So, how did Jesus help Peter match his perception to his reality? Peter was the object of a divine setup.

First, notice that satan asked permission to sift Peter as wheat. Jesus determined that satan would be used to bring Peter to the maturity level both Jesus and Peter really desired. And Jesus was praying that Peter would pass the test. Jesus told Peter that he would deny Him three times that very day. Peter could not believe what Jesus was saying.

Sometimes the lessons we must learn are very painful. This experience was necessary in Peter's life. It was necessary to purge Peter from his sin of self-righteousness. This very lesson would allow Peter to come face to face with his own misperception of where he was in his relationship and devotion to Jesus. When he was forced to confront this, it nearly broke him apart. He wept bitterly once he realized he had done just as Jesus had predicted.

This confrontation with reality is necessary at times in our lives. Do not be surprised if Jesus allows you to experience some painful circumstance. You may be the subject of a divine setup designed to bring you to a greater maturity level in your walk with Jesus. It may not be a fun experience when you go through it, but you will, like Peter, become a leader whom God will use to lead others.

November 7

The Value of Hard Places

So then, death is at work in us, but life is at work in you.
2 Corinthians 4:12

Being forced into hard places gives us a whole new perspective on life. Things we once valued no longer hold the same value. Small things become big things, and what we once thought big no longer holds such importance.

These hard places allow us to identify with the sufferings of others. It keeps us from having a shallow view of the hardships of others and allows us to truly identify with them. Those who speak of such trials from no experience often judge others who have had such hardship. It is a superficiality of Christian experience that often permeates shallow believers.

Those who have walked in hard places immediately have a kinship with others who have walked there also. They do not need to explain; they merely look at one another with mutual respect and admiration for their common experience. They know that death has worked a special thing in them. This death leads to life in others because of the hard places God has taken them through.

It is impossible to appreciate any valley experience while you are in it. However, once you have reached the top of the mountain, you are able to appreciate what terrain you have passed through. You marvel at what you were able to walk through. The valley of the shadow of death has yielded more than you ever thought possible. You are able to appreciate the beauty of the experience and lay aside the sorrow and pain it may have produced.

Death works in you for a greater purpose. If you are there today, be assured that God is producing something of much greater value than you will ever know.

November 8

Hindrances to Christ's Rule

The weapons we fight with are not the weapons of the world. On the contrary, they have divine power to demolish strongholds.

2 Corinthians 10:4

The Bible says when Christ comes to live in your heart, old things are passed away, all things become new (see 2 Cor. 5:17). The Lord has put a new Spirit in us. Previously, I could not understand why so many of us who proclaimed Christ had such little impact on the kingdom of darkness. It seemed to me that our culture should be impacted much more if His children walked in the light as Jesus did. Jesus impacted His culture like no other man.

I saw many businesspeople, who proclaimed Christ, living no differently than a person who had not claimed Him as Lord. These men and women had a form of religion, but little power that reflected Christ's rule in their lives. Then one day God took me through a time of testing that led to a discovery of generational influences that impacted the way I viewed people and circumstances on a subconscious basis. I discovered this was a stronghold that had been implanted many generations earlier. Because the stronghold operated on a subconscious level, it was not easily recognizable. Strongholds keep us from being free to reflect Christ in and through our lives because they require allegiance until they are dealt with. Strongholds can often be so hidden that we would not even identify them as evil. A stronghold of fear, control, rebellion, insecurity, idolatry, pride, or bitterness may be hidden until it is revealed through circumstances.

All strongholds are built in our lives as a result of seeking to meet one or more of seven basic needs God has created in us. Once we believe a lie that God cannot meet a need without our effort, we open our spirit to a stronghold. The more lies we believe, the more we invite these strongholds to take root in our lives.

Are you ineffective in your Christian experience? Are there besetting sins that seem to recur in your life? You may find that satan has built a fortress in your heart that has been there many generations. You must ask God's forgiveness for entertaining this stronghold, and you must renounce it. Then as Christ renews your mind and heart, you will see Christ's power released in your life like never before.

November 9

God's Proving Ground for Faith

He did this only to teach warfare to the descendants of the Israelites who had not had previous battle experience.   Judges 3:2

God brought the nation of Israel into the Promised Land of Canaan through Joshua. After Joshua, there came an entire generation who had very little experience in fighting battles like the ones fought by Joshua. Training and testing God's people is one of God's important strategies that enable His children to succeed in spiritual warfare. This is why we do not live a life free of trials. These trials are sent specifically to see if our faith is real or simply empty words.

"They were left to test the Israelites to see whether they would obey the Lord's commands, which He had given their forefathers through Moses" (Judg. 3:4). God allows circumstances to develop around your life to give your faith opportunity to be proven. It is only when we are tested in battle that we become skilled warriors. You can be confident God will allow trials to come your way through situations like an unreasonable boss, a vendor who refuses to pay, a false assault on your character, or a difficult relationship that requires unconditional love. These battles are sent your way to test what you know in the mind in order that they might become part of your heart.

You will discover if you have passed the tests or if you need more battles that will give you the opportunity to learn the art of spiritual warfare. Do not fear these battles that are before you. God has already given you the victory if you choose complete dependence and obedience to Him. Then you will become one of God's greatest warriors, skilled in spiritual warfare.

November 10

How God Makes Fishermen

"Come, follow Me," Jesus said, "and I will make you fishers of men."
Matthew 4:19

Our calling has three distinct stages, which we can see in the lives of many called before us, to become mature fishers of men who greatly impact God's Kingdom. First, there is the gestation period. This is the development stage of our lives. It may involve years of normal work experiences. You may be a Christian during this time, or you may be following after worldly success as a non-Christian. Paul spent years in religious and political training, persecuting believers most of his early life. Moses spent years in the court of Pharaoh and 40 years tending flocks in the desert. Jesus spent 33 years living at home and working in His father's carpentry business. However, all these years were part of their preparation.

Next is the crisis stage. Sooner or later, God calls you into relationship with Him. For many, like Paul, it comes through dramatic encounters like being knocked off a horse, blinded and spoken to personally by God. Some people are more difficult than others to reach and so require this level of crisis. This is a time when major changes are required by God so that you follow Him fully. It can be a time in which God harnesses years of experience for a new life purpose. Paul's earthly experiences would be used in his calling to the religious and political leaders of his day. For Moses, the burning bush experience would begin his journey in which he would discover his ultimate calling after years of preparation. For Peter, it was his denial of Jesus three times that allowed him to face his shallow commitment to Christ. For Jesus, it was the cross. These were the benchmark turning points for men who made an impact on their world.

Last is the fruit-bearing stage. In it, God's power is manifested in your life like never before. God takes all your experiences and uses them to build His Kingdom in and through your life. Your obedience to this final call results in fruitfulness you could never imagine without the long preparation process. For Abraham, it resulted in becoming the father of many nations. For Paul, it resulted in bringing the gospel to the

Gentiles. And for Peter, it meant becoming the rock the Church was built on. For Jesus, it was salvation for the entire world.

What does God want to achieve through your life? God has a plan that is so incredible you cannot comprehend it. It requires only that you love Him and follow Him. Then you will become fishers of men like the world has never known.

November 11

Receiving Only From God

I will accept nothing but what my men have eaten and the share that belongs to the men who went with me—to Aner, Eshcol and Mamre. Let them have their share. Genesis 14:24

Abraham's nephew was a man named Lot. Lot was part of Abraham's household until the land on which they fed their flocks could no longer support their growing families and herds. Abraham allowed Lot to choose the land where he wanted to live. Lot chose the land of Sodom.

Afterwards, Sodom was invaded by four kings, and Lot's family and goods were taken into captivity. When Abraham learned of this, he immediately gathered his best fighting men and pursued the armies to free Lot and his family. He was successful in freeing Lot's family and the families of Sodom. The king of Sodom was grateful to Abraham for what he did and wanted him to keep the goods he recovered. Abraham had made a decision before the battle that he would only keep what he recovered for his nephew Lot, and goods as payment for the men who fought.

Abraham understood the principle of receiving from God. He was a man with great integrity in God. He did not want to be known as someone who became wealthy because of the kindness of a wicked king. He wanted others to know that whatever prosperity he gained was a result of the blessing from God's hand alone. Abraham understood an important principle of receiving from God.

Jesus also modeled this principle by receiving only what His Father wanted Him to receive. God's will for Jesus was to receive based on a carpenter's wage even though He was the God of the universe who had access to all things. Imagine the discipline Jesus had to have, knowing what He could have had. He upheld His own financial integrity in God.

Each of us must discern what comes from the hand of God rather than the hand of man. As businesspeople, there are situations that allow us to manipulate, sweat, and toil our way to profit. There is also profit as a result of hard work done in obedience to our calling to the marketplace. Knowing the difference in these two concepts is a sign of integrity before God. Only God receives glory when we receive what God wants us to receive. Are you receiving the fruit of your labor in God? Ask God to show you the difference of these two concepts for your own life.

November 12

Created for His Good Pleasure

> *For we are God's workmanship, created in Christ Jesus to do good works, which God prepared in advance for us to do.* Ephesians 2:10

Eric Liddell was an Olympic runner from Britain who won a gold medal in the 1924 Paris Olympics. He was a man who had a deep commitment to the Lord and had future plans of being a missionary. In the meantime, he knew God had given him a special gift to run, and he often said, "I feel God's pleasure when I run."

He spent years training for the Olympics. He passed each hurdle and qualified for the Olympics. Finally, the day came for him to run in the games that were held in Italy. There was only one problem. One of his running events was held on Sunday. Liddell refused to run on Sunday, believing it dishonored the Lord's Sabbath. He held to his convictions and brought great persecution on himself. He made a decision that even if it meant losing his opportunity to compete, he would not run. God's laws were greater than man's applause. Just when the circumstances seemed hopeless, another situation arose that allowed Little to run on a different day.

So often this is the case in the spiritual realm. God tests our hearts to see if we will remain faithful to Him at the cost of something important to us. Once He knows where our loyalty lies, He opens a new door that meets the desires of our hearts.

God takes pleasure in seeing His creation used for His glory. Liddell understood why he was made to run; he used his gift of running to bring pleasure to his Creator. Later, Eric Liddell went on to serve God on the mission field.

Does your life work bring pleasure to the Lord? Do you understand that God instilled certain gifts and talents in you so that He might find pleasure in His creation of you? Take pleasure in the gifts God has given to you this day. And let His glory shine through you.

November 13

Prosperity in Afflictions

> *The second son he named Ephraim and said, "It is because God has made me fruitful in the land of my suffering."*   Genesis 41:52

When Joseph was elevated to rule over the Egyptian kingdom, he revealed some profound truths gained from the experiences of his years of adversity. He named his first son, Manasseh for, he said, "God has made me forget all my trouble and all my father's household" (Gen. 41:51b). His second son was named Ephraim because, "God has made me fruitful in the land of my suffering."

Whenever God takes us through the land of affliction, He will do two things through that affliction: 1) He will bring such healing that we will be able to forget the pain, and 2) He will make us fruitful from the painful experiences.

God does not waste our afflictions if we allow Him the freedom to complete the work in us. His desire is to create virtue that remains during the times of testing so that He can bring us into the place of fruitfulness in the very area of our testing. He has never promised to keep us from entering the valleys of testing, but He has promised to make us fruitful in them. He is the God who turns the Valley of Achor (trouble) into a door of hope (see Hos. 2:15).

If you are in the valley of affliction, now is the time to press into Him. When the time comes to bring you out of this valley, He will heal your memories and bring fruit from this very time.

November 14

Sold Out

> *But whatever was to my profit I now consider loss for the sake of Christ.*   Philippians 3:7

George Mueller was a man known for building orphanages by faith in the mid-1800s. He raised literally millions of dollars for his orphanages, yet died with little in his own bank account. When asked about his conversion experience he commented,

I was converted in November of 1825, but I only came into the full surrender of the heart four years later, in July 1829. The love of money was gone, the love of place was gone, the love of position was gone, and the love of worldly pleasures and engagements was gone. God, God alone became my portion. I found my all in Him; I wanted nothing else. And by the grace of God this has remained, and has made me a happy man, an exceedingly happy man, and it led me to care only about the things of God. I ask affectionately, my beloved brethren, have you fully surrendered the heart to God, or is there this thing or that thing with which you have taken up irrespective of God? I read a little of the scriptures before, but preferred other books; but since that time the revelation He has made of Himself has become unspeakably blessed to me, and I can say from my heart, God is an infinitely lovely Being. Oh, be not satisfied until in your own inmost soul you can say, God is an infinitely lovely Being! [Basil Miller, *Man of Faith and Miracles* (Minneapolis, Minnesota, Bethany House Publishers, n.d.)]

Many will never get to the place where George Mueller was in his spiritual life, because we are unwilling to release control of these areas of which he speaks. If we do release control, it usually is due to a process that God brings us through. Paul got knocked off a horse and was spoken to personally before he was willing to listen and follow completely. Peter had to live with Jesus three years and he still denied Him. It was only later, after he denied Jesus and realized how weak he was in his own faith, that he became fully committed to the Savior.

What will it take for you to fully surrender? You will know that you have given full surrender when power, money, and position no longer have meaning in your life. Paul said he came to a place where his life was the life of Christ only. It is a sacrificial life, but it is also a life of freedom, purpose, and meaning. Let God take full control and see His life lived fully through you.

November 15

Real Customer Service

While they were going out, a man who was demon-possessed and could not talk was brought to Jesus.　　　　Matthew 9:32

Years ago, it was not uncommon to have your milk delivered to your home. Doctors made house calls. And when you made a call to a company to discuss a problem, you actually spoke to a human being. Those days of personal serivce are gone, and if we are not careful, we will follow the same trend in how we share the gospel.

So often we are encouraged to bring people to church. Yet, we see no examples of where Jesus brought people into the synagogue to get them saved or healed. The miracles happened more often in the marketplace because that was where Jesus could be found. Jesus had less response and found more resistance in the synagogue than in the marketplace. He took the gospel to and modeled the gospel in the marketplace. That is where the power of God was manifested. This is not to say we should not bring people to church, only that our priority should be to bring the Church into the marketplace, not bring the marketplace into the church.

Paul understood this when he said,

> My message and my preaching were not with wise and persuasive words, but with a demonstration of the Spirit's power, so that your faith might not rest on men's wisdom, but on God's power (1 Corinthians 2:4).

Paul understood that it wasn't words that impacted people; it was the power of God manifested through him.

When is the last time someone saw something happen through your life that could not be explained other than God working in your life? When you begin to see this happen, you will be modeling ministry as Jesus modeled it. You will be bringing the Church to the people, not the people to the church. Pray that God makes you a vessel of His power, not simply a vessel of words.

November 16

The Ultimate Franchise

> And He said unto them, How is it that ye sought Me? Wist ye not that I must be about My Father's business?   Luke 2:49 KJV

Earth is God's business. He has set up many franchises (churches) designed to send His representatives (Body of Christ) into the world to make known the best product ever given to mankind (Jesus). His branch managers (pastors) have been given the responsibility to teach and support those in the field. God's goal is to establish a franchise in every nation, state, and city. It is the ultimate business because when you introduce someone to His product (Jesus), you receive a reward from the home office (Heaven). God has promised that His representatives will have all the tools and customer support needed to accomplish their strategic plans.

Jesus knew that He was to be about His Father's business. He knew He was sent to earth not to enjoy the pleasures of lowly man, but to accomplish a task for which He alone was sent. When He had accomplished His mission, He was to entrust this mission to other representatives into whom He poured His life for three years. This field training allowed Jesus to mentor, model, befriend, and demonstrate firsthand the model for a successful business to be launched and sustained.

God has big plans for His franchise. He wants every human being to partake of His product; however, even God knows that not everyone will. Nevertheless, this does not thwart His efforts in seeking to make it known among His audience.

You have been called to be part of the ultimate franchise. How many new recruits have you been responsible for bringing into the franchise lately?

November 17

Product Testing

His master replied, "Well done, good and faithful servant! You have been faithful with a few things; I will put you in charge of many things. Come and share your master's happiness!" Matthew 25:21

Testing allows one to discover how well a product is made when placed under extreme stress. Increasing the pulling pressure between two objects reveals the amount of tension that can be withstood in a chain link. Eventually, the "choking" point occurs. In sports, we ascertain the "choking" point for athletes by putting them into a pressure situation. At what point will the athlete lose concentration and collapse under the pressure? It is under these stressful times that we discover how well we have been trained to withstand the pressure and make right decisions regardless of outside influences.

November 17—Day 321

In my younger days I played sports. I came to observe that we fail under pressure usually because we reach a point where our ability to focus on execution yields to concern about outcome. This worry about outcome forces us to lose our concentration. The fear of failure begins to rule our emotions and actions, which ultimately results in our failure. What we fear has come upon us. It becomes a self-fulfilling prophecy.

In life, we see giving in to pressure in the form of compulsive behavior, withdrawal, anger, abuse, moral failure, and dishonesty, to name just a few manifestations.

Jesus never yielded to pressure. He never made decisions based on outcome. He always made the right decision. He always performed the same no matter what the circumstance. He lived a life based on absolutes, not circumstances. He never gave in to "situational ethics."

As God entrusts us with more and more responsibility, He brings more and more pressures into our lives to "test the product," to make sure that He can give even more responsibility to us. This process helps us see where we are in our maturity and determines our level of future responsibility.

Are you a product that can withstand the product test? Will you perform as the Maker designed no matter what outside pressures come? Know that you cannot perform well unless you are continually in relationship with and obedient to the one who made you. Trust the product developer today. He has made you to perform well under pressure.

November 18

Fulfilling Vows

When you make a vow to God, do not delay in fulfilling it. He has no pleasure in fools; fulfill your vow.   Ecclesiastes 5:4

Have you ever had a business relationship with someone who made a commitment but later said, "Well, things changed, so I cannot honor our original agreement." Sometimes this may be the case, but often it is simply an opportunity to avoid fulfilling an agreement. God is big on fulfilling vows. God's nature is righteousness and truth. You will always see God honor His Word. He expects the same of His people.

God says there are consequences when we do not fulfill our vows. Subsequent Scripture verses reveal the following:

> *It is better not to vow than to make a vow and not fulfill it. Do not let your mouth lead you into sin. And do not protest to the temple messenger, "My vow was a mistake." Why should God be angry at what you say and destroy the work of your hands? Much dreaming and many words are meaningless. Therefore stand in awe of God* (Ecclesiastes 5:5-7).

God tells us that He will destroy the work of our hands for failure to fulfill vows. That's pretty strong language. It gives us an indication of how important fulfilling vows is to God. He will not prosper our work if there are unfulfilled vows in our lives

Are there any unfulfilled vows in your life that may be hindering your projects? Vows show up in many areas of our lives—marriages, businesses, personal friendships. Unfulfilled vows in any one of these could be the reason your work may be hindered.

Ask God today if there are any unfulfilled vows in your life. If so, begin today to make them right so that you may be successful in whatever God calls you to do.

November 19

Are You a Romans 8:14 Christian?

> *For if you live according to the sinful nature, you will die; but if by the Spirit you put to death the misdeeds of the body, you will live, because those who are led by the Spirit of God are sons of God.*
> Romans 8:13-14

Joshua and Caleb are described in Scripture as men who had a different spirit. They were two of the 12 spies sent into the Promised Land to determine if it could be taken, as God had promised it to them. The other ten gave a bad report that instilled fear in the people, which ultimately caused a rebellion. This resulted in an entire generation dying in the desert. Joshua and Caleb were the only two who were led by the Spirit of God, versus the spirit of fear. They were the only ones to enter the Promised Land from their generation.

Are you a person led by the Spirit? The verse above tells us that those who are led by the Spirit are sons of God. "But because My servant Caleb has a different spirit and follows Me wholeheartedly, I will bring him into the land he went to, and his descendants will inherit it" (Num. 14:24). Caleb was a Romans 8:14 man! The Spirit led him. He was not led by fear.

Many of us have failed to enter into our own Promised Land because we have failed to be led by the Spirit rather than by fear. Fear prevents us from entering into what God has promised for each of us. God has reserved an inheritance for us that is exceedingly good. God described the Promised Land as a land of milk and honey. Our own Promised Land is the same. But you must be led by the Spirit to enter in. You cannot be led by fear, reason and analysis, or even skill. The Spirit must lead you.

Commit yourself to being a Romans 8:14 man or woman. Then you will enter into the land God has promised for you.

November 20

Starting Over

The brother in humble circumstances ought to take pride in his high position.   James 1:9

Do you find yourself in humble circumstances? If so, James tells us that we are to take pride in this "high" position. These two things would seem to be an oxymoron. Most of us would not consider humble circumstances a high position. Successful business tells us that being on top means being wealthy, attaining favor and status, or having power to influence. However, Jesus influenced not from power, but from weakness.

J.C. Penney is a name synonymous with department store. He first launched his chain of "The Golden Rule" stores in 1907. In 1910 his first wife died. Three years later, he incorporated as the J.C. Penney company. In 1923 his second wife died giving birth to his son. In 1929 the stock market crashed and he lost $40 million.

> By 1932, he had to sell out to satisfy…creditors. This left [Penney] virtually broke. …Crushed in spirit from his loss and his health suddenly failing, Penney wound up in a Battle Creek, Michigan sanitorium. One morning he heard the distant singing of employees who gathered to start the day with God: *Be not dismayed, whate'er betide, God will take care of you….* Penney followed the music to its source and slipped into a back row. He left a short time later a changed man, his health and spirit renewed, and ready to start the long climb back at age fifty-six.

> By 1951 there was a J.C. Penney store in every state, and for the first time sales surpassed $1 billion a year. [John Woodbridge, ed., *More Than Conquerors* (Chicago, Illinois: Moody Press, 1992), 340-343.]

The success of J.C. Penney can be traced to God's mercy in his life to bring him out of his humble circumstance. Do you find yourself in a humble circumstance? God is the only one who can help you see your humble circumstance from His viewpoint—a high position. It is a high position because of what God is going to teach you in this place. He does not intend you to stay there; it is merely a stopping place to learn some important things you would not learn otherwise. Press into God and trust Him for the outcome to your circumstances.

November 21

A Business Problem Leads to a Call

Now the donkeys belonging to Saul's father Kish were lost, and Kish
said to his son Saul, "Take one of the servants with you and go and
look for the donkeys."   1 Samuel 9:3

The people of Israel wanted a king. God finally agreed. Samuel was the prophet of Israel who was to anoint the man God had chosen. God selected a young man to be the first king of Israel—his name was Saul.

It is interesting to look at the circumstances in which God called Saul into his new vocation. It seems that Saul's father had a business that used donkeys. During these times, donkeys were often used for commerce. It was obviously important to the father to find these lost donkeys, so he sent Saul and his servant out to find them.

They went from region to region, unable to find the donkeys. Finally, Saul told his servant that they should go back. He thought that his father would be worried.

But the servant replied, "Look, in this town there is a man of God; he
is highly respected, and everything he says comes true. Let's go there
now. Perhaps he will tell us what way to take" (1 Samuel 9:6).

Saul took his advice. Near the town they met some young girls who told them that Samuel had just come to their town that day.

When they arrived, they met Samuel who told them that the donkeys were safe and he would also tell Saul the next morning all that was in his heart. He then informed Saul of his new calling to be the next king of Israel.

Can you see what circumstances led to Saul's receiving his call? It started with a business problem—lost donkeys. It led to connecting Saul with Samuel through a number of divine appointments and circumstances. God still does this today.

God will provide the necessary circumstances to accomplish His purposes in your life. You must realize that a business problem may lead to a new calling for your life. Saul had no idea lost donkeys would be the instrument used to change his life. So, too, we must realize God's ways are not our ways.

November 22

A Question of Ownership

Whoever finds his life will lose it, and whoever loses his life for My sake will find it. Matthew 10:39

Otto Koning was a missionary in New Guinea. He worked among a native tribe that had known only their village ways. One of those village ways was stealing from others. When Otto and his wife arrived and moved into a hut, the natives often came by to visit. The Konings would notice that after the natives left the missionaries' home, various household items had disappeared. They saw these items again when they went to preach in the natives' village.

The only fruit Otto could grow on the island was pineapples. Otto loved pineapples, and he took pride in the pineapples he was able to grow. However, whenever the pineapples began to ripen, the natives would steal them. Otto could never keep a ripe pineapple for himself. This was a frustration, and he became angry with the natives. All during the seven-year period in which this took place, Otto preached the gospel to these natives, but never had a conversion.

The more the natives stole, the more angry Otto became. Finally, one day Otto had a German Shepherd dog flown in from another missionary to protect his pineapple garden after other frustrated efforts failed. This only further alienated the natives from him.

Otto took a furlough to the United States and attended a conference on personal rights. At this conference, he discovered that he was frustrated over this situation because he had taken personal ownership of his pineapple garden. After much soul searching, he gave his garden to God. Soon the natives started having problems among their tribe. They discovered that Otto was the reason for their problems because he gave his garden to his God. The natives saw a correlation between what Otto had done and their own lives being affected by calamities in their village. When Otto gave his garden to God, he no longer got angry and was free from worry. The natives started bringing him fruit from the garden because they didn't want any more calamities to come into their village.

The light came on one day when a native said to Otto, "You must have become a Christian, Otto. You don't get angry anymore. We always wondered if we would ever meet a Christian." They had never associated Otto with the kind of person he was preaching about because his message did not line up with his life. Otto was broken in spirit when he realized he had been such a failure.

At the end of seven years, he witnessed his first conversion, and many began coming to Christ once he fully gave his garden to God. The fruit grew so abundant that Otto began exporting it and growing other types of fruit, such as bananas. His village became the most evangelized in the whole region, yet for seven years he had not one convert.

Otto realized something each of us must realize: To gain your life you must lose it, along with your possessions. It was only when he gave all his possessions to God that he became free from them. God measured back to him manyfold once He had complete ownership.

Do you have some possessions that you need to give up to God today? Let God have all that you have. Become a steward, not an owner. You will be surprised at how well God can take care of His possessions.

November 23

Good Things Versus God-Things

Because those who are led by the Spirit of God are sons of God.
Romans 8:14

The greatest sign that you and I are maturing in our walk with God is when we can discern the difference between "good things" and "God-things." When the people of Israel journeyed out of Egypt through the desert, they were led by the cloud by day. They could move only as fast as the cloud. If they went ahead, they went without God's presence. If they lagged behind, they also lost God's presence.

Each of us must have the discernment to know when God is leading in a matter, or if it is simply a good idea. There are so many things in which you and I can be involved, and the more successful you become, the greater the temptations to enter into things where God has not called you. Entrepreneurs are especially prone to see all the opportunities.

I recall one time when I entered into a project that I thought was a great idea. It would help many people. After two years, the project had to be discontinued. It was a great lesson on understanding what projects have God's blessing on them. There are some projects you and I might get involved in that result in little fruit compared to the investment put into them. That is because they may never have been birthed by the Holy Spirit.

As sons of God, we are called to be led by the Spirit. This requires a level of dependence on God in which many of us really do not want to invest. It requires listening, waiting, and moving only when God's Spirit tells us to move. Businesspeople are "action" people. We know how to get things done, but our greatest strength can be our greatest weakness.

Today, ask God to make you a Romans 8:14 man or woman who is led by the Spirit of God. Pray against lagging behind or moving ahead. Ask God to reveal whether the next project you consider is a "good thing" or a "God-thing."

November 24

Check Under the Hood

> *But now you must rid yourselves of all such things as these: anger, rage, malice, slander, and filthy language from your lips.*
> Colossians 3:8

"The root issue you are dealing with is fear. The physical symptom is control, and when you cannot control, you get angry because of unmet expectations." These were the words I spoke during a conversation in a restaurant to my friend who was separated from his wife. He described his anger and how he never saw some of these characteristics in his life until he entered this marriage.

A friend once said to me, "Anger is like the lights on a dashboard. They tell you something is going on under the hood. You must find out the source of the problem." Whenever we have expectations of another person and those expectations do not materialize, our tendency is to get angry. The source of the anger is often the fear that the unmet expectation will negatively impact us. We fear that our finances, our well-being, our image, or any number of things may be impacted by the unmet expectation. My friend's wife had not met his expectations in many areas of his life, so then, many times it resulted in harsh words that damaged his wife's self-esteem. Now, it was leading to a marriage crisis.

Jesus often spoke of living as though we were dead. How can you live as though you are dead? "In the same way, count yourselves dead to sin but alive to God in Christ Jesus" (Rom. 6:11). It is a choice each of us must make. Once you become dead to that which stirs an emotion in you, God is free to change that situation. Until then, you can expect God to allow that situation to remain until you reckon yourself dead to the effects of the issue that causes you to struggle.

Is there something that causes anger within you? Ask God what the source of that anger is. You might be surprised at what you find. Then ask God to give you the grace to reckon yourself dead to that issue. You will find new freedom in your relationships and your own peace of mind.

November 25

Enlarging Your Territory

> …*"Oh, that You would bless me and enlarge my territory!…."*
> 1 Chronicles 4:10

He is mentioned only once in a brief description in the Old Testament, yet what he says and what his life bespeaks could fill volumes. He was a man whom God saw as worthy of a request that had significant consequences for him and his family. His name was Jabez. Here is how the Scripture describes him:

> *Jabez was more honorable than his brothers. His mother had named him Jabez, saying, "I gave birth to him in pain." Jabez cried out to*

the God of Israel, "Oh, that You would bless me and enlarge my territory! Let Your hand be with me, and keep me from harm so that I will be free from pain." And God granted his request (1 Chronicles 4:9-10).

When you think of territory, you probably think of land or some area in which you have dominion. Jesus often spoke about giving responsibility based on what we do with the little things first. Jabez must have been a very responsible person. God describes him as honorable. Jabez must have understood what it really means to be blessed by God. He was a man who knew what it meant to press into God and ask for God's favor with passion. God saw the heart of this man and gave him his request. His borders were enlarged! He lived a life free from pain. Imagine that!

The only reason God will enlarge a person's territory is that He knows that person will use it responsibly. He will steward what is given in light of God's Kingdom. God truly wants to increase our territory to have greater influence in the world around us. That territory can mean personal influence and/or physical territories.

It is rare to have a life without pain. Pain is often necessary to mold us and shape us. This is the only exception I have seen in Scripture. Jabez must have been quite a man with incredible integrity and purity of heart.

Are you this kind of person? Can God enlarge your territory and entrust you to use it for His purposes? Ask God today to enlarge your territory. Ask Him to make you the kind of man or woman who is worthy of such trust.

November 26

Freedom and Boundaries

Now the serpent was more crafty than any of the wild animals the Lord God had made. He said to the woman, "Did God really say, 'You must not eat from any tree in the garden'?"　　　Genesis 3:1

God is big on giving man freedom and boundaries—freedom to manage what He has entrusted to us, boundaries to protect us from evil.

T G I F　345

November 26—Day 330

The boundaries in the Garden of Eden were not set for the purpose of limiting Adam. Man got into trouble when he questioned those boundaries. God had provided everything he would need for life. He also entrusted man with responsibility to manage and work the Garden. God gave him freedom in that responsibility. God knows we were made to express ourselves creatively through our work.

Each of us must have freedom and boundaries in our work life. Whenever you are hired for a job, you must have the freedom to make certain decisions. You must have the authority to manage things within your area of expertise. You must also have limits within your area of responsibility. You need to know where those limits are and stay within them. Both freedom and boundaries are always under the umbrella of God's authority and our authorities at work.

Jesus understood these boundaries. When He was tempted for 40 days by the devil after being baptized, He was challenged by satan to go outside His freedom and boundaries. (See Matthew 4:1-11.) Satan said that He had the power to turn a stone into bread. Jesus was hungry and easily could have justified using His power to feed Himself. However, Jesus understood He could do nothing outside the boundaries of God's will for His life. It was God's will for Jesus to be tempted and to withstand the temptation. God was showing His Son that "man does not live on bread alone, but by every word that comes from the mouth of God" (Mt. 4:4b).

You and I are tempted every day to go beyond our God-ordained boundaries. Whether it is solving financial problems that have arisen through debt, making wrong decisions due to pressure, or manipulating someone in order to achieve our ends, it all represents rebellion toward God.

Ask God to show you His freedom and boundaries for your life. These are meant to enhance your life, not hinder it.

November 27

Staying Connected

Let the morning bring me word of your unfailing love, for I have put my trust in You. Show me the way I should go, for to You I lift up my soul.   Psalm 143:8

Two of the greatest inventions of my time has been the laptop computer and e-mail. The laptop means I no longer have to stay in one place to be productive in my business life. E-mail has allowed me to stay connected to people all around the world with the touch of a button.

My greatest frustration is when either of these does not work. Sometimes e-mail cannot be used because I can't get a connection. Sometimes I cannot use my laptop because I have not properly charged it, and then the charge runs out while I am on an airplane. Both of these situations mean I am unable to tap into the resource that allows me to fulfill my calling in my work to the fullest.

The morning time with God is much like these situations. God pours His Word into my spirit, and I am recharged. This recharging has an important effect on my day. It allows me the greatest opportunity to hear the small voice that directs my steps. If I refuse to "get connected," I risk following my own ways of fulfilling the duties of my day. It sets forth the opportunity for God to speak into my spirit what He desires for me each day. It allows me to focus on God's purposes, not mine.

The only way to know someone is to spend time with him or her. The only way to discern the voice of another is to hear that person's voice. David, the author of this psalm, was a warrior, king, and businessman. He understood this principle of connecting with God in the morning. His morning allowed him to connect with God's love, renew his trust in Him, and hear His directions for his life. Shouldn't you and I do the same?

November 28

Signs and Wonders Today

The whole assembly became silent as they listened to Barnabas and Paul telling about the miraculous signs and wonders God had done among the Gentiles through them.   Acts 15:12

"I was a pastor for 19 years before I went into business," said the man sitting across the table from me as we were sharing lunch together. What led him from being a pastor to a businessman was both a move of God and an attack from the enemy.

"I was a pastor of a particular denomination that did not embrace all of God's Word. It was a time in my life when I was experiencing many physical problems. I was on the verge of being admitted to the hospital. I had been seeking God about whether He was truly a God of healing and whether His Word was applicable in all areas of life as it was in the early Church. I was to go into the hospital the next day. That night I cried out to the Lord. I confronted God about His Word. I asked Him if He still did miracles today. Just then, I turned on my TV and saw an evangelist preaching. At that very moment, he stopped preaching, looked into the TV camera, and said these words: 'There is a man in the viewing audience who has been a pastor for many years and is struggling to know whether God heals today. His own denomination does not believe He does. [He even named his denomination.] God is healing you right now to demonstrate to you that His healing is for today, and you are to know that His Word is true for today just like it was for the early Church.' "

My friend was shocked. The TV evangelist could not have described him more accurately if he had been sitting in the same living room with him. God healed him that very night. He was not admitted to the hospital. He was forced to go before his church and witness to God's power in his life. He was soon fired as pastor of this church, and this is what led him into business.

So often when we experience God in greater and deeper ways, the persecution comes not from the world, but from those who are closest to us. Jesus was persecuted by the religious community. He was betrayed by one of His own disciples. However, we must realize this betrayal was necessary for God to accomplish His work through Jesus.

God will bring each of us to a crisis of faith to test what we really believe. For my friend, he had to experience God in a new way. Then he had to be tested in that belief to the point of losing his job.

Have you experienced God in all of your life? Are there areas in which you believe God does not operate today? Before you discount God, seek Him with a whole heart. You might be surprised at what you will find.

November 29

A Heavenly Strategic Planning Session

And the Lord said, "Who will entice Ahab into attacking Ramoth Gilead and going to his death there?" One suggested this, and another that. 1 Kings 22:20

There are few times we get a glimpse of what goes on in Heaven. Here is one instance when the angels were conferring with the Lord about the judgment of King Ahab for his sin and who was going to set up Ahab for this judgment.

If God wanted to use you to impact your world for Jesus Christ, what circumstances would have to be created in order for you to respond to His call? Would prospering you materially encourage you to this end? Would a major change in what you are presently doing be necessary? What would your response be should God and the angels conclude that the only way to move you into a position of fulfilling God's purposes was to remove some things that might be very dear to you? Would you agree with their plan if you knew this would be the only way you would achieve the purposes for which God made you? Hard questions, aren't they?

This is the very thing God does in many who have been called for a special mission. Moses had to be stripped of his royal position in the family of Egypt and sit in the desert for 40 years. The apostle Paul had to be knocked off his horse, blinded, and receive a personal visitation from Jesus. The 12 disciples had to leave their jobs for three years to follow Christ. Imagine what kind of disruption this had on their lives. There are many examples of God bringing major upheaval in the lives of those He called for His purposes. Why?

The reason is that we do not seek God with a whole heart in times of prosperity and comfort. Prosperity and comfort tend to breed complacency and satisfaction. It is rare to find the man or woman who seeks God with a whole heart who does so simply from a grateful heart. We often must have pain or crisis to motivate us. Eventually, that crisis bridges us to a new calling, and we embrace that calling if we are open to the Holy Spirit's work in us. We can actually thank God for the change that was required to get us to this place, but it is not without anguish of heart.

Would you be willing to sit in the strategic planning session for your life and agree with the plans God has for your life? Could you give God complete freedom to implement that plan, no matter the cost? Ask God to give you the grace and trust in His love for you to say "yes."

November 30

Obedience-Based Decisions

> *We are witnesses of these things, and so is the Holy Spirit, whom God has given to those who obey Him.* Acts 5:32

So often we as a society equate numbers with success. The larger the conference, the more successful we deem it. The larger a church, the more we believe that God is blessing. And so on. I recall planning a conference one time. Registrations were not where I felt they needed to be a few weeks before the date of the event. It wasn't long before I began to get "under the pile" about the level of attendance. My friend, who was organizing this conference with me, called and asked how I was doing.

I had to confess where I was. He immediately reminded me of my own teaching in this area. We are all called to be led by the Spirit, not by outcomes. "If God called us to put on this conference, then the outcome is up to Him if we have done our part." He went on to explain how he learned this lesson in a similar way a few years earlier.

He and a friend were led to host a Bible study group. His friend was to speak. It was nine o'clock and they were the only two people there. His friend was discouraged and was ready to leave.

"No," said my friend. "We have done what the Holy Spirit directed." He then stood up and began to welcome people as though there were many in the room. (No one was in the room.) He introduced his friend and they began the meeting. A few minutes later, people began to straggle in. By the time the meeting was over, ten had shown up, and one man in particular was impacted by the meeting.

Being led by the Spirit often means we must not use the world's standard for success as our measuring stick. You never know what an act of obedience will yield at the time. We must leave results to God. Our role is to obey. His role is to bring results from our obedience.

Do you make decisions based on the potential outcome or by the direction of the Holy Spirit in your life? Do you overly evaluate the pros and cons without consideration to what the Holy Spirit might be saying deep inside? We are all prone to make decisions based on reasoning alone. Ask God to give you a willingness and ability to hear the Holy Spirit and to obey His promptings.

December 1

Living Forward, Understanding Backward

The one who calls you is faithful and He will do it.
1 Thessalonians 5:24

When I was in my 20's, I participated in a wilderness training course in a desert and mountain area. For our "final exam," we were blindfolded, placed in the back of a pickup truck, and taken to a remote area. We were dropped off and told to meet back at the camp in three days. We did not know where we were. We had to determine our location with our compasses. It was a frightening experience for four young people who had learned to navigate through the use of a compass only a few days earlier. With our food and water on our backs, we began our trek. It had just snowed that morning, so the way was difficult. We walked through valleys, canyons, snow-covered hills, and forests. In all, we walked more than 60 miles in three days. There were times when we did not think we could go another foot. Exhaustion and frostbitten feet were taking their toll. However, we finally made it to our base camp successfully, and to our surprise, we were the first ones among the other patrols to make it back.

At the conclusion of our journey, we were able to stand on top of a ridge, look behind us and see the beautiful terrain that we had just scaled. The pain of what we had just endured seemed to subside. We could not believe we had actually walked through those valleys and snowcapped hills. There was a sense of accomplishment.

Life is very much like this. It is often lived forward, but understood backward. It is not until we are down the road a bit that we can appreciate the terrain God has allowed us to scale and the spiritual deposits He has made in our life as a result. When you begin to realize some of this, you sit back and breathe a sigh of relief because you know that God was in control all along. It didn't seem like it at the time, but He was.

Are you in the midst of a difficult journey that seems almost impossible to continue? Be assured that God is providing grace even now to equip you for that journey. There will be a time when you can say, "Wow, look at what God has done because of what I gained through that valley." Trust Him with the outcome of where you find yourself today.

December 2

Special Callings

Nevertheless, each one should retain the place in life that the Lord assigned to him and to which God has called him.

1 Corinthians 7:17a

God's calling to believers has been misunderstood over the centuries. In the Catholic era of the Church, the holistic view of the gospel changed, and there became a dualistic expression as it relates to faith and work. This became known as the "Catholic Distortion." It was shortly after this time that Protestants also bought into this same reasoning. This is why so many of us even today hear the term, "full-time Christian work" in expressing the distinction between one who is "full time" in God's service and the person who is in "secular" work. This implies an elevation to the vocational calling. This distortion is the worst form of dualism, because we are suggesting that there is a more nobler calling than our "secular" work if we are truly committed to God and His service.

Each of us is called to relationship with God through Jesus Christ. We are called by Him, to Him, and for Him. Once we enter that relationship with Christ, we are called into the physical expression of that relationship. This is where our vocations are manifested as a result, not as an end in themselves.

Additionally, there are examples of special callings in the Bible in which individuals have a direct communication from God to do a specific task for Him. Moses, Paul, Peter, and many others had direct communication about what God was calling them to do. Not everyone receives this "special" calling. This is not to say God is not personal with each of us. Some have had extraordinary supernatural encounters with God that led to their calling being specific to a task ordered by God. All of us have been called to follow Christ and live our lives in obedience to Him. Many of us have a sense to go in one direction or another based on our life experiences and giftedness. This, too, is God's calling.

Calling goes beyond our work and includes our relationships to others: our wives, our children, our neighbors—and our coworkers. We must remember this in order that our "work calling" does not become elevated at the expense of the other important aspects of our lives. This is the holistic approach to the gospel in which God made all of life equally important.

Therefore, the next time someone says, "I was called into the ministry" or "I am in full-time Christian work," stop them and tell them we are all in full-time Christian work. There is no secular and religious in the economy of God. I have a dear friend who often says, "I am a servant of the living God masquerading as a dentist." So, too, are you first a servant of the living God.

December 3

The Spirit of Competition

I in them and You in Me. May they be brought to complete unity to let the world know that You sent Me and have loved them even as You have loved Me.   John 17:23

A story is told about F.B. Meyer, the great Bible teacher and pastor who lived a century ago. He was pastoring a church and began to notice that attendance was suffering. This continued until he finally asked some members of his congregation one Sunday morning why they thought attendance was down.

A member volunteered, "It is because of this new church down the road. The young preacher has everyone talking and many are going to hear him speak."

His name was Charles Spurgeon. Meyer, rather than seeking to discourage this, exhorted the entire congregation to join him and go participate in seeing this "move of God" as he described it to his congregation.

"If this be happening, then God must be at work."

Meyer, even though he was an accomplished preacher and teacher, recognized where God was at work and joined Him in it. [The author heard this on a radio show from Key Life Ministries with Steve Brown, based in Orlando, Florida.]

Can you imagine this story taking place in our competitive world today? Competition has penetrated the Church so much that many churches and Christian organizations approach ministry like a sports event. They view their mission as a business that seeks to gain market share among Christians—donors, members, influence—all under the name of God. I am sure God looks down at us and asks, "Whatever happened to John 17:23?" Sometimes we must remind our fellow servants that we are all on the same team! We should be seeking to impact the Kingdom of God, not increase our own market share.

When Jesus made this statement about unity in John 17:23, it represented the key to bringing salvation to many. He was saying that when His Body is unified, the non-Christian would be able to see who Jesus really is—the Son of God. Are you contributing to unity in the Body of Christ? Or are you contributing to a spirit of competition? Ask God where you can be an instrument of unity in His Body.

December 4

Anger Born of the Spirit

When Saul heard their words, the Spirit of God came upon him in power, and he burned with anger.　　　　　1 Samuel 11:6

There are occasions in which righteous anger is justified by God. It is a type of anger that does not lead to sin, but fulfills God's purposes.

Saul had just been crowned as the new king of Israel. His first battle was upon him, and he had to bring a new nation together to fight the Ammonites. The Spirit of God fell on Saul and resulted in righteous anger against God's enemies. God led him to send an unusual "direct-mail" package to all the regions where the people lived. He cut up pieces of oxen and sent the pieces throughout Israel with a warning—"Join the army or your oxen will be as these!"

Sometimes God uses strong measures to accomplish His purposes. In this case, fear and intimidation were used to motivate the army of God to be as one. God must have felt this is what was needed to drive this army to become a unified force.

December 4—Day 338

God knows the only way to achieve success is if the army is one. A house divided cannot stand. What will it take to unify your company, your church, and your family to be one? Unless you are one, you cannot win the battles you will face. Ask God to make you and those you walk with to be one in mission and one in spirit.

December 5

Belief or Unbelief

> ..."*Abraham believed God, and it was credited to him as righteousness.*"
> Romans 4:3

Each morning we awake and go about our day based on one of two beliefs: Either we believe in God and our every action is motivated by this central value, or we do not really believe and our actions reflect so.

You can be a believer yet act as though there is no God. Whenever you fret over life circumstances, you immediately demonstrate unbelief. Whenever you move out of fear or anxiety, you believe a lie about God's nature.

Each day your actions affirm or convict you of your belief system. It reveals who the central focus of your life really is—you or God. It reveals who you place your ultimate trust in—you or God. It is one of the great paradoxes for believers. One day we can believe Him to move mountains. The next day we can question His very existence.

- Peter believed God and walked on water.
- A sick woman touched the hem of His garment and was healed.
- A Canaanite woman believed and freed her daughter from demon-possession.

In what circumstances do you act as an "unbeliever"? Ask God to increase your level of trust so that your actions match up with one who believes every day.

December 6

Disappointments

Hope deferred makes the heart sick, but a longing fulfilled is a tree of life.   Proverbs 13:12

Life is filled with disappointments. Many of God's greatest servants experienced deep disappointment in their journeys of faithfulness to God. Joseph, after spending years as a slave and in jail for crimes that he did not commit, revealed deep disappointment when he was forgotten another two years in prison. John the Baptist, when awaiting execution, doubted whether Jesus was, in fact, the Christ because he was sitting there awaiting his death. Elijah, losing all hope and despondent to the point of death, asked God to take his life in the desert; and Peter, who left his fishing business and invested three years of his life only to watch his Savior crucified, wondered whether the purpose of those three years could be justified.

When life doesn't add up, it leaves the heart sick. When we have done all we know to do and the formula has not worked, it leaves us questioning. These are times that try the very souls of men. There is no human sense to be made of it. We are left with a choice: to cling or not to cling. There are times when holding on to our Master's robe is all that we can do. It is all that He wants us to do.

The heights by great men reached and kept
Were not obtained by sudden flight;
But they, while their companions slept,
Were toiling upward in the night.

Standing on what too long we bore,
With shoulders bent and downcast eyes,
We may discern—unseen before—
A path to higher destinies!

Longfellow

There is only one answer to life's disappointments. Like the psalmist, we must "Find rest, O my soul, in God alone; my hope comes from Him. He alone is my rock and my salvation; He is my fortress, I will not be shaken" (Ps. 62:5-6).

December 7

Equipped for the Marketplace

May the God of peace, who through the blood of the eternal covenant brought back from the dead our Lord Jesus, that great Shepherd of the sheep, equip you with everything good for doing His will, and may He work in us what is pleasing to Him, through Jesus Christ, to whom be glory for ever and ever. Amen. Hebrews 13:20

"We've spent too much time equipping our businesspeople to do our ministries rather than equipping them to do the ministry God has called them to in the workplace," said a third-world pastor to a large group of businesspeople.

Over 70 percent of our time is spent in the workplace, yet our training and teaching focuses on areas where we spend much less time. The workplace is the greatest mission field of our day, yet we do not train businesspeople how to effectively integrate their faith into their workplace. The wall between Sunday and Monday still exists. Most businesspeople do not understand that all of life is spiritual, not just life on Sunday.

A recent study found that 50 percent of Christians have never heard a sermon on work; 70 percent have never been taught a theology of work; and 70 percent have never heard a sermon on vocation. Why do we focus on the fringes rather than the center where most people spend most of their time—the workplace?

God is removing the wall of separation by speaking to pastors and businesspeople all over the world. A pastor recently shared how his church ordains their businesspeople for their calling to the workplace. Another pastor described their church's commitment to integrating training for their businesspeople on the theology of work. Another told how they began a marketplace ministry within their church for their businesspeople, and even integrated Sunday school programs specifically geared to help businesspeople understand their calling in the workplace.

We are entering a new era in the Church when businesspeople are seen as a remnant of the Body of Christ who need to be mobilized and trained for the work of the ministry to their own mission field—the marketplace. Are you one of the men and women God is raising up for this task? Pray that God will help pastors understand and affirm this calling, and that they will respond by training the people of their churches for their own ministry to the workplace. When we reclaim the 70 percent, the remainder will be reclaimed automatically.

December 8

No Manna Stores

Then the Lord said to Moses, "I will rain down bread from heaven for you. The people are to go out each day and gather enough for that day. In this way I will test them and see whether they will follow My instructions." Exodus 16:4

When God took the nation of Israel through the desert, there was one thing the people simply could not do outside of God alone: They could not provide for themselves. They could not plant. They could not harvest. They could not manufacture. It was a place and time where nothing but complete dependence was the rule. God gave manna one day at a time. The manna spoiled the day after, so they could never store it. They could not go to the manna store to get more. They couldn't start a manna business to capitalize on all the free manna. I can tell you from personal experience that when God takes you to the desert, there is nothing you can do to change it until He wants to change it, so do not strive against God in the desert place.

What was the purpose of this restrictive time in their lives? Why did God have to keep them from using any of these abilities to earn on their own? It was a season to build trust and reliance on God. They had relied on the "manna" of Egypt for so long that He needed to change their whole nature of looking to Egypt as their provider to looking to God as their provider. This boot camp was to be only for a season. However, what should have been less than a 30-day journey took 40 years because of the hardness of their hearts. They never passed the test God gave them.

Has God taken you into the desert? Is He forcing you to depend wholly on His provision? Pray that you will learn the lessons God desires you to learn in the desert place. He will bring you out when He has accomplished all He wants to build in your life. Remember that it is a season; you will not be there forever. He understands that no one can stay in a desolate place forever.

December 9

The Role of Intercession

> *Coming over to us, he* [Agabus] *took Paul's belt, tied his own hands and feet with it and said, "The Holy Spirit says, 'In this way the Jews of Jerusalem will bind the owner of this belt and will hand him over to the Gentiles.' " When we heard this, we and the people there pleaded with Paul not to go up to Jerusalem.* Acts 21:11-12

In my own personal spiritual pilgrimage, God has allowed me to come into relationship with those in the Body of Christ who are called to a greater level of intercessory prayer. God calls each of us to be intercessory prayer warriors, but there are individuals in the Body of Christ who are called to be frontline warriors and who are more skilled in the area of intercession. These individuals often can have a gift of prophecy as part of their intercessory anointing. Such appears to be the case of Agabus in the Book of Acts.

Agabus seems to have received a word from God, and by way of a physical demonstration, tied his belt around Paul to let him know that he would be bound in Jerusalem if he went to this city. Agabus and the others immediately drew a conclusion that he was not to go to Jerusalem. Paul disagreed and proceeded to Jerusalem where he was, in fact, bound and beaten after giving testimony to the people and religious leaders of Jerusalem.

God calls intercessors to the role of *seeing*. He calls leaders to the role of *interpreting actions*.

God allows intercessors to see a more complete picture. However, actions are never left for the intercessors to determine. Conversely, leaders need to get the spiritual picture of what they are dealing with. This is why they need gifted intercessors. They must not make the mistake of believing they can see the entire picture without the intercessors. Once they have the intercessors' insights, they must determine the right course of action. This is their role. Conflicts arise when either tries to fulfill both roles.

Paul knew he was to go to Jerusalem, even if it meant being beaten. He did go and was beaten. However, we sense that he made the right decision based on Jesus' comments to him in Acts chapter 23, verse 11: "The following night the Lord stood near Paul and said, 'Take courage! As you have testified about Me in Jerusalem, so you must also testify in Rome.' "

Pray that God will bring intercessors and leaders into your life. He wants you to have a complete picture of the situations you face each day and to know the actions necessary for fulfilling His will for your life.

December 10

Hungering for God

God looks down from heaven on the sons of men to see if there are any who understand, any who seek God.　　　　　Psalms 53:2

"Are you coming to the conference?" I asked my friend.

"I really don't understand why I should come to this. How can I really benefit?" was his response. At that moment, I realized that I was wasting my time with this man on whom I had invested much throughout his Christian walk. He was often like a roller coaster—up one minute, down the next.

"You simply aren't hungry enough," I commented to my friend.

Whenever someone must always rationalize and examine whether the things of God are beneficial to them, you know that they are not hungry enough for God. I recall one time when I was in a difficult place. I received an audiotape from a man who gave me some insights into my problem. I was hungry enough to book a flight to a city 500 miles away just to meet him and find out more. My finances were at a very low point, so it took some real faith to do this. That meeting turned out to be a divine appointment and became a turning point in my life.

God is looking for men and women who hunger to know Him. When we believe that we know all we need to know, we are in a dangerous place. God has placed men and women in the Body of Christ who have had different experiences and gifts that can be helpful in our own spiritual pilgrimages. It requires humility of heart to realize that we can learn from others. We can easily rationalize our business pressures and time commitments to discount such opportunities.

December 11

Paul's Personal Mission Statement

> *I want to know Christ and the power of His resurrection and the fellowship of sharing in His sufferings, becoming like Him in His death, and so, somehow, to attain to the resurrection from the dead.*
> Philippians 3:10-11

We hear a lot these days about planning and goal setting. Proponents of planning say, "If you aim at nothing, chances are you will probably hit it." They say that to wander aimlessly through life is like sailing a boat without a sail and rudder. You end up wherever the wind takes you.

Paul understood his personal mission, which should be the personal mission of every believer in Jesus Christ. It is the one summary statement that best describes the purpose of our existence on earth and the goal of our Christian experience. It can be reduced to three important characteristics.

To know Christ.

To know and experience His power.

To identify with His sufferings.

All that flows from these three objectives becomes a by-product. Salvation is a by-product. Miracles are a by-product. Christlikeness is a by-product. Paul's focus was on relationship. He understood that the deeper the relationship, the more power he would experience. He also understood that as he grew in this relationship, there would be suffering. Whenever the Kingdom of Light confronts the kingdom of darkness, there is a battle, and this often results in casualties. Christ confronted these earthly kingdoms and suffered for it. If we are living at this level of obedience, we, too, will face similar battles; it simply comes with the territory.

Does this sound like your personal mission statement? Is your focus in life centered on knowing Christ and the power of His resurrection? If not, press into Him today in order to begin experiencing Christ more intimately.

December 12

The Finger of God

> *When the Lord finished speaking to Moses on Mount Sinai, He gave him the two tablets of the Testimony, the tablets of stone inscribed by the finger of God.* Exodus 31:18

Throughout the Bible, the word *testimony* is used in many ways. *Testimony* comes from the Hebrew word *eduwth*, which means "witness." The Ark of the Covenant contained the Ten Commandments, written and inscribed personally by God and given to Moses on Mount Sinai. These became known as the *testimony*. The Ark was a divinely inspired structure that was to be used as a witness to the people of Israel and the whole world of God's power and majesty. These divinely created tablets were a witness of God's activity on earth with man.

December 12—Day 346

Throughout the Bible, God looked to create testimonies with His people. At the Red Sea, He created a testimony through Moses. God created a testimony through Joshua when He parted the Jordan River and allowed the people with the Ark to cross on dry land. When Lazarus lay dead for days, Jesus came and created a testimony of His ability to raise the dead.

Jesus is still looking for those who are willing to have a testimony created through their lives. One of the major characteristics of a God-ordained testimony is for something to happen that cannot be explained in the natural. In other words, if you can make it happen through your abilities, it is not a testimony about God, but about you.

One time, I was invited to go to South Africa to a major conference, but I did not have the funds to go. I sensed that I was to attend this conference, but refused to use a credit card to fund the trip. I waited and waited. Finally, on the day of the registration closing, a man came to my office and said I was to go to this conference and he would fund the trip. He took out his checkbook and wrote a check for $2,500. That has become a testimony of God's activity in my life.

God wants to create a testimony in every aspect of your life—your family, your work, your church, and in your community. He is waiting to put His finger on your next endeavor to reveal His power through your life. Look carefully at the events where God might want to create a testimony out of an impossible situation. He delights in using His children for this purpose because it brings Him glory.

December 13

God's Chosen Few

> *But those who suffer He delivers in their suffering; He speaks to them in their affliction.* Job 36:15

He was born with cerebral palsy in South Africa. He barely survived his birth. He did not walk until he was four years old. One leg was longer than the other and he could not speak well. For most of his life, his hands shook and he had little control over them. Feelings of rejection and bitterness at his plight were common occurrences during his growing-up years. During his school years, he was chastised by kids and generally rejected by society.

At age 17, his father felt led to take his son to a healing service. That night, the young boy's leg divinely grew two inches. He no longer walked with a limp. Bradley met the Savior and began to grow in his intimacy with Him. God began to speak to him and show him things. Prayer became his source of comfort and strength. God gave him insights about people and situations, bringing blessing to all who encountered him. Today, this young man travels around the world as an internationally known intercessor and founder of a school of intercessory prayer. Literally hundreds of hours of knowledge about the way God speaks to His children have been birthed in and through this young man.

One evening Bradley walked forward in a meeting of about 40 businesspeople and handed a note to the leader during a Christian business conference. The note was for someone in the room, but Bradley did not know whom it was for. It was the last day of a 40-day fast for this writer. The message gave a specific description of what I had been experiencing the two years leading up to that night. Nobody would have known such details. I knew it was for me. It was a miraculous "telegram from God" that provided confirmation and encouragement of where God was taking me. God used one broken man to speak to another broken man.

God's ways are not our ways. His preparation of His warriors seems cruel and hurtful at times. His ways are much higher than ours. Trust the God of the universe that He can orchestrate the events of your life when they seem the darkest.

December 14

Hearing God's Voice

Now Samuel did not yet know the Lord: The word of the Lord had not yet been revealed to him.   1 Samuel 3:7

Samuel was born to Hannah, a woman who had a deep commitment to God. She was barren, but she cried out to God for a son. The Lord gave her Samuel, whom she completely gave to the Lord for His service. After weaning him, she took him to the house of the Lord to be reared by the priests. Eli was the priest of Israel, but he was not a godly leader. He had allowed much corruption, including the sins of his sons, in God's house. God was not pleased with Eli and later judged him and his household.

Samuel grew up in the temple serving God. He also grew up seeing the hypocrisy of Eli's household, yet this did not change the young man. God was with him. We learn that even though young Samuel had a belief in God, he had not yet experienced a personal relationship with Him. God called to Samuel three times, but Samuel thought it was Eli, the priest, calling him. Finally, Eli told him to say, "Speak Lord, for your servant is listening" (1 Sam. 3:9b). This is what Samuel did, and God began telling Samuel important things to come.

Many of us grow up in religious environments. We go to church every week. We have a head knowledge of God, but we do not recognize God's voice in our lives. There comes a time when we must recognize God's voice for ourselves. God does not want us to have a religion; He wants us to have a two-way relationship with Him. Samuel was never the same after this encounter. He would know God's voice and would respond to Him in obedience.

Do you know God's voice? Can you recognize it when He speaks? In order to hear God's voice, you must be clean before Him and listen. Listen to God's voice today and follow His plans for you.

December 15

Desert Preparation

Nor did I go up to Jerusalem to see those who were apostles before I was, but I went immediately into Arabia and later returned to Damascus. Galatians 1:17

The apostle Paul tells us in the first chapter of Galatians some of the facts surrounding his own conversion. He tells us that he clearly understood the call Jesus placed on his life. He did not have to consult other men about this calling. But before he was released to begin his own mission, He went to Arabia for three years. Why did Paul have to go to Arabia for three years before he ever met another disciple of Jesus Christ?

The Scripture does not tell us plainly why Paul spent three years in Arabia. However, based upon many examples of God placing special calls on people's lives, we know it often requires a time of separation between the old life and the new life. No doubt, Paul had plenty of time to consider what had taken place in his life and time to develop an intimate knowledge and relationship with the newfound Savior. His life was about to change dramatically.

So often, when God places a call on one of His children, it requires a separation between the old life and the new life. There is a time of being away from the old in order to prepare the heart for what is coming. It can be a painful and difficult separation. Joseph was separated from his family. Jacob was sent to live with his uncle Laban. Moses was sent to the desert.

When God began a deeper work in my own life, it required a separation from all I had known before. He removed all that I had placed confidence in up to that point. It was very painful and very scary since I was in my mid-40's. In my mind, it was not the time to start life over. I had been making plans for early retirement. God had a different idea. He removed all my comforts and security in order to accomplish a much greater work than what I could see at the time. The picture is clear now. I understand why it was necessary, but I didn't at the time.

Perhaps God has placed you in your own desert period. Perhaps you cannot make sense of the situation in which you find yourself. If you press into God during this time, He will reveal the purposes He has for you. The key is *pressing into Him*. Seek Him with a whole heart and He will be found. God may have a special calling and message He is building in your life right now. Trust in His love for you that He will fully complete the work He has started in you.

December 16

A Candy Maker

For God so loved the world that He gave His one and only Son....
John 3:16

A candy maker in Indiana wanted to make a candy that would be a witness of his faith. He incorporated several symbols for the birth, ministry, and death of Jesus Christ. He began with a stick of pure white, hard candy—white to symbolize the Solid Rock, the foundation of the Church and the firmness of God's promises.

The candy maker made the candy in the form of a "J" to represent the name of Jesus, who came to earth as our Savior. It could also be thought to represent the staff of the Good Shepherd with which He reaches down into the ditches of the world to lift out the fallen lambs who, like all sheep, have gone astray.

Thinking that the candy was somewhat plain, the candy maker stained it with red stripes. He used three small stripes to show the stripes of the scourging Jesus received, and by which we are healed. The large red stripe was for the blood shed by Christ on the cross so that we could have the promise of eternal life.

The candy became known as the candy cane—a decoration seen at Christmas time. But the meaning is still there.

During Christmas, do you reflect on the real meaning of the season? It is one season we can use like no other to bring the focus on Christ. Ask God to give you opportunities to share Christ with someone this Christmas.

December 17

Elevated From the Pasture

Now then, tell my servant David, "This is what the Lord Almighty says: I took you from the pasture and from following the flock to be ruler over My people Israel." 2 Samuel 7:8

Have you ever heard someone say, "He is a self-made millionaire"? They are stating that this person accomplished everything through his own efforts. His achievements were a result of his hard work and street smarts.

David was nearing the end of his life. The prophet Nathan was responding to David's idea to build a temple where the Ark of the Covenant would stay. God reminded David of his roots and where He had brought him. God took David from the fields of pasturing sheep to pastoring a nation. God reminded David that He cut off all of David's enemies. (David never lost a battle.)

Have you ever felt tempted to look at your accomplishments with pride as if you were the reason for your success? Have you ever thought your prosperity was due to your ingenuity? Has your material success been a testimony to others that God is the ruler of all aspects of your life, even the material side?

Joseph's greatest test was not his temptation to be bitter against his brothers. It wasn't the sexual temptation that came inside Potiphar's house. It wasn't even the discouragement of years of imprisonment for being wrongfully accused. It was the temptation of prosperity and ownership. Once he was elevated, he was given choices that he never had before. It was totally up to him as to which choice he would make. Stewardship reveals what we believe about God and ourselves.

Not every man can carry a full cup. Sudden elevation frequently leads to pride and a fall. The most exacting test of all to survive is prosperity.—Oswald Chambers

Do you have a proper understanding of who you are? Do you understand that it is God who has given you the ability to work and achieve? He is the source of all good things. Ask God today if your life models this belief.

December 18

Betrayals

If an enemy were insulting me, I could endure it; if a foe were raising himself against me, I could hide from him. But it is you, a man like myself, my companion, my close friend. Psalm 55:12-13

"You will always be attacked in the place of your inheritance," said the man sitting across the breakfast table. "God has called you to bring people together and to impact other people's lives as a result of this anointing in your life. You must make sure that you seek to maintain righteousness in all of your relationships." Those words came from someone who had the wisdom and authority to speak them to me.

I have had a number of close relationships that ended in betrayal. I am very loyal to my friends and those with whom I have covenant relationships. Yet there are times that no matter how righteous you are, when someone means to betray you, he will do it. Loving those who betray you is "graduate-level Christianity." The religious community and one of His closest friends betrayed Jesus. Those who were closest to David betrayed him. Joseph's own family betrayed him. Loving our enemies cannot be accomplished by mustering it up. It can only happen when we have come to a death in ourselves so that Christ can love through us. It is truly one of those acts of identifying with the cross.

If you are a leader, you can be sure God will allow you to experience betrayal. It is one of those courses in the Kingdom that may not be required until God has seen that you have successfully passed other tests. It is the most difficult and most gut-wrenching of all tests. A godly response goes against all that is in us. Our natural response is to protect, retaliate, and retain unforgiveness and bitterness. Our natural response is satan's most powerful weapon; to overcome it requires much grace from God. Ask God to build His nature in you now so that when such attacks come, you will be aware that it is a test and you will respond in righteousness.

December 19

Seeking His Face

Since then, no prophet has risen in Israel like Moses, whom the Lord knew face to face.   Deuteronomy 34:10

One of the great differences between Moses and any other character in the Bible is how God describes Moses. Moses was a friend of God, and he met God face to face. "The Lord would speak to Moses face to face, as a man speaks with his friend" (Ex. 33:11a). So often, we view others for what they can do for us, instead of who they are. There is a difference between being a servant and being a friend. There is a difference between being an employee and being a son.

Do you seek God's face, or do you find that you spend more time seeking His hand? God wants us to seek Him for our every need. However, there is a higher calling for every believer. That is to seek God's face, and to see Him for His love and tenderness toward us as His children. He can provide for our physical needs, but when we see Him face to face, we are changed. We no longer see Him as one to be feared as much as one to know intimately. We no longer view Him for what He can give to us, but for what He already has given for us.

When we see Jesus face to face, we are no longer slaves, but friends. We do not fear Him as a slave fears his master. We have entered a new kind of relationship—a relationship that has mutual respect and care.

Today, Jesus is calling you to seek His face, not just His hand. When you seek His face, you will know His provision and His mercy in all aspects of life. Seek His face today and become a friend of God.

December 20

One Flock, One Shepherd

I have other sheep that are not of this sheep pen. I must bring them also. They too will listen to My voice, and there shall be one flock and one shepherd.   John 10:16

A friend of mine told me a story about an experience he had in Israel. They were in the country visiting some of the famous biblical sites when they saw a group of sheepherders. A shepherd brought his flock of sheep into a round pen for the night. Then, a few minutes later, another shepherd brought his flock into the pen. Then, a few minutes later, yet another shepherd brought his sheep into the pen. There were three groups of sheep in the pen with no identifying marks among any of them. My friend wondered how in the world they would separate their sheep the next day.

The next morning, a shepherd came over to the pen and made a comment to his sheep. One by one, the sheep filed out to follow him. Only his sheep followed his voice. My friend said it was an amazing scene to see only that shepherd's sheep follow him and the others remain in the pen. What a picture of Jesus' words spoken centuries earlier.

Hearing and responding to Jesus' voice is the key to having a two-way relationship with God. It is the difference between having religion and a relationship. Can you recognize God's voice in your life? Are you listening to the Shepherd's voice? Do you respond when He calls? Ask Jesus to help you increase your ability to hear. Give more time to spending quiet moments in His presence to hear His voice. He wants to be your Good Shepherd.

December 21

Living for a Cause Greater Than Yourself

He who is kind to the poor lends to the Lord, and He will reward him for what he has done.　　　　　　　　　　　　Proverbs 19:17

If you were God and you wanted to send one of your servants to help the less fortunate in the world, how would you train your servant for this task? Our ways are not God's ways. We find an interesting story in the case of Brigid, a woman born in the early 400's in Ireland.

Brigid was born from a sexual encounter between an Irish king and one of his slaves. She was raised as a slave girl within the king's household and was required to perform hard work on the king's farm. From the beginning, Brigid took notice of the plight of the less fortunate. She would give the butter from the king's kitchen to working boys. She once gave the king's sword to a passing leper—an act about which the king was enraged. The king tried to marry her off, but to no avail. One day, Brigid fled the king's house and committed herself to belonging only to Christ.

Brigid sought other women who also wanted to belong only to Christ. Seven of them organized a community of nuns that became known as the settlement of Kildare, a place where many thatch-roofed dwellings were built, and where artist studios, workshops, guest chambers, a library, and a church evolved. These and other settlements became little industries all to themselves, producing some of the greatest craftsmanship in all of Europe. Many of the poor had their lives bettered because of Brigid's ministry to them.

Brigid became a traveling evangelist, helping the poor and preaching the gospel. When she died in 453, it is estimated 13,000 people had escaped from slavery and poverty to Christian service and industry. Her name became synonymous with the plight of the poor. She was a woman who turned a life of slavery and defeat into a life lived for a cause greater than herself. She became a nationally known figure among her people, and the Irish people still recognize her each February 1.

God has called each of us to live for a cause greater than ourselves. If God asked you what you had done for the poor, what would you say? Jesus had a special place in His heart for the poor. Ask God how you might use your gifts and talents to improve the plight of the poor in your community.

December 22

The Gospel of the Kingdom

This, then, is how you should pray: "Our Father in heaven, hallowed be Your name, Your kingdom come, Your will be done on earth as it is in heaven."   Matthew 6:9-10

Imagine that you have never driven a car. You are not aware of all the features of a car. Up to this point, you have had to walk everywhere you go. All you are told is that you are about to receive something that will get you anywhere you need to go. The day arrives and you are given a brand new car. You get in and drive the car. However, the emergency brake is on, preventing you from going faster than 20 miles per hour. No one tells you that you should unlock the brake. Regardless, you are excited because you no longer have to walk to your destination. You are not told that the car has lights, which would allow you to drive at night. Neither are you told about the many other wonderful features of the car. You just know you have a new car that will get you anywhere you want to go at 20 miles per hour. For the rest of your life, you drive this incredible car during the daytime only at 20 miles per hour.

Why would Jesus pray that things in earth would be like they are in Heaven if it were not possible? When Jesus came to earth, He came in order to penetrate the very kingdom of darkness with light. He came to bring healing to sickness, replace sadness with joy, and fill meaninglessness with purpose. He came to change things for the better for a world that had no hope outside of God.

Using the illustration above, Jesus did not come to merely give us a ticket to Heaven (a car that you drive only in the daytime at 20 miles per hour). He came to bring us much more—the Kingdom of God on earth. Nowhere in the Bible will you find the term, gospel of salvation.

The Church does not exist for Heaven, but for earth. If it existed only for Heaven, then each of us would immediately be taken to Heaven. There would be no reason for us to remain on earth. So why has God allowed us to receive this new birth and remain on earth? It is so that we might bring the Kingdom of God into our world—our families, our workplace, and our communities.

God wants you to bring the Kingdom of God into the territory He has given you so that His will can be done on earth as it is in Heaven. Your domain is your workplace, family, and community. Ask God to show you how He wants to penetrate the darkness of your domain with His light. Then you will see and experience all the features of this gift that has been given to you.

December 23

Unlocking the Power

I in them and You in Me. May they be brought to complete unity to let the world know that You sent Me and have loved them even as You have loved Me. John 17:23

There have been certain breakthroughs in the world that have changed the course of history: electricity, the automobile, the atom, and the telephone, to name just a few. If we never recognized the applications of these inventions, we would still be sitting around in the dark, riding horses, and communicating by Pony Express. However, we have seen the opportunities and the applications, so the world is a different place now.

Jesus made a profound statement that has the potential to change the world if we simply apply the truth. What if I told you that this one truth would allow people to see Jesus and respond to the gospel like nothing we have ever experienced? It is the key to unlocking the door of salvation to so many that remain lost. Yet it is the one thing we, as His children, fail at the most.

December 23—Day 357

What is this one thing? It is unity. Lack of unity among His Body of believers prevents Christ from being revealed to so many. Efforts have been made, but our Body remains fragmented and weak. Consider that there are more than 24,000 Christian denominations in the world today and five new ones beginning each week, according to the 1999 September issue of *Moody Magazine*. Does this sound like unity?

God has called each of us individually and corporately to represent Christ to the world, but our independence, pride, and ego prevent us from becoming unified in the purposes of Christ.

Are you a catalyst for unity in His Body, or an instrument of division? Are people seeing Jesus because of the unity they see in your family, your church, and among your workers? The old adage, "United we stand, divided we fall," is not just a good battle cry; it is a spiritual truth that will determine the fate of many souls. Pray that God will allow you to be an instrument to unify His Body.

December 24

The High Places

> *Blessed are you, O Israel! Who is like you, a people saved by the Lord? He is your shield and helper and your glorious sword. Your enemies will cower before you, and you will trample down their high places.*
> Deuteronomy 33:29

One of the most successful movies of our time has been *Star Wars*, a futuristic movie where the forces of good battle the forces of evil in a far-off galactic solar system. In order for the forces of good to win their battle, they must enter the airspace of their enemies and find the central power source inside the enemy space station. Their fighter jets must locate this central nervous system and fire a laser missile into its heart in order to destroy the power source. The final scene shows the hero sending a last-minute laser missile into the power source and blowing up the space station and all the evil characters who live on it.

Throughout history, cultures have recognized idols on the high places, on the tops of hills or mountains, as their power sources. God said these high places are an abomination to Him. When God brought the people of Israel into the Promised Land, He instructed them to destroy all the high places. Many times through history, God had to judge Israel for their failure to destroy the high places.

Today, every major cult or evil spirit has its own high place that must be destroyed first before a righteous foundation can be laid. It may not mean you can physically destroy this high place, but you can tear it down through spiritual warfare and intercessory prayer.

High places are anything that is elevated above God and is worshiped. Are there any high places that take the place of God in your life? Are there any high places where you live that must be dealt with through spiritual warfare to allow the Kingdom of God to reign? You must destroy the high places in order for God to reign completely. Ask God to show you the high places so that you can elevate the one true God.

December 25

Business as Usual

And she gave birth to her firstborn, a son. She wrapped Him in cloths and placed Him in a manger, because there was no room for them in the inn. Luke 2:7

Imagine if the God of the universe decided to visit planet earth as a new baby and you were given the opportunity to host His first night—in your hotel! Think of the future promotional possibilities..."God stayed here His first night!" You could sell tickets to see the room where He was born. What an opportunity to make history as a small-business owner!

God had need of a business owner's establishment one night 2,000 years ago. But there was no room for God in this business that night. There was no room for the unexpected miracle, no awareness of what was taking place in the heavenlies, no sign that God might be reaching out to this businessperson to be used like no other in all of history.

Every day God has need of some businessman or woman's business. He wants to demonstrate miracles in their business. But there is no room in their business for Jesus. He is not asked to participate.

That night God slept in a stable. That night a business opportunity from Heaven was missed. It was business as usual.

May we all have spiritual eyes and ears to know when our Master is needing what He has entrusted to us for His purposes.

December 26

Working Wholeheartedly

> *In everything that he undertook in the service of God's temple and in obedience to the law and the commands, he sought his God and worked wholeheartedly. And so he prospered.* 2 Chronicles 31:21

Hezekiah was a godly king. He was also a very talented businessman and builder. He was responsible for many noteworthy projects that are described in detail in the Old Testament. We discover from the passage above that King Hezekiah had two major attributes that contributed to his success and prosperity: He sought God, and he worked wholeheartedly upholding God's laws.

Godly success involves a partnership between you and God. Success in God's economy means achieving the purpose for which God made you. That purpose can never be discovered without seeking Him with a whole heart. You may achieve great things without seeking God, but you will never achieve the things God set out for you to achieve without seeking Him. Unless you seek Him, you may find yourself one day climbing to the top of the ladder only to find it leaning against the wrong wall.

What does it mean to seek God? It means creating time to sit before His throne in quiet places. It means reading His Word in order to know

Him more intimately. It means developing an ear to hear His voice so that we know when to turn to the right or to the left. God desires to know you.

Are you willing to take the time to know Him? If so, you can be sure He will guide you into those things that will bring success to every aspect of your life.

December 27

Kings and Priests

And hast made us unto our God kings and priests: and we shall reign on the earth. Revelation 5:10 KJV

The Bible describes two distinct roles in the Old Testament—kings and priests. Kings were the rulers; priests were the religious leaders. The New Testament reveals we all are kings and priests because of the redemptive work of Christ.

Today, kings are most often represented by business and political leaders, while pastors represent the priestly roles. God calls each of us to fulfill both roles in our lives today. However, our vocational roles often create a division that is misunderstood by both businesspeople and pastors. These misunderstandings have led to a weakened and less effective Church.

Pastors have been guilty of viewing their businesspeople as dollar signs. They sometimes see them for what they can contribute to *their* ministries instead of equipping them to use *their* gifts and talents to impact the businessperson's mission field—their workplace.

Businesspeople have tried to get pastors to operate their churches like businesses, and have used their worldly ways for spiritual purposes. They often view the pastor as the primary ministry worker instead of taking on the responsibility themselves to do the work of the ministry.

This is a grievous sin that exists in the Body of Christ, and it requires repentance from both groups. Unless we recognize this, we will never see the reality of revival that God wants to bring to the business community, and pastors will fail to gain an ally to fully complete the work of the Church in their community.

Are you a pastor who has failed to see the calling that businesspeople have received to the workplace? If so, ask God to forgive you for viewing your businesspeople as those to be used for your own purposes.

Are you a businessperson who sees your church as another business to be run based on worldly measurements? Do you see the pastor's role as one who is primarily responsible for the work of the ministry? If so, you must repent and ask God to forgive you of this unbiblical view. God has called both of you to fulfill His purposes together through your gifts and talents.

December 28

Management by Force

> *"Take the staff, and you and your brother Aaron gather the assembly together. Speak to that rock before their eyes and it will pour out its water. You will bring water out of the rock for the community so they and their livestock can drink."* Numbers 20:8

Moses and the people had been traveling for days without water. The people were thirsty. They were complaining and grumbling about their plight, and Moses became the object of their complaining. Moses sought the Lord for wisdom on how to handle the situation. The Lord instructed him to speak to the rock and water would flow. This would be a sign that God was still in control, that Moses was still the leader, and that God was their provider.

When it came time to speak to the rock, Moses' disgust with the people became so great that instead of speaking to the rock, he angrily addressed the people and then struck the rock twice. The water came out, in spite of Moses' disobedience. But the Lord was not pleased with Moses.

This was a time for Moses to operate at a higher level. No longer was he called to touch things with his staff to perform miracles; it was a time for him to speak to the problem. His very words would have changed the situation. Moses' staff represented two things—his physical work as a shepherd of sheep and his spiritual work as a shepherd of the people. God was calling him to move into a new dimension of using his staff. Up to now, Moses had always been commanded by God to touch something to perform the miracle. Now it was time to speak God's word to the problem.

However, Moses made the mistake many of us make. He used his instrument with force to accomplish something for God. He took something God wanted to be used in a righteous manner and used it in an unrighteous manner. He used force to solve the problem. This disobedience cost Moses his right to see the Promised Land.

Have you ever been tempted to use your power, skill, and ability to force a situation to happen, perhaps even out of anger? God is calling us to use prayer to move the face of mountains. The force of our ability is not satisfactory. God is calling each of us to a new dimension of walking with Him. Pray that God will give you the grace to wait on Him and not take matters into your own hands. Then you will not be in jeopardy of failing to move into the Promised Land in your life.

December 29

A Rhema Word

For you will have a covenant with the stones of the field.   Job 5:23a

When I first met my wife, I was impressed to do something rather strange. I decided I would send her a rock in a box with a Scripture verse that describes how God used stones in the Bible. I was going to send it anonymously from a company called Significant Moments. I was going to do this for six months. The final month I planned to send the last rock with a note that said, "The most significant moment was the day I met you." I was going to sign my name on the last mailing. However, before this could happen, the plan was spoiled.

December 29—Day 363

I was helping my wife (just a friend at the time) move her furniture. We were exchanging stories about our lives. She began to tell me the story of how she got her name. Her father was an orphan in England, and in England they give orphans different names from their given names. They named her father "Staines." *Staines* means "place of stones." Not only that, he discovered later that his real name was Malcolm Stones. I nearly drove off the road when she told me this story. My plan was foiled! But my faith was advanced light years. I told her my plan since it would be too obvious now. We both looked at each other in amazement.

A month later, I went on a trip. She sent a little gift package along with me with a card that quoted a Scripture from Job. "For you will have a covenant with the stones of the field" (Job 5:23a). It was a *rhema* word for both of us. God used these times to confirm our relationship.

The Bible speaks of the Word of God as living. *Rhema* is a Greek word meaning "living." Sometimes the Holy Spirit speaks through the living Word regarding a specific situation in which we find ourselves. It is one of those mysteries that God does from time to time.

As you read your Bible, be aware of the *rhema* Word of God. He may speak to you in specific ways you never thought possible.

December 30

An Intercessor's Gift

Surely you have heard about the administration of God's grace that was given to me for you, that is, the mystery made known to me by revelation, as I have already written briefly. Ephesians 3:2-3

My wife and I had a very unusual courtship with many serendipitous moments that God used to confirm our relationship. When we were engaged to be married, she went to a wedding shower given by many of her friends in a town where she used to live. One of her friends was known for her intercessory prayer life.

When my wife arrived at the shower, her friend apologetically handed her a gift bag and said, "I have an unusual gift in there for your husband. I don't know why I felt led to buy it for him. My husband thinks I'm crazy for giving such a gift as a wedding present, but I was so impressed to buy this for him. Here it is."

My wife looked in the bag and pulled out a furry creature. When she saw what it was, she burst out laughing! It was a beanie baby named "Ostrich."

"How did you know?" exclaimed my wife.

"Know what?" asked her friend.

"My pet name for Os is 'Ostrich'!"

They both were amazed at God's sense of humor.

Sometimes we do not believe God can speak through others to encourage, and even humor us in miraculous ways. God wants to demonstrate His loving, and even light humor, in His relationship with us. Develop your intimacy with God and experience Him in the very intimate aspects of your life.

December 31

A Gift Basket From Heaven

> *I will betroth you to Me forever; I will betroth you in righteousness and justice, in love and compassion. I will betroth you in faithfulness, and you will acknowledge the Lord.*   Hosea 2:19-20

My wife came to know Jesus in the workplace when her boss led her in the sinner's prayer to receive Christ. She was 29 and had no idea who God was. She was a professional single woman who had always had a boyfriend. When Christ came into her life, He gradually began to change her life in very significant ways—especially in the area of relationships. As she began her first Bible study, she read in Matthew 7 that if she asked, she would receive (see Mt. 7:7). She prayed for a husband

and the Lord spoke to her through His Word. The next verse in her study was "Be still, and know that I am God" (Ps. 46:10a).

Over time, the Lord began to show her that He wanted to become her Husband. After two and one-half years without a boyfriend, she asked the Lord to show her how to fall in love with Him. Days later, she received a phone call from someone asking her if she could go on a three-day retreat. She instantly knew God was answering her prayer. He showed her that she could have the same kind of intimacy with Him that she could have with a human husband. She thought this to be strange for the obvious reasons most would think it strange. However, God began to demonstrate to her a level of intimacy that she never thought possible.

It was Valentine's Day, and she would normally leave such occasions to the married couples to celebrate. However, on this occasion, her church was having a Valentine's Day dinner. She felt impressed to go as a single. Actually, she knew the Lord was her escort. Because she had made a decision not to date in order to develop her intimacy with the Lord, she no longer received perfume as gifts. *Lord, I know You would not take me to a Valentine's Day banquet without giving me a gift*, she thought to herself. That evening, there was a drawing, and Angie won a beautiful gift basket full of fragrances.

On another occasion, she went to a company banquet alone. She was considered by this time rather weird for her commitment not to date. She often joked, "If it weren't for back rubs, I would never have need of a man." (You have to know Angie to appreciate that statement.) That evening, she won a gift certificate for a massage. Her friends looked at her and said, "How do you do that?"

Intimacy with God is not a fairy tale God teases us with in the Bible. He really desires to have intimacy with you and me. Ask God to reveal Himself to you in personal and intimate ways. He desires to do this.

Index

Index—Adversity

Index—Calling

Index—Faithfullness

Index—Perservance